CONGOTAY! CONGOTAY!
A Global History
of Caribbean Food

congotay 1 *n* Usu. In the expression, *One day, one day, congotay,* indicating that the oppressed will one day be freed, that one day justice will prevail (prob. < One day will be Congo's day) . . .

2 *n* A children's song game ... a long line of chickens protected by a "mother" from an individual saying "I must have a chick."

concontay . . . congotay . . . n A thick paste-like meal made from cassava . . . *Congotay* . . . was traditionally used as a ritual food at ceremonial dances where it is served with a goat's head sacrificed for the ancestors.

From *Dictionary of the English/Creole of Trinidad & Tobago: On Historical Principles,* edited by Lise Winer (Montreal: McGill-Queens University Press, 2008).

CONGOTAY! CONGOTAY!
A Global History
of Caribbean Food

CANDICE GOUCHER

M.E.Sharpe
Armonk, New York
London, England

For Hyla, Joseph, and Kosa

The EuroSlavic fonts used to create this work are © 1986–2014 Payne Loving Trust.
EuroSlavic is available from Linguist's Software, Inc.,
www.linguistsoftware.com, P.O. Box 580, Edmonds, WA 98020-0580 USA
tel (425) 775-1130.

Cover images: *(top, left to right)* flying fish and ships, 1707 *(John Carter Brown Library, Brown University)*; ackee *(Heidi Savery)*; fishing boats, Cape Coast, Ghana *(Candice Goucher)*/*(bottom, left to right)* food market, Antigua *(Candice Goucher)*; making pottery, Ghana *(Candice Goucher)*

Library of Congress Cataloging-in-Publication Data

Goucher, Candice Lee.
  Congotay! Congotay! : a global history of Caribbean food / by Candice L. Goucher.
    pages cm
Includes bibliographical references and index.
ISBN 978-0-7656-4215-8 (cloth : alkaline paper)—
ISBN 978-0-7656-4216-5 (paperback : alkaline paper)
1. Food—Caribbean Area—History. 2. Cooking, Caribbean—History. 3. Cooking, Creole—
History. 4. Food habits—Caribbean Area—History. 5. Intercultural communication—
Caribbean Area—History. 6. Caribbean Area—Civilization—African influences.
7. Caribbean Area—Social life and customs. 8. Caribbean Area—Social conditions. I. Title.

TX360.C35G68 2014
641.59729—dc23   2013018365

Contents

List of Illustrations and Map

List of Recipes

Preface

Much of my research career as historian and archaeologist was focused on two distinct academic fields: African studies and world history. As an Africanist, I have investigated the history of African metallurgists, digging their furnaces and slag mounds, listening to the music of their forges, where men were cooking metals. As a world historian, I have been most fortunate to partner with friend and colleague Linda Walton. In the most delicious of collaborations, we worked together on books and multimedia projects that framed our understanding of the historical forces of globalization between the intimate folds of families and kitchens, and the political, environmental, and economic structuring of individual and collective lives. These two paths have brought me to the crossroads, where Caribbean women were cooking meals.

The research for this project has simmered on a back burner for decades. Across those years I have traveled, eaten, cooked, and read widely. In the course of consuming and producing these meals and words, I have accumulated many debts. I am grateful to my family, friends, and many colleagues, who shared their stoves, their pots, their ideas, and their recipes: the late Andrew Salkey, John Rickford, Joseph Lambert, Ken Harry and family, Kwaku Mensah, Kofi and Monica Agorsah, Linda Walton, Doreen Simon and family, Bernice Yearwood, the late Alma Devonish and Adele Kendall, Oscar Jones, the late Marjorie Cowie, June Edwards, Thomas Cuthbert, Iya Makeda Joan Cyrus, Viviane Madacombe, Henry Drewal, Jacques Depelchin, Hollis Liverpool, Ray Holman, the Kendall family, the late Gregory Gaskin, Lee Theisen, the late Rick Harmon, Heidi Savery, Wolde Kristos, Jessica Harris, Evan Schneider, Barbara Traver, Adam Carpinelli, Desiree Hellegers, Pavithra Narayanan, Armando García de la Torre, Miguelito Bernal, Amitava Chowdhury, Aditi Sen, Maria de Lourdes Silvestre dos Santos, and Kimberly Mullen. I appreciate the assistance of many institutions and libraries, including the staffs of the National Maritime Museum, Greenwich, UK; National Library of Jamaica; University of the West Indies; Ministry of Culture, Trinidad and Tobago; University of Guyana; Barbados Museum and Historical Society; Newport Historical Society; British Library; Merseyside Maritime Museum, Liverpool; Library of Congress; John Carter Brown Library, Brown University; and Fernando Ortiz Institute, Havana. Two institutions have supported research travel and project components: Portland State University and Washington State University, where the Center for Social and Environmental Justice provided intellectual space that combined collegiality with interdisciplinary validation over the course of nearly a decade. Finally, for guidance in bringing this project to the table, I thank M.E. Sharpe's superb team, especially executive editor Steve Drummond, editorial coordinator Irene Bunnell, and project editor Henrietta Toth.

This book is dedicated to three people, who are my three hearthstones, supporting and sustaining my labors: to my mother, Hyla Goucher, who taught me that cooking food and love of family were intertwined; to my partner, Joseph Lambert, who first opened the door to the Caribbean and continues to share my kitchen; and to our son, Kosa Goucher-Lambert, who enthusiastically ate curries, salt fish, and cassava pone as a child and whose love of food adventures and commitment to sustainability as an adult give me hope for the future.

Introduction
The Creole Continuum of Foodways

Conversation is the food of ears.

—Nineteenth-century Creole proverb from Louisiana[1]

*It was in language that the slave was perhaps most successfully
imprisoned by his master; and it was in his (mis-)use of it that
he perhaps most effectively rebelled. Within the folk tradition,
language was (and is) a creative act in itself;
the word was held to contain a secret power.*

—Edward Brathwaite, *Folk Culture of the Slaves in Jamaica*[2]

Food and speech share space in the human mouth. Just ask Anancy, the
trickster spider-hero of African-Caribbean cultures. In one of the beloved
Anancy tales collected before 1880 by William Musgrave, the son of the
colonial governor of Jamaica (who had learned the stories told to him by
his Antiguan nurse), Anancy has permission to eat an entire heap of yams,
but only if he discovers the yam's "true" (African) name from his mother.[3]
To his dismay, the gluttonous Anancy remembers the name only when one
yam remains to be eaten. The magic word was *nyampinya*, or *nyami* in
other versions, from a West African word for "yam" that also means "to
eat." Borrowed by the Spanish and Portuguese, the word became "yam" in
the English-speaking Caribbean. *Inyame* still means to "stuff down" food
in the circum-Caribbean. Speech provided more than the names for foods
brought from Africa or culinary lessons that survived the Middle Passage.
Language change helps explain the complex historical processes of cultural
resistance and transformation.

Creole Culture in the Caribbean Crucible

The Caribbean crucible contained the earliest morsels of our globalized experience of a common humanity. Since 1492, the distinct cultures, peoples, and languages of four continents met in Caribbean waters and intermingled in wave after wave of post-Columbian encounter. Foods and their styles of preparation were among the most consumable of cultural elements undergoing transformation. African peoples, cuisines, tastes, and styles also resided at the heart of a complex, dynamic, and creative transfer and mixing process sometimes referred to as "creolization." Whether applied to words or foods, languages or other cultural components, creolization was a response to the global forces that brought disparate peoples together. In this book, I argue that Caribbean cuisine and culinary practices provide historians with critical kitchen-based lexicons for the study of global historical processes and patterns, the "grammatical" rules governing the shape of human interactions, in which Africans played a primary role.

Creole language studies have revealed the myriad ways in which the relative power of African and European participants occupied a continuum.[4] Since enslaved Africans constituted the largest number of immigrants into a European-dominated world, their influence was both universal and contradictory. John Rickford has defined the initial appearance of a pidgin language as an opportunistic means of communication among speakers of mutually distinct languages. Creoles eventually emerge from pidgins as the native-born or first language of their speakers and as a fully fledged system transmitted across generations.[5] Creoles are thus the linguistic product of longer, sustained interaction. Creoles appear to arise in the particular contexts of trade, colonialism, and plantation life common to the Caribbean. Because the shifts in the structuring of discrete culinary components were determined by control over cognitive realms, it follows that the domains of food knowledge would reflect similar historical processes of interaction. Allsopp, in his classic work on Afrogenesis, noted the conceptual unity of creoles with cognitive contributions from speakers of African languages. Furthermore, creoles emerge from "systemic transfers." According to Allsopp, "indisputable correlates" point to the conclusion that "there was an underlying common African way of putting things, a broadly pervasive experience of life-view."[6]

This patterned creolization resulted in cases of linguistic (and cultural) interaction that many scholars feel to be uniquely situated in the Atlantic world's plantation societies of the seventeenth and eighteenth centuries. In their creolized interactions, primarily Europeans and Africans engaged in processes of adaptation, assimilation, mingling, and borrowing through which they negotiated a nuanced, ordered restructuring of their common ground. Creolization occurred on both sides of the Atlantic, initially in the maritime contexts in which ships provided sites that were fundamental to their linkage into a single system of transportation and transformation. Creolization restructured not only language, but also other cultural elements, including foodways, along the way.

The term "creole" was first applied in the sixteenth century to people, meaning the native-born descendants of Africans, Portuguese, and Spanish in the islands and coastal colonies of the Caribbean, Atlantic, and Indian Oceans, places where the earliest interactions of Europeans and non-Europeans occurred. It is thought to have originated with the Portuguese word *crioulo*, a person raised in the house, especially a servant (from which the Spanish *criollo* and *criar*, meaning "to create or beget," and French *créole* are derived). The terminology was extended to language for the first time in the writings of the French official Michel Jajolet, sieur de la Courbe, in his *Premier voyage du sieur de la Courbe fait a la coste d'Afrique en 1685*. La Courbe was a company administrator for the Compagnie du Senegal, and he traveled in areas that previously were controlled by the early Portuguese merchants and their descendants. His travel description used the term to refer to a Portuguese-based language that was spoken in coastal Senegal before the French arrived.[7]

Linguists have since studied examples of the historical interaction of mutually unintelligible languages in order to identify the rules of engagement in processes of creolization. Who and what was considered "creole" shifted over time and across the territory we call the circum-Caribbean. Besides providing an explanatory premise for sourcing components, the creole concept also masks multiple processes of erasure and mixing. By the nineteenth century, "creole" again came to mean "locally born," this time excluding newly arrived Asians. Yet the processes were unstoppable and Asian cuisines entered the kitchen lexicon. Why do some grammars and structures win out over others? How does the degree of marginalization or control over cognitive domains shape the selectivity of participant choices and shared end products? Answers to these questions have revealed highly contested issues at the core of the globalization processes that beget modernity. They are also relevant to the task of erecting a framework for understanding food history in the Caribbean.

Creole Cuisine

The writer Lafcadio Hearn is usually credited with the earliest exposition of creolization in relation to foodways. An emigrant to the United States from Greece, Hearn was a writer who lived in New Orleans between 1877 and 1887, followed by two years in Martinique and many more in Asia. Chastising "the extravagant servant," Hearn ignored the role of Africans and instead credited the frugal (white) housewife's artistry in the creolization process:

> Economy and simplicity govern "La Cuisine Creole"; and its many savory dishes are rendered palatable more as the result of care in their preparation than any great skill or expensive outlay in the selection of materials. The Creole housewife often makes delicious morceaux from the things usually thrown away by the extravagant servant.[8]

Despite his early (illegal) marriage to an African-American woman, Hearn did not escape the racist analysis common to his day. For Hearn, "la cuisine créole" had become the sophisticated product of *terroir*, (of the soil) of its New Orleans birthplace, "which is cosmopolitan in its nature, blending the characteristics of the American, French, Spanish, Italian, West Indian [devoid of African!], and Mexican." Interestingly, the multilingual Hearn gleaned much from his understanding of the local in what he identified as six distinct Creole dialects. He even published a small collection of proverbs called *Gombo Zhebes*, mixing food and language metaphors.

The soup or stew called *gombo* (gumbo) has become the quintessential poster child of culinary creolization, and no fewer than nine versions are provided in the cookbook Hearn assembled. The dish's name is thought to originate from the Central African (Angolan) term for okra, *ki ngombo*, but its foundational roux relies on fat and flour in a distinctively European style of preparation. Only two years later, Hearn's ideas about creole food underwent a further transformation when Hearn became resident on the French Caribbean island of Martinique. There he finally recognized the role of Africans and their descendants in creating creole cuisines, the mainstays of which he found were nearly identical to those of Louisiana, revealing that "By *mangé-Créole*, I refer only to the food of the people proper, the colored population, for the cuisine of the small class of wealthy whites is chiefly European, and devoid of local interest."[9]

A Global Historical Narrative

The following chapters use food as a means of mapping the contours of Caribbean history and, by association, the cultural and social dimensions of the planet's longest narrative of globalization. The Caribbean past was the product of global forces that brought together the appetites of four continents. We view globalization through the window of Caribbean cuisine by examining the power of people and knowledge in the early cultural confluence of Europeans, Asians, Africans, and the indigenous peoples of the Americas. What was the interplay of local and global as their stories unfolded?

Beginning in 1492, early European visitors and colonizers found new plants and animals common to the tropics of the Western Hemisphere. From the time of Columbus, foods circulated in the Atlantic world within the globalized context of maritime trade. The Columbian Exchange, a term coined by historian Alfred Crosby, emphasized the multidirectional and mutually transformative nature of these transfers. New lifestyles and cuisines also evolved from the movement of plants, animals, and microbes in the Atlantic. Not all effects were positive. Indigenous populations were decimated, even as the newest immigrants consumed their food knowledge and borrowed their foods.

This narrative pays particular attention to the African heritage of enslaved peoples during the Atlantic slave trade era, when their numbers eventually came to dominate the Euro-Caribbean colonizers. Foods and foodways were thus introduced both as a result of commercial interests and also, surreptitiously, as a means of resistance. Mapping the critical era of globalization must also include mapping capital, since the Atlantic period witnessed the earliest commoditization of global exchanges.[10] In the seventeenth and eighteenth centuries, new forms of domination and economic exploitation emerged with the plantation system designed to grow sugar.

Not only indigenous peoples, Europeans, and Africans were involved in culinary exchanges. Enslaved Africans dominated the cuisines. They brought Wolof, Bambara, Fulani, Akan, Ewe, Yoruba, Kongolese, and many other culinary traditions to the Caribbean table. Encounters included, first, the foods from Asia and, later, Asian cooks. The circulation of new wealth, arising particularly from the silver trade between the New World and East Asia, also knit together food communities spanning Pacific and Atlantic worlds, linking such disparate places as Indonesia and the Philippines with Cuba, India, Mauritius, Jamaica, and Trinidad. After slavery began to be abolished in the early nineteenth century, indentured laborers from South Asia and China were introduced, completing the global reach of culinary traditions brought to Caribbean waters from both east and west.

Enslaved Africans obviously were disadvantaged in their interactions on plantations, yet often managed to dominate the creole continuum. African vocabularies and foodstyles were exposed to similar social constraints. Africans held both the opportunity and motivation to maintain the structure of transplanted food preparation and the meaning assigned to new borrowings and old retentions. Their successful creation of unique Caribbean foodways through the dynamic processes of transformation and creolization reflected a surprisingly robust control over the cognitive domains of culinary practice, perhaps in part because cooking food was so embedded in aspects of non-material life, such as ritual, belief, and gendered relationships, and grounded in linguistic categories of social interaction. Shared foodways reiterated the conceptual unity of disparate African origins, fostered intergenerational links, and shaped variation into commonalities useful for covert resistance to slavery and oppression. Moreover, African-dominated cuisines were equally embedded in local environments, often not unlike those of the cooks' African homelands. Locally based creole cuisines characterized an adaptation to place-bound lives in the Caribbean. Thus the African-derived domains of local food knowledge provided resilient strategies of sustainable practices that resisted globalization and stood in sharp contrast to European vulnerability. Owing to a reliance on global imports, the poles of hunger and plenty continuously shaped the region's foodways.

Finally, a note about the title of this book: *Congotay* is a name given to the cassava porridge that sustained generations of Caribbean people. In some parts of the Caribbean, it is also a children's game and song wrought with moral lessons. *Congotay! Congotay!* in its varied meanings thus evokes the family transmission of African-derived foodways. Throughout the book, I have tried to read this kitchen lexicon "against the grain," suggesting the ways in which a hidden history of Caribbean women intimately shaped the earliest global encounters of our planet. Culinary knowledge and empowerment through consumption were early antiglobalization forces that argued for situating the critical meanings of historical experience in the local, everyday, and most basic gestures of shared humanity.

Notes

1. Collected between 1877 and 1885 by Lafcadio Hearn, *Gombo Zhebes: Little Dictionary of Creole Proverbs* (New York: Will H. Coleman, 1885).

2. Quoted in Andrew Salkey, *Anancy's Score* (London: Bogle-L'Ouverture, 1973), 8.

3. W.A.B. Musgrave, quoted in J.B. Andrews, "Ananci Stories," *Folk-Lore Record* 3, no. 1 (1880): 53–55.

4. John R. Rickford, *Dimensions of a Creole Continuum: History, Texts, and Linguistic Analysis of Guyanese Creole* (Palo Alto: Stanford University Press, 1987); see also Verene A. Shepherd and Glen L. Richards, eds., *Questioning Creole: Creolisation Discourses in Caribbean Culture* (Kingston, Jamaica: Ian Randle, 2002).

5. John R. Rickford, "Pidgens and Creoles," in *Oxford International Encyclopedia of Linguistics*, ed. William Bright, vol. 3 (1991): 224–228.

6. Quoted in John R. Rickford, "Preface and Editing of Two Papers by S.R. Richard Allsopp, 'The Case for Afrogenesis' and 'The Afrogenesis of Caribbean Creole Proverbs,'" *Society for Caribbean Linguistics Occasional Papers*, nos. 33–34 (2006): 3–52.

7. Michel Jajolet, sieur de la Courbe, *Premier voyage du sieur de la Courbe fait a la coste d'Afrique en 1685* (1688).

8. Lafcadio Hearn, *La Cuisine Creole: A Collection of Culinary Recipes From Leading Chefs and Noted Creole House-Wives, Who Have Made New Orleans Famous for Its Cuisine*, 2nd ed. (New Orleans: F.F. Hansell, 1885), Introduction.

9. Lafcadio Hearn, *Two Years in the French West Indies* (New York: Harper, 1903), 271.

10. "Mapping capital" is a term used by my Washington State University colleague Desiree Hellegers, who has applied it to the experiences of indigenous peoples in the Americas.

Map of the Caribbean
(Courtesy of University of Texas Libraries)

CONGOTAY! CONGOTAY!
A Global History
of Caribbean Food

ONE

Gastronomic Voyages

Magical Foods of the Atlantic World

During our passage, I first saw flying fishes, which surprised me very much; they used frequently to fly across the ship, and many of them fell on the deck. . . . The clouds appeared to me to be land, which disappeared as they passed along. This heightened my wonder; and I was now persuaded more than ever that I was in another world, and that every thing about me was magic.

—Olaudah Equiano, *The Interesting Narrative of the Life of Olaudah Equiano, Written by Himself*[1]

. . . For ordinary food, at its most sumptuous and exciting, was often illusion.

—Caroline Walker Bynum, *Holy Feast and Holy Fast*[2]

In the beginning, the Caribbean world *was* a magical world not only because fish could fly. The first peoples living on its shores imagined the sea to be inhabited by unseen spirits and ghosts, a gateway to the dead. The indigenous people of the Caribbean, like many Africans and Europeans across the Atlantic, envisioned a land of the dead across the vast waters. The western Atlantic Ocean moved in deep, dark, and mysterious currents, in contrast to the clear, calm, and protected turquoise waters of the Caribbean. Only the island of Barbados withstood the ocean's full fury from its position surrounded by Atlantic waters. The residents of other Caribbean islands, together with those living on the outer shores of the circum-Caribbean region, moved easily from one land perch to the next in their giant canoes dug out of grand silk-cotton trees. These carved vessels could hold seventy-five or eighty men and women as they maneuvered swiftly across the great distances between islands. Over the course of thousands of years, oceanic voyages had linked the Caribbean with Mesoamerica and with the South American mainland.

Flying fish and ships, 1707
(Courtesy of the John Carter Brown Library, Brown University)

South American peoples and their foods began to arrive in the region by about 6,000 years ago. Since about 500 BCE, voyages had interconnected the islands of the Lesser and Greater Antilles and brought farming to most island homes. The Taino of the Greater Antilles brought ideas of voyaging to their understanding of the cosmos. The underworld was a place of subterranean waters. Aquatic birds were representations of the Taino water goddess, Coatrisquie, who might unleash her powers in destructive ways. Even the night sky's stars and constellations were imagined as marine creatures: alligator, fish, crab, lobster, and mollusk swam in the sky. While they were at sea, the island Caribs of the Lesser Antilles would blow a great shell to announce their arrival with friendly intentions. Food offerings would be thrown overboard to remember those Caribs who had perished and now lived in huts under the sea. The saltiness of seawater came from the sweat and urine of the spirit Zemeen, who also dwelled there.[3] The Caribs in Dominica believed that two small rock islets off their coast turned into great canoes at night and carried the souls of ancestors out to sea.[4] They conceived of death itself as a voyage of the soul to islands of the afterworld, a place the European explorer Christopher Columbus claimed to know and offered to show to the people he mistakenly called Indians. But the Caribbean encounters between the indigenous peoples, their marvelous sea spirits, Columbus, and the Africans and Europeans who followed in his wake were anything *but* magical.

For the European sailor, the dark Atlantic waters had for centuries produced nightmares of monsters in boiling seas and a fear that a sailing ship that ventured too far might drop off the end of the earth itself. Phantoms were commonplace sightings by sailors, such as the Venetian merchant Alvise da Cada'mosto who made two voyages to Africa (1455–1456). He and other ship captains routinely believed they had observed mermaids and sometimes mermen. Captain Christopher Columbus claimed to have seen three such creatures off the coast of Hispaniola in 1493, when he wrote that they "came quite high out of the water."[5] Such sightings were not enough to deter sailors. Viking sailors and probably Basque fishermen had reached across the Atlantic at least half a millennium before Columbus, to establish communities in Newfoundland and possibly further south. The remains of Viking encampments and settlements dotted the shores of lands that would later be known as Greenland and Newfoundland.[6] From these northern reaches, fishermen provided Europe with a steady supply of dried and salted Atlantic codfish. Later the codfish was introduced to the enslaved Africans aboard slave ships, and salted cod became a staple food in New World cuisines after 1492. Salted cod was a favored food item that endured in Caribbean diets throughout the twentieth century. The popular presence of cod both in European religious foods and later in African diasporic cuisines provides testimony to the profound economic interests rooted in the mysterious North Atlantic waters five centuries before Columbus.

The western and central Atlantic waters were also respected and feared by the many Africans along the continent's western shores. Some envisioned the green ocean as a deity to be acknowledged by sacrifice and ritual. Rough waters, sandbars, and rocky coasts afforded relatively few safe harbors in West Africa. Atlantic waves broke hard on African shores and discouraged travel in the open seas. The southern Ijebu Yoruba, in what is contemporary Nigeria, recognized a group of water spirits called *awo* who could give birth to human children and were believed to affect the well-being of coastal communities. Those spirits lived in wondrous houses beneath the sea. Furthermore, words for fish and for history shared the same phoneme in several West African languages, emphasizing the interrelated ideas of continuity and change and also their association with watery realms.[7]

While the Edo and Yoruba, other Nigerian cultural groups, reckoned with the forces of Olokun and Yemaja, god and goddess of the sea's fertility and wealth, Fante fishermen farther west on the Gold Coast (today's Ghana) made promises to the sea by building shrines. The sea's powers inspired groups of warriors called *asafo*. Indeed, the Atlantic became a symbol of Fante military aggression and conquest, just as the sea challenges the land in the movements of the waves. A Fante proverb asserted that "the sea came to find the rocks already there."[8] For other Africans living southeast of the Yoruba, the expanse of dark, central Atlantic waters was thought to be so great that no human could ever cross it to reach a land of the dead. They were not the only ones to conceive of the place of the dead "beyond the waters." The Mende of Sierra Leone believed the abode of spirits to be underwater. So did the Bini, whose sixteenth-century divine ruler's powers were symbolized by legs portrayed as mudfish, a creature with the extraordinary ability to both walk and swim, thus moving easily between the realms of the living and the ancestors.

The sea brought the Portuguese and other Europeans, who attracted wealth and power from the spirits. Other coastal Africans on both sides of the Atlantic came to recognize and even worship the beautiful, but seductively dangerous Mami Wata, a water spirit honored in shrines filled with the exotica from overseas.[9] The sea represented a meeting site and a place for the transformation of self. It is perhaps in the earliest fifteenth-century Euro-African encounters that Mami Wata emerged from mermaid imagery for active duty as mesmerizing spirit/deity.[10] The Ibo (Nigerian) shrines to the water spirit Mami Wata reflected a configuration that combined local and borrowed, familiar and foreign, in its images, powers, and peoples. Water spirits like Mami Wata were often thought to accumulate great wealth in their aquatic kingdoms. No wealth was greater than that derived from the sea.

The Europeans who sailed the seas to reach the African continent and then the Caribbean in the fifteenth century were first imagined to be magical beings from this watery world beyond the living. After 1508, the voyages of European slave ships across the unknown Atlantic would trace what would be known as the Middle Passage. These voyages would harbor, for African and European imaginations alike, still darker and more unspeakable secrets of the dead in the horrors of the floating traffic in human beings. The movement of ships from Europe to Africa and across the Atlantic to the Caribbean eventually marked the outlines of latitude and longitude. It mapped the evils of the Atlantic slave trade and created the first diaspora or dispersal of cultures from Eurasia and Africa. More than anything else, these Atlantic "highways" linked the globe's continents by transporting peoples and their foods as commodities and cultures.

Gastronomic Voyages

First the Iberians (Portuguese and Spanish), then others (Dutch, French, English, Danes) made the voyages. The ships increased in size and their landings in the Caribbean irrevocably changed the local landscapes and the worlds they entered. By the eighteenth century, a global experience had been created from the Caribbean encounters. Ned Ward, who ran the King's Head Tavern near Gray's Inn in London between 1699 and 1731, called the eighteenth-century ship the "great Wooden Horse of Nature . . . to ride in post-haste from one World to the other."[11] The patterns of these voyages made the Caribbean a kind of global meeting place over and over again. The cultural networks and trading systems of land and sea met in the Caribbean. These encounters were heard in the creolized words spoken, just as they were evident in the foods that the peoples of the Caribbean tasted. Their flavors and aromas were experienced in the global varieties of culinary expression that joined Caribbean island daily life. Improvised foodways held on to the familiar and embraced the new, transforming taste and technique. Through expanding global encounters, the peoples of four continents cooked and ate meals in which cultural meanings were created, shared, and sustained across generations. Metaphorically and materially, the culinary magic of the Caribbean itself took place in the great cauldron of imagined modernity.

The Caribbean was reached via a complex network of water highways or shipping lanes, as they would be known. Mixing metaphors of land and sea, the Europeans were to notice that the ships' masts in the harbors were like "forests."[12] The fish were stacked in the harbor ports and looked like stacks of wood, cut planks. While limited and sporadic contacts between the far reaches of the Atlantic world may have preceded Columbus, it was the late fifteenth-century European voyages that would forever alter the Western Hemisphere's peoples and cultures, including their cuisines. Although our popular concept of world history conjures up land-based battles over territory, kings and commoners in field and factory, and communities connected by cities and states, our shared maritime past was universally more influential in knitting together what historians have been able to identify as humanity's global experience. How this happened first in the Caribbean, the roles that food played in the formation of a global community, and the culinary consequences of early encounters are the focus of this book. While few historical narratives can convey the tastes and flavors of the past, the story of food comes closest to the task of reconstructing lived history.

In the Wake of Columbus

When Admiral Columbus "sailed the ocean blue" in 1492, the Atlantic crossing was hardly a voyage to be remembered for its culinary delights. The sailors on board the *Niña*, *Pinta*, and *Santa Maria* were served a monotonous diet typical of late fifteenth-century seafaring. The basic foodstuff was the horrid but essential sea biscuit, a twice-baked bread of wheat flour that became so hard and so infested with weevils that its consumption could become nearly as injurious as the alternative of persistent hunger. Indeed, wrote the admiral's son, "And what with the heat and the dampness, even the [sea] biscuit was

Ship's biscuit, c. 1784
(Courtesy of the Maritime Museum, Greenwich, London)

so full of worms that, God help me, I saw many wait until nightfall to eat the porridge made of it so as not to see the worms."[13] Notwithstanding the critics of maritime cuisines, these ship's biscuits would eventually be mass-produced by the Royal Navy's bake houses, providing each sailor with a pound per day in the eighteenth century. The weevils did not disappear; they would be known affectionately as "bargemen."[14] And sea biscuits became an essential ingredient of "lobscouse," the maritime hash. In the French world, the *pain de mer* (hardtack) would be produced as colonial travel food using steam-powered flour mills in Nantes.[15]

At the start of his voyages, Columbus took on barrels of the biscuits produced by Genoa bakers, plus water, red wine, olives, olive oil, molasses, goat cheese from Gomera (in the Canary Islands), honey, raisins, rice, garlic, almonds, various dry legumes (chickpeas, lentils, and black-eyed peas), tough, pickled and salted pork and beef, salted sardines, and dried salt cod. The crew supplemented their preserved meat ration on board by purchasing rats (called "millers") from the ship's rat catcher, by catching flying fish and sharks when waters were calm, and by capturing the generally detestable seabirds when finally close to shore. Historians have closely examined the culinary remains of sunken ships, such as the *Mary Rose*, which sank in 1545 and contained hard biscuit, salted meat, peas, hard salted cheese, and presumably many drowned rats. More than 200 years later, the daily rations at sea differed only slightly: hard biscuit, peas, salted fish and meat, butter, cheese, oatmeal, and beer were still the fate of every sailor on board His Majesty's ships in 1815.[16]

The food was stored in the driest part of the damp and leaking ship's hold until it was time for it to be prepared in the ship's galley. There in the galley or above board, ovens were set in sand in an open firebox called a *fogon*. A screen protected the backside from harsh winds. Since there was no chimney, the flavors of almost everything cooked below deck were smoky and dark. Food was mostly boiled in large copper kettles and iron cauldrons and served to the sailors in large communal wooden bowls. Meals were eaten with the hands, not with forks and spoons. Each Spanish sailor carried a personal knife to cut large pieces of meat, which were relatively rare. At the end of the nineteenth century, knives and spoons were still prohibited by the British navy, which feared disgruntled crew members' use of them as weapons.

European tastes and food practices were centered on the experience of a meal as communion. Food was shared and not eaten with strangers. Trade with the Mediterranean and Eurasia had brought spices to the European table. European Catholic diets during the Middle Ages and Renaissance were restricted in the consumption of meat, a "hot" food thought to heat up the body and the mind, thus leading one to stray from the spiritual path. For the purpose of fasting, fish was considered a "cool" rather than a "hot" food, and consequently Wednesdays, Fridays, and Saturdays, plus the forty days of Lent and other holy days, all became fish days. Sexual intercourse and the eating of meat were forbidden during such times. Two main meals were served daily, except during the religious fasts of the church calendar, which numbered nearly half the days of the year. Their purpose was not only spiritual or social but economic as well; fish days were intended as a boon to the fishing economy. Fishing the waters of the Atlantic thus reinforced the dietary restrictions of most of Europe.

Fishing African Shores

Preserved fish was also a fundamental part of the West and Central African diets. Hot smoked, dried, fermented, and salted fish were used as flavoring in the wet cooking of stews that accompanied almost every form of starchy staple. Preservation techniques inhibited the growth of mold and bacteria, allowing the fish to be traded inland from the ocean and outward from river environments. Archaeological excavations have revealed the widespread consumption of large quantities of fish from streams, channels, pools, swamps, and reedy estuaries. In the African empires of the tenth century, fish was a key component of the cuisine.[17] This reliance on fish would have allowed an easy transition to new dietary restrictions brought by the spread of Islam between the twelfth and fourteenth centuries.

At the time of the Muslim Moroccan traveler Ibn Battuta's journey to Mali in 1353, fish was part of the daily diet. Along the Niger and other great riverine systems of the continent, Nile perch and carp (tilapia) were common, but subjected to a variety of preparation and cooking techniques. Both dried shrimp and fish were also ground into a powder that was used to thicken soups and stews. The smoking and drying of fish was generally the activity of specialized households and categorized as women's work in coastal West Africa. Among the Ga-Dangmes of the Gold Coast (Ghana) today, canoe fisheries and processing activities are still cemented through kinship relationships that support the production of the herring-like sardinella. Women smokers, who own ovens for smoking, also rent them to younger family members, who obtain fish from husbands or other relatives. Centuries before, the Dutch trader Willem Bosman described several of the species of fish (in this case, shark) caught for inland trade:

> The third sort [are] *Hayes* or *Requiens*, by some (though utterly wrong) named Sea-Dogs; for they are not in the least like them. They are very thick as well as very long, some of them betwixt twenty and thirty foot; their Head is broad, flat, and their Snout very sharp-pointed; as to the rest they are very ugly. This Fish is the *Negroes* best and most common Food. They are daily taken on the Gold Coast in great shoals. The *Europeans* never eat them, by Reason of the toughness of their Flesh; to remedy which the *Negroes* lay them a rotting and stinking seven or eight Days; after which they are greedily eaten as a delicacy, and a great Trade is driven in this Commodity to the In-land Country.[18]

Bosman also noted the early use of fish for flavoring along the Gold Coast, where "Their common Food is a Pot full of Millet boiled . . . over which they pour a little Palm-Oyl, with a few boiled herbs, to which they add a stinking Fish."[19] Along Senegambian waters, the white grouper (known locally as false cod or *thiof*) was similarly preferred for flavoring and processed for inland trade. Today thiof is a threatened species due to commercial overfishing. None of the African Atlantic fish could compare with the impact of cod.

Fishing boats, Cape Coast, Ghana
(Photograph by Candice Goucher)

Sailing with Salted Cod

The trade in codfish was especially lucrative because the 200 or more species of Atlantic codfish were abundant and could be easily and successfully preserved. The cod eventually became a Christian symbol, an ancient sign of membership in the faith and associated with the baptismal immersion in water. While the Vikings and Norsemen had hung the fish out to dry in the frosty winter air, allowing it to become as durable as a wooden plank, to be chewed like hardtack, the Basques salted the cod before drying, with the notable result that it lasted longer than most men at sea. In Europe, the fish also became a symbol associated with departure and travel.[20] Most codfish live in cold waters, in contrast to the tropical seas of the South Atlantic Ocean. More specifically, they spawn and feed where the cold waters meet warmer currents, such as where the Gulf Stream mingles with Arctic and Labrador waters. The maritime search for codfish preceded the voyages of Columbus and lasted well into the twentieth century. Eventually the codfish trade would support the purchase of enslaved Africans, who ironically would be fed the salted fish as a mainstay of slave food. Scholars disagree on the origins of the words for codfish. In the Caribbean, the older French word *morue* (meaning "prostitute") is used, or the Portuguese *bacalhau* (Spanish *bacalao*). Salt fish, as salted cod came to be known on Anglophone islands,

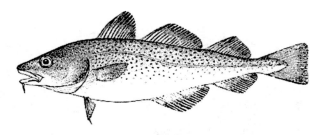

Atlantic cod
(Courtesy of the US Department of the Interior, Fish and Wildlife Service)

carried double meanings associated with the taste and smell of female genitalia.[21] In the English, French, and Spanish Caribbean, salt fish held sexual and spiritual connotations.[22] Restored by soaking and boiling, the fleshy, but preserved codfish flaked apart and then was further enlivened by spices and sauces of each cook's choosing—a kind of symbolic but secular transmutation.

The growth of the Atlantic slave trade paralleled the growth of the trade in salted cod. New Englanders in North America joined the Newfoundland, French, and Basque fishermen in supplying dried and salted cod to foreign markets. The evolution of their market destinations was neither simple nor straightforward. The history of the North American cod fishing industry involved the complex narrative of competing business interests and conflicts between the French, Spanish, Portuguese, Dutch, and English and their colonies. Facing trade restrictions initially, British merchants were allowed to sell salt cod directly to foreign ports by the end of the sixteenth century. After the world's first global conflict, the Seven Years' War (1756–1763), the French lost their Newfoundland fishing rights and New Englanders became the international commercial powerhouses. Eventually salted cod became "the Meat of All the Slaves in All the West Indies."[23] As Richard Vines had observed earlier (1647), "[In the Caribbean] men are so intent upon planting sugar that they had rather buy food at very dear rates, then produce it by labor, so infinite is the profit of sugar works."[24] Salted cod could be sold to African ports or to merchants on the Caribbean islands in exchange for sugar, molasses, or slaves, sometimes legally and at other times as contraband. Consumed on plantations or ships, the preserved cod became a mainstay of maritime and slave diets. Not only salted cod but also pickerel filled in for the "chronic scarcity of fresh and tender flesh" in New World diets, including those of early European communities.[25] In parts of New England, nearly half of all the population between the ages of sixteen and forty-five were engaged in fishing and processing of fish, much of which took place in floating fish factories. Some 45 percent of all exports went to the West Indies, despite West Indies cod having taken on a reputation for being poor in quality. Known as "Jamaican" or "Barbados" cod, the inferior trash fish was smaller, sometimes broken, and imperfectly processed, only partially dried and oversalted for the humid tropical destinations.

Yet this maligned fish was traded for another foodstuff, the valuable molasses, which was the by-product of the refining of sugarcane. Merchants brought molasses back to New England. There in the dozen or more distilleries of Rhode Island and Boston, molasses was made into rum and eventually sold to West Africa in exchange for slaves destined for the Caribbean sugar plantations. Cod and rum soon joined gold as local currencies in West Africa. The voyage itself was far from pleasant; indeed, in the words of the merchant Dalby Thomas of the Royal African Company, it was "a filthy voyage as well as a laborious one."[26] Once the ships reached Africa, the transactions brought profits. For example, on the eighth day of June in 1733, a New England ship bought "A Man Boy" for two pieces of cloth, three pounds of sugar, two and a quarter barrels of gunpowder, and ninety-three gallons of rum at the Gold Coast port of Anamabo.[27] On the other side of the Atlantic (on the Caribbean island of Antigua), a young male slave might sell for "six heads of rum and nineteen barrells [sic] of sugar and one large bag of cotton."[28] Codfish also traveled on these ships, feeding sailors and slaves. The cod became a symbol of capitalism and its image adorned state seals, town emblems, postage stamps, coins, and every sort of public and private furnishing in North America. Just as the known world doubled in size during the sixteenth century, the amount of codfish caught and exported increased by fivefold thereafter. The global appetite for the salty fare was born.

African Salt Production

Trans-Saharan exchanges in West Africa included a vigorous trade in salt. Salt was valued as a commodity and, when mined in blocks, was a currency from ancient times. In 1352, Ibn Battuta arrived in the salt-mining town of Taghaza, situated at the site of a dry, salt lake bed. People there constructed buildings out of salt. Ibn Battuta also described the salt mines worked by slaves. A load of salt (two slabs) would be loaded on camels and exchanged for gold.

Salt was used as a flavoring and food preservative. Ancient Egyptians and peoples on both sides of the Mediterranean, including the Basque cod fishermen, had long traded salted fish. Egyptians used salt in the form of natron, thought to be a divine salt, for salting fish and fowl and for their mummification of human bodies. In Africa's tropical and arid regions, salts were needed for survival; rock salt became a precious commodity used to replenish the body's salts that were easily lost in sweating. The many dried salt lakes and salt mines produced a variety of salts, with varying flavors. Lake Chad offered a particularly abundant source of natron to West and Central Africans.

Africans in coastal regions also recovered salt from the sea at places in the Senegambia, Gold Coast, and elsewhere along sub-Saharan Africa's shores. The evidence from historical linguistics suggests that the salt trade was an important factor in creating interregional networks of trade between the coast and interior.[29] Early European travelers observed its manufacture and trade. Seawater could be boiled away, leaving the salt to be collected. Solar evaporation also was used to trap the crystals from the ocean water, capturing the salty crust left behind. Pressed between grass mats, this salt was shaped into cakes. Finally, potash salts could be made from leaching plant or wood ash soaked in water. All of the salts produced were valued, sometimes mixed together, and traded long distances to flavor local foods. Africans carried their techniques for salt production across the Atlantic.

Caribbean Salt Production

The centrality of salted fish and meats in the Caribbean trade meant that salt production would be critical to the success of local industries. The Portuguese, who may have observed West African salt producers in the fifteenth century, reported that some groups in the Senegambia had never seen or tasted salt due to its high value on the coast. During the seventeenth century, the Dutch took the lead. So central were they in preserving food that the Dutch word for brine, *pekel*, slipped into common usage. The Dutch harvested sea salt on the island of Bonaire using enslaved African labor and expertise. A solar production facility owned by Cargill (an international producer of salt and other foods) still exists there. On the island of Inagua, the southernmost piece of land along the Bahamian archipelago, millions of pounds of salt are still recovered annually from salt ponds. As the water in the pools of captured seawater evaporates in the sun, the heavy brine solidifies overnight and then melts during the day, leaving behind a crystallized bed. Salt islands of earlier centuries also included Turks and Caicos, Anguilla, and Tortuga. Their proximity to the cod-fishing regions of the North Atlantic made the islands valuable possessions. Treating local and imported foodstuffs by salting, brining, or pickling helped preserve the foods brought across the seas while creating a taste for salty or sour foods in Caribbean cuisines. Soon other sauces and gravies were made from peppers, fruits, and vegetables, swimming in heavily salted solutions with vinegar added. The endeavors to preserve fish and meat were not the only struggles for preservation.

Salt solar evaporation pans, Bonaire
(Courtesy of WorldWide TravelGuide b.v., The Netherlands)

Maritime Encounters

Shared maritime culture remained at the heart of an increasingly globalized modernity. Ships carried people and foods as commodities. Voyages were central to shaping a shared experience of food, technology, and culture. Atlantic history became a history of gastronomic encounters between Europeans, indigenous peoples of the Americas, and Africans, both free and enslaved. From the time of Columbus in the late fifteenth century, thousands of large and small ships continually searched across the Atlantic for treasures as valuable as cod. Early journeys were dangerous, and the stakes needed to be high enough to attract participants. Pound for pound, more valuable than pearls or precious metals were the much-sought-after spices. The search for wealth was a treasure hunt for spices, the taste of the faraway, and other goods. The journeys took ships and their crews into the dark Atlantic waters, despite the stories of boiling seas and mermaids, and delivered them to the turquoise Caribbean.

Even before the passengers reached distant shores, dangers awaited them on board. Diseases, fevers, and pathogens of all sorts were invisible passengers on the ships. The most dreaded sailor's disease was scurvy. Ironically, it was dietary in nature, caused by inadequate consumption of ascorbic acid (vitamin C)—often the result of long sea voyages. Afflicted sailors suffered swollen gums, wounds that failed to heal, lethargy, and a malady that one sixteenth-century sailor described as the eating away of the "flesh of the legs [when touched by] a man's fingers, the pit remaining without filling up in a good space." Scurvy was regarded as a "strange and cruell disease" on the long sea voyages during the sixteenth century.[30] Its cause in vitamin C deficiency was not identified through a controlled clinical study until 1747. The cure would be a couple of lemons or, in the mid-nineteenth century, the somewhat less successful substitution of West Indian lime juice, which had a lower vitamin C content. Henceforth, the sailors in the British navy would often be called "limeys."[31] Maritime food traditions spanned the broad reach of European voyagers, from Spanish and Dutch to English, French, and Danish sailors charged with keeping crew and cargo alive. Their concerns about diet and nutrition helped shape the culinary pantry of Caribbean kitchens.

Other medicinal cures were brought on board to treat the fevers, disease, and motion sickness that inevitably struck during the voyage. These medicines included sugar as well as ginger and other tropical plants. Other dangers lurked in the casks used to store liquids on board ships. Lead poisoning from the fittings of stills used to manufacture drinks contaminated the concoctions consumed by sailors, causing "dry bellyache." As late as the eighteenth century, nearly half of those seafaring Europeans leaving the continent for Africa and beyond would never return, despite the measures they took to protect their health and well-being. Lack of food was said to be a major reason for defection to piracy. Sailors who had suffered shortages of their rotten provisions followed the pirate's path, in part by eating and drinking "in a wanton and riotous Way."[32]

The dangers experienced by sailors were more than matched by the epidemiological devastation the Europeans would inflict upon the indigenous populations with whom they came in contact. Peoples of the Western Hemisphere, as it turned out, had absolutely no immunity against such European diseases as swine flu. Eventually more than 90 percent of local populations would be decimated by the contact. The historian Alfred Crosby coined the phrase "Columbian Exchange" to describe the mutuality of movements of diseases, plants, and animals between hemispheres, perhaps underplaying the inherent violence in the relationships that were constructed in the wake of Columbian voyages.[33] Yet the earliest encounters were remarkably peaceful, causing Columbus and others to muse that the seemingly docile, friendly, and trusting demeanor of the Indians could work to the advantage of their conquerors; and so it sometimes did. Although the indigenous people of the Caribbean too often became victims of genocide, they also shaped the encounters and patterns of settlement and subsistence in significant ways.

All manner of fruits and vegetables, meats and spices brought forth new tastes and unfamiliar ideas. Even before its use as a preventative against scurvy, citrus fruit had a magical reputation. In Roman North Africa, tradition says that a certain king discovered that limes consumed prior to poisoning by a deadly snake protected a man otherwise destined for death. Romans began to preserve the fruit in earthenware jars filled with salt. The lime was also known as an aphrodisiac, and some West Indians still believe that burning its rind will bring back love lost. This was probably not the sort of magic the Spanish colonial governor Nicholas Ovando had in mind when he planted the first citrus trees on the island of Hispaniola. His plan was to establish a refreshment station for ships on their way to the real Indies, not to the "West Indies," Columbus's mistaken attribution.

The European contact with coastal Africans presents a different story. There the Europeans were disadvantaged by their inability to withstand tropical heat and disease. Unlike Africans, who—once they survived infancy and childhood—developed some degree of immunity, adult European sailors had acquired no immunity to such maladies as malaria and sleeping sickness, and many died quickly of these and other unidentified fevers. By contrast, Africans had been exposed to most of the same Old World diseases known to Europeans and, like Europeans, had developed immunity by the time they reached adulthood. Thus, Africans had less to lose on the epidemiological front. Moreover, the Africans' immunity to tropical and Old World diseases no doubt contributed to their survival as enslaved peoples brought to the New World to replace the labor once supplied by decimated Native American populations. Essential for successful African resistance were the culinary partnerships with the peoples they replaced.

The First Voyagers: Indigenous Cuisines

The indigenous peoples of the Caribbean, among them the Arawaks, Tainos, and Caribs, subsisted on diets that included foods fished, farmed, hunted, trapped, and gathered from their varied and often lush island environments.[34] They were also immigrants—their ancestors having journeyed 1,000 to 5,000 years earlier by sea from the South American mainland, the Central American coasts, and possibly even the far reaches of North America. From prehistoric times Caribbean peoples exploited plants, together with land creatures and water species from shallow marine and intertidal sites. The precolonial Tainos were especially fond of the manatee and iguana and may have eaten the giant galliwasp (a large lizard) to extinction on some islands. Fish and bread were among the first local foods Columbus encountered. On Thursday, December 13, 1492, while anchored off the coast of Hispaniola, Columbus described the Caribbean gifts of food in his log:

After they were calmed down, they all went to their houses and each one brought food. They brought the bread of niamas [or manioc], which are tubers and look like large radishes. These are planted in all their fields and are their staff of life. They make bread from them and boil and roast them, and they taste like chestnuts—anyone who eats them will say that they taste like chestnuts. They gave my men bread and fish and whatever they had.[35]

The royal physician appointed to accompany Columbus's second expedition, Diego Alvarez Chanca, was also the first to write extensively about the flora, fauna, and peoples. He wrote of Cuba: "Always the land was of the same beauty and the fields very green and full of an infinity of fruits, as red as scarlet, and everywhere there was the perfume of flowers and the singing of birds, very sweet."[36] Chanca observed a native fishing technique that employed a certain fish fastened at the tail with cords and thrown in the water, whereupon the fish would attach to another fish with its suckers, before the hunters pulled it back aboard their canoe.

Two centuries later, Jean Baptiste Labat (a Frenchman who lived and traveled in the Caribbean between 1694 and 1705) described the Caribs of Dominica cooking coffer-fish, "set [directly] across the fire between the wood and the embers in higgledy-piggledy fashion."[37] (This meal was served with the local fare of hot cassava bread and stews of crab and pepper sauce.) In addition to fish, the Caribs also ate turtles, dogs fattened on fish, tame birds such as herons and ducks, rabbits, pigeons, bread, and fruits. The island staples were brought originally from the mainland of South America to the fields of the Tainos and Arawaks: cassava (*Manihot esculenta*), sweet potato (*Ipomoea batatas*), arrowroot (*Maranta arundinacea*), tannia or cocoyam (*Xanthosoma sagittifolium*), and yampi (*Dioscorea trifida*), another type of yam. Most foods were mixed with either cassava or maize gruel or baked into cakes. Home gardens produced squash or pumpkins (*Cucurbita spp.*), beans (*Phaseolus spp.*), peanuts or groundnuts (*Arachis hypogaea*), tomatoes, pineapples, avocados, and chili peppers (*Capsicum spp.*).

Having employed the Mesoamerican agricultural techniques of slash and burn, Native Americans in the Caribbean developed technologies for fertilizing the soil and building dams and artificial fish ponds, thereby enhancing their more regular food supplies of snails, shellfish, barnacles, grubs, gull and turtle eggs, and tropical fish. Life revolved around garden cycles. Planting was accomplished using a sharpened digging stick. Stone alignments found in gardens in the Turks and Caicos and in the Dominican Republic were used to track solstice and star movements that, in turn, guided the planting regimens.

Because the circum-Caribbean was a transitional zone between the tropics of South America and the temperate lands to the north, the food plants of both regions found their way into island cuisines. Peruvian potatoes were more difficult to grow outside of their mountain homelands, but crops such as the South American sweet potato were widely cultivated. Cocoa was highly valued as a beverage, and the beans even served as a medium of exchange in some parts of the region. Cassava or taro (manioc) was a staple from Brazil that yielded more food per acre than any other crop wherever it was planted. Its roots, when ground, were used to make a flour, and the pulp could be used to produce an alcoholic beverage. The writings collected by Richard Hakluyt about Sir Francis Drake's stopover in the West Indies (1585–1586) described the "Cassavi bread, made of cassava roots, very white and savourie."[38] Like the other members of the *Euphorbiaceae* family, the cassava root contains a poison (toxic levels of cyanogenic glucosides) that protects the bitter plant from insect attack and is released when the root is cooked or exposed to the air. The poison must be removed by methods of grating and squeezing before the plant becomes edible. In the case of cassava beer, women also prepared the pulp by chewing it and taking care to spit it out and not swallow the juice, thus adding saliva to the brew. In fact, with the exception of corn—called *maiz* by the Taino and introduced from the mainland by about 110—all of the staple crops of the pre-Columbian Caribbean grew underground. Early sustenance came from roots, not grains, and food mostly foraged and hunted, to complete a diet of small game, mollusks, turtles, and fish.

Fishing the Prehistoric Caribbean

Human groups were present in the Caribbean by 4000 BCE or earlier (the island of Trinidad was connected to the mainland until about 6000 BCE). Many archaic diets are inferred on the basis of stone tools and ceramics, carbonized remains of flora and fauna, and shell middens. In some parts of the Caribbean, such as the Bahamas, marine fish constituted more than 80 percent of the local (Lucayan, in this case) diet as discovered in archaeological sites. The early prehistoric diets, which were incomplete without meat, gave way to marine-based culinary traditions, as human populations increased and indigenous land mammal populations declined in the millennium before Columbus. The sea that delivered early peoples to their island homes was not forgotten. It is probable that the peoples whom Columbus encountered also preserved their own local fish by salting. We know that the Mayan salt-fish industry contributed to the region's trade in fish, some of which was also sun-dried, roasted, or smoked. The origins of the Taino can be traced to northern South America, where archaeologists have unearthed clay cooking pots, dating from at least 5,000 years ago, suggesting that at least some food was boiled—cassava gruel, for example. These people carried their cooking pots with them, down the Orinoco River, through the Guianas to the Lesser Antilles and all the way to Puerto Rico, by 100 BCE. Many food items were smoked, including meat and chilis, foods that were also wrapped in plant leaves with insecticidal qualities. Liming (soaking or cooking in an alkaline solution) was another technique of preservation employed in maize-dough production. Both meat and fish were high-status items in the diet. Some meals might also be liquid, such as drinks of fermented maize and water, known from the period of European contact and chronicled in later times. Seafood included a kind of catfish, mullet, herring, mackerel, shark, rayfish, dogfish, crayfish, shrimp, mussel, clam, oyster, crab, conch, and turtle. In Dominica, as Labat observed, "[apart from crabs] they eat nothing that is cooked in water; everything is roasted or smoked."[39] Techniques for grilling fish and meats were prized culinary arts.

Early European Chroniclers

The Europeans first encountering the new species of fish and animals in the Caribbean often renamed the strange creatures in order to associate them with familiar home foods. The new fish became "mountain mullet" or "salmon of the West Indies" and found favor. Flying fish and snapper were good fish (fatty and sweet), whereas the early settlers found crabs and shark (thought to be predators and scavengers) most disagreeable.[40] The term "buccaneer" (*boucane, boucanier* in French) came from the Arawakan word *buccan*, a wooden frame for smoking meat, and was used to describe European hunters, some of whom sailed the Caribbean as privateers outside the control of colonial authority. Buccaneers lived on the unclaimed islands and coasts, where they often hunted the green sea turtles (*Chelonia mydas*) and the hawksbill (*Eretmochelys imbricate*) for their meat and for the valuable tortoise shells destined to adorn European trinkets and cutlery; by the mid-nineteenth century, these species were nearly extinct on some beach habitats, even as turtle soup became the rage in European taverns. Buccaneers and others relied heavily on indigenous knowledge of local marine and terrestrial life. The Europeans observed the Taino Indians eating "large, fat spiders, white worms that breed in rotten wood, and other decayed objects." The agave worm was a plump delicacy, as was the flying ant. The local zamia bread, made of cassava roots, was allowed to become blackened, wormy, and fermented, the Europeans observed, as a means of ridding the plant of its harmful toxics. Columbus had noted how the versatile maize was "most tasty, boiled, roasted, or ground into flour," and he may have carried kernels back to Europe as seeds.[41] The creature called iguana (a large tree lizard) was likewise approved for consumption during Lent and on Fridays, because it was sometimes found around water and therefore considered a "fish." Columbus's sailors reportedly found iguana to be "white, soft and tasty." During the next century, sailors on Drake's West Indian voyage responded similarly to the turtles and "guanos" on the island of Cuba. These creatures and the "little beastes like cattes" were pronounced "verie good meate."[42] Some meat had no European counterpart. Yet the coatimundi, armadillo, quam, currasow, cockrecoes, paca, and curlews might find favor as a "peculiar delicacy" among meat-eating buccaneers, for whom meat was an expensive luxury and closely associated with masculinity.[43] While the Europeans commonly looked down upon the cuisines they encountered, after a century the native peoples were still providing the "visitors" with water, "Cassado" bread, potatoes, and plantain fruit.[44] The Taino cassava bread would come to be called the "bread of the conquest," as native peoples supplied labor and foods as tribute, thus forcibly contributing their foodways to the hungry colonial cultures.

Magical Fruits of Paradise

Europeans tasted various fruits for the first time during Columbus's voyages. Pineapple (*Ananas comosus*) was described by the admiral, and later its virtues were extolled by Fernandez de Oviedo, who called it the most beautiful fruit he had ever seen. By the early sixteenth century, green pineapples were being packed on ships and, with good sailing, reaching European shores nicely ripened for the delight of kings and nobles. The Spanish king Ferdinand II declared the one and only pineapple he ate (in 1516) to be the best thing he had ever tasted. On the other hand, Charles V of France refused to taste a pineapple, although he reported favorably on its wonderful fragrance. The pineapple eventually became extremely popular, as witnessed by the number of wooden chairs and other furnishings on both sides of the Atlantic that were carved and decorated with pineapple motifs that symbolized the tropical abundance and hospitality afforded the "visitors." Other fruits first encountered by the Europeans in the Caribbean included papaya (*Carica papaya*), mamey (*Mammea americana*), and guava (*Psidium guajava*); vegetables included both common beans (*Phaseolus vulgaris*) and lima beans (*Phaseolus lunatis*), as well as the ubiquitous corn. The early Europeans eagerly ate some of the Caribbean foods and fed others to their pigs.

None of these Native American foodstuffs attracted the attention of the Europeans more than spices. Spices were rare ingredients in culinary flavoring and were also used medicinally. Known to Europe as a luxury import from tropical Asia, sugar was one such "spice." There were many others, highly sought for their real and imagined properties. Not all foodstuffs were what they seemed. Thinking he had reached the East Indies, Columbus claimed to have found Chinese rhubarb, a plant used medicinally, and he even brought back to Europe some cuttings of the roots of the common garden rhubarb plant that he had mistaken for the rare medicinal one. On his second voyage, Columbus also claimed to have found "different kinds of wild spices that could be brought to perfection by cultivation, such as fine-colored cinnamon (though bitter to the taste), ginger, [and] pepper."[45] In fact, Columbus found neither aromatic cinnamon nor ginger; both spices were native to the East Indies, not the West.

Columbus's expectations and limited knowledge of plants influenced his impressions. He complained that the trees were "as different from those of our country as day is from night, and the same may be said of the fruit, the weeds, the stones and everything else."[46] The fruits of *Capsicum*, called peppers of the Indies, became pervasive food items that significantly altered cuisines around the world. Originally grown as wild plants in the Americas as early as 5000 BCE, at least four varieties of these chili peppers had been domesticated by Native Americans by the time of Columbus's arrival. Europeans and others found that chilis were cheap and easy to grow, and they spread initially in the popular rather than the elite cultures of Africa, Europe, and Asia. Once they took hold, peppers remained.

Only one of the chili pepper species, the *Capsicum chinense*, also known as Scotch bonnet (now thought to be a cousin of the habanero, which has a different pod type), was found originally in the Caribbean (in Cuba). The others spread to the islands from South and Central America, though how early is not known. Early voyagers may have brought them in their canoes, but it is also possible that birds, not people, spread the wild cultigens. By 1492, indigenous people living in the Caribbean had domesticated multiple species of the native plant of tropical South America. The active (pungent) ingredient in the fruit obstructs the perception of sour and bitter, thereby further altering tastes around the world. But chilis were not only used in food; they were employed as weapons as well. During the attack on Columbus's fort in Santo Domingo, chili smoke was thrown into combat areas as the chief ingredient in a kind of chemical weapon. Mostly without violence, the unforgiving heat of the chili pepper would conquer the cuisines of five continents, where today it is eaten daily by more than one-quarter of the world's peoples.

The genus *Capsicum* is of the family *Solanaceae*, which also includes the tomato (*Solanum spp.*), a fruit probably first encountered by Europeans in their contact with Aztec cooks. The *Capsicum* provided but a few of the provocative flavors of this family. Others family members were spices such as *Pimenta dioica*, or "allspice," a plant that Jamaica planter Bryan Edwards called "one of the most elegant productions in nature," and vanilla (*Vanilla planifolia*), which comes from the cured black pod of a tropical orchid native to Mesoamerica.[47] The outer coating of seeds of the *anatto* (*Bixa orellana*), gave a distinctive red coloring and flavoring to many foods. It later became a substitute food coloring for transplanted Africans accustomed to seeing their stews take on the reddish color of the palm oil in which meat was originally cooked on the African continent.

Early European sailors encountered many strange and magical substances. Tobacco (*Nicotiana rustica*) was smoked or ingested as a religious drug. Gonzalo Fernández de Oviedo y Valdés observed the substance called tobacco and wrote about it in 1535 in the first commissioned history of the New World, the *General and Natural History of the Indies*: "This plant is very prized by the Indians, and they grow it in their gardens and farms. . . . They believe that the use of the plant and its smoke is not only a healthy thing for them, but a very holy thing."[48] The Arawak word for tobacco was *coyiaba*, which meant "prayer." Columbus encountered cacao beans carried by a Mayan trading canoe near Honduras and likened them to almonds. Like tobacco, cacao was also reportedly a substance consumed in religious or privileged and ceremonial contexts on the mainland. Often Native American women were prohibited from consuming cacao, as were the men and women of lower classes. Cacao was usually sweetened with honey or spiced with pepper.

Both tobacco and cacao were brought back to Europe, where they were sometimes used for their medicinal qualities but often looked upon with considerable suspicion. The two plants had little cultural impact on European society initially, in contrast to their eventual worldwide importance as cash crops after the seventeenth century. Islanders traditionally ingested other substances as medicines. If, in the end, their magic failed, they were forgotten for centuries.

Cooking with Salt Cod

No food represented the magical art of preservation more than salted codfish. The most ubiquitous recipes of early sailing days are the numerous versions of salted fish. Whether served at Basque, Portuguese, Italian, or English tables, on land or aboard ship, salted codfish was prepared in basically the same manner throughout the fifteenth and sixteenth centuries. The wood-like plank of dried fish, almost 80 percent protein, was boiled to remove the salt, skin, and bones and to rejuvenate the fish's flaky texture. The white fish could then be stewed with pepper and drizzled with olive oil, or prepared with wine, almonds, and garlic, with mustard sauce, with ginger, egg yolks, and milk, or with butter and parsley. Caribbean cooks added lime juice, tomatoes, and various peppers, replacing the olive oil or butter with coconut or palm oil. Some went a step further and incorporated the fish into small fried fishcakes, dumplings, or fritters. In Jamaica, the national dish became salt fish and ackee, neither of which was native to the island. Ackee, a poisonous fruit when unripe, crossed the Atlantic from Africa with the enslaved sometime before 1778, when Europeans first noted the fruit. William Bligh eventually carried the plant along with breadfruit to the Royal Botanic Gardens in Kew on the *Providence* in 1793. The relatively bland flavors of both the salted North Atlantic cod and the West African ackee were spiced with peppers, onions, and garlic and sometimes colored with a few berries of the reddish anatto bush.

Portuguese Bacalhau

The European version of the salted cod recipe was simply cod, olive oil, and black pepper. The most time-consuming part of this recipe was preparation of the dried, salted fish. Two methods were employed to remove the salt and reconstitute the fish to its original flaky texture. Soaking overnight was the surest way to clean the fish and debone it. If possible, cooks changed the water several times, desalting the fish. After a final rinse, the cook placed the fish in a pot with clean water and boiled it for a few minutes. After cooling the fish, the cook could remove any remaining bones and skin. The fish was then ready to flake into small, white pieces. The process removed much of the salt, but not all. After the flaked fish was thoroughly heated in olive oil, the only seasoning required was freshly ground black pepper, perhaps the grains of paradise traded to Europe from West Africa.

Caribbean Salt Fish

Salted codfish was and is ubiquitous in the Caribbean. Caribbean portion sizes of salted codfish today are usually small, as the imported fish has become expensive. The salt fish is often served as a side dish with a subtle cook-up (rice cooked with meat scraps and vegetables), with fried rice, boiled banana, or with the fairly bland ackee, a plant native to West Africa. In Puerto Rico, salt fish is boiled (bones and all) with white rice in a dish known as *mira bacalao* ("look for the salt fish"). In the French Caribbean, salt fish is sometimes cooked with diced potatoes and capers and served as a salad or appetizer. Codfish is used in fritters and finds its way into coconut milk stews. It can be fried in oil with peppers and onions and served with *sada roti* or bake, a fried bread. Peppers are always present.

Besides the salted cod that arrived on European ships on nearly every Caribbean island, herring, shad, and mackerel were also salted and traded as slave provisions. The wealthiest plantation owners controlled the distribution

SALT FISH

1 pound salt fish (cod or haddock)
juice of 1 lime
2 green onions or scallions, finely chopped
    (or 1/2 small yellow onion, finely chopped)
1 large green, red, or orange pepper, finely chopped
1 tablespoon canola or peanut oil
2 cloves of garlic, finely chopped
1 tomato, finely chopped

Prepare the salt fish as in the previously described Portuguese traditional manner for *bacalhau*. De-salt to taste by rinsing with cold water or boiling briefly. Once the right taste is achieved, flake the fish by hand into bite-sized pieces. Marinate the prepared fish in lime juice and set aside while cooking the remaining ingredients. Sauté the chopped onion and pepper in 1 tablespoon of canola or peanut oil until they start to soften and become translucent. Add garlic and then tomato, cooking until they just begin to soften. Add the salt fish to complete the stew, cooking until just heated. This produces a wetter, softer salt fish dish than the original, fried Mediterranean version. Serve with baked or fried bread.

of salt fish. Codfish was rationed to enslaved communities and served in the plantation great house on mahogany dining tables. African cooks embraced its use in soups; as had been customary for the dried shrimp and fish in West and Central African cuisines, salt fish was used sparingly with other provisions. A source of protein, the dried and salted cod was added to wet stews as another layer of flavoring for bland greens and seeds. Together with salt pork and salt meat (usually beef), the salted cod was used to flavor local foods. Its techniques of preservation and the reconstitution engineered at the kitchen hearth were at the symbolic heart of the Caribbean experience.

Pepper Pots

The dish called pepper pot follows the one-dish tradition shared by peoples of Native America, Africa, and Europe. Its premise was also preservation-oriented. There are basically two versions of Caribbean pepper pot. One is a stew whose basis is the syrup (cassareep) derived from bitter cassava, a plant that reached Venezuela and Columbia by 3000 BCE; the other is a soup whose flavors are dominated by a lively medley of greens and vegetables—sometimes called callaloo, if dasheen or some other greens became the centerpiece of the soup. This version is found on many islands, including Jamaica, Antigua, Anguilla, Montserrat, Haiti, Guadeloupe, Martinique, and St. Vincent. Its etymology is possibly from the Spanish *calalu*, derived from a Carib or West African language; its food origins appear to be West African, although the soup was also known as Congo soup. The cassareep version appears notably in today's Barbados, Grenada, and Guyana, where indigenous cultural influences persisted longest. Meats from the bush were readily available because of the proximity of the rain forest. The tough wild meats benefited from the sweet-and-sour cassareep flavor. Both the term and process of preparation seem to derive from Arawak traditions of food preservation. Cassareep was produced in a laborious process of removing the poisonous prussic acid from the bitter cassava fruit. The juices were boiled until they became the thick, dark-brown, harmless syrup. Cassareep also helped preserve the meats in the cook's pot, whose own flavors for decades augmented the standard "house pot" from which a meal would be eaten one day and restarted from its dregs the next day with the addition of new meat. The reheated stews sometimes lasted the lifetime of the cook.

Many other African-derived soups were built around the widespread use of greens, first mentioned in the seventeenth-century accounts of plantation life. By 1760, a pepper-pot soup was identified with the West Indies, "that most delicate Pallat-scorching Soop call'd *Pepper-pot*, a kind of Devil's Broth," and a vegetable version of the greens-based pepper pot appeared about half a century later in an early Jamaican recipe for black crab pepper pot, recorded as "very good indeed" in an 1802 diary entry of an elite white woman living in Jamaica: "a capon stewed down, a large piece of beef and another of ham, also stewed to a jelly; then six dozen of land crabs, picked fine, with their eggs and fat, onions, pepper, ochra, sweet herbs, and other vegetables of the country, cut small; and this, well stewed, makes black crab pepper-pot."[49] Another Jamaican estate owner, "Monk" Lewis, writing in 1834, recorded that slaves prepared their pepper pot with salt fish.[50] These pepper pots were not unlike the "Philadelphia pepper-pot," which George Washington reputed to have requested in order to raise the morale and "heat" of Continental army troops in 1777 at Valley Forge during a time of scarcity and deprivation.[51] Since no recipe was written down until later in the eighteenth century, it is likely that the actual cook, who successfully mingled the flavors of tripe, scraps of meat, and peppers, was African-American and perhaps even West Indian.

John Lewis Krimmel, *Pepper-Pot: A Scene in the Philadelphia Market,* 1811
(Courtesy of the Philadelphia Museum of Art)

By the time of Richard Briggs's American cookbook, published in 1792, the peppery soup had become "West Indian" to American audiences. All versions rely on Scotch bonnet peppers for their spicy flavoring.[52]

Along the Creole Continuum

The soups of many elements convey the most obvious mixing of traditions that became common practice across the Caribbean. Spanish communities in the New World became the first sites of early Creole cooking. "Creole" as used

GUYANA PEPPER POT

4 pounds meat, with bones (cow heel and tail, or any beef, pork,
venison, or other game)
salt and black pepper to taste
1 tablespoon cooking oil
2 onions, chopped
2 Scotch bonnet peppers
2 cups cassareep

Season the meats with salt and pepper. Braise slightly in 1 tablespoon of cooking oil in a heavy stew pot. Add the onions, peppers, and cassareep. Some commercially available versions of cassareep are flavored with pepper and thyme. Add water to cover and bring to a boil; reduce heat and simmer until the meats are tender (about 2 hours). Cooks sometimes add several cloves and a cinnamon stick to the stewing meat. Add salt and pepper to taste. Serve with slices of homemade white bread to sop up the thickened sauce.

in the sixteenth century was a term that referred to those of European descent *born* in the Caribbean (*criollo* in Spanish and *créole* in French). Later the term referred to any admixture of different cultural elements in the New World, sometimes with connotations of race, color, or cultural style. That mixing had a long and violent history. After the accidental sinking of one of Columbus's ships, about forty sailors became the first European residents of the New World. Their clashes with the indigenous inhabitants in Hispaniola (today's Haiti and Dominican Republic) resulted in disaster and death, although we do not know why or how, since no sailors had survived by the time Columbus returned later. The indigenous peoples in the encounter had escaped to inaccessible parts of the interior. Eventually escaped African slaves relied on indigenous knowledge of the local environment and its foods in order to establish successful Maroon communities and create the provision grounds that sustained communities.

Archaeological evidence documents the mutually beneficial and cooperative interactions between enslaved Africans and indigenous people, beginning in the earliest Spanish period. Subsequent interactions were marked by European greed, remembered in the abundant evidence of cultural divides, including culinary, separating Europeans and the "other." Resistance against the imposition of European tastes also left its mark. The application of the term "Creole" could be derogatory, as explained by the plantation manager Lovell (in a 1735 letter to Abraham Redwood) in Antigua: "My wife would have done the same [written to you] but she is too much of the Creole/ I mean too Lazy/."[53] A London cartoon from about 1800 described the creolization process in the arrival of a European planter, "Johnny New-Come," in Jamaica, his overconsumption and illness, his struggle to "domesticate" under the watchful eye of his African cook (holding soup bowl, spoon, and drinking vessel), and finally, his eventual death. However, false expectations and racist attitudes were not the only obstacles to re-creating cultures in the New World.

Growing European crops in the Caribbean tropics was not as simple as it might have seemed to the early European agriculturalists. The Spanish tried unsuccessfully to grow wheat and barley on the islands they settled, despite wanting desperately to reproduce their familiar cuisine that was dependent on cereal grains. They did manage to introduce oranges, lemons, and limes. Crops such as olives and grapes failed. The Spanish may have helped spread tropical American plants, including cocoa, coconut, avocado, and chocho (*Sechium edule*), into new regions. There were also unfortunate stowaways— rats and mice. In addition, the Spanish brought horses and chickens. The most invasive foods brought by Europeans were four-legged. Pigs, cattle, goats, and sheep greatly altered the fragile environments of the islands, where livestock destroyed native crops by trampling and overgrazing. Pigs ate the sea turtle nests. Feral goats were a threat to vegetation. The mongoose, a diurnal creature, was introduced to rid Caribbean cane fields of rats and poisonous snakes, which unfortunately were nocturnal.[54] Some islands, such as Haiti, never fully recovered from deforestation associated with European livestock. After the invasion of the Europeans, Aztec poets would speak for the hemisphere when they wrote, "Weep my people . . . The water has turned bitter, our food is bitter."[55]

The participants intentionally constructed some of the culinary encounters, whereas others were the unintended consequence of randomly linked events. Indigenous women and enslaved Africans were forcibly drafted as cooks on expeditions. Together they provided meals for soldiers and settlers using local cooking techniques and familiar ingredients. Local foods were listed among the tribute items given to European conquerors. Although wheat and other European foods such as olive oil, lettuce, carrots, radishes, turnips, broad beans, and Asian spices were regularly imported, New World maize and cassava prepared by indigenous women eventually became the accepted staples, supplementing the imported supplies of beef and pork. (Early European military expeditions in the New World actually marched with herds of pigs, whose sense of smell detected unseen enemies.)

Preserving Food and Flavor

The ships that brought new culinary traditions to the Caribbean used preservation techniques from the ancient worlds of Africa and Eurasia. They relied on salt, brining, pickling, and fermentation. Salt beef, salted codfish, and salt pork were imported in vats and barrels. Wines often tasted like vinegar by the time they reached the Caribbean and they could be used for pickling or drinking. Meats and breads were traditionally cooked outdoors by Native American men on what the Spanish called *barbacoa*, a framework of green sticks over an open fire built in a pit. Otherwise, in early Spanish territories the indigenous hunters were forbidden to trade, slaughter, or sell pigs.[56] The Old World animals (including pigs and dogs) frequently escaped into Caribbean terrain, where the later buccaneers hunted them down. Their taste for animal fat may have originated on board ships, where cooks skimmed off the fat from the vats of boiling meat and sold it to some diners. Lard was an acquired taste shunned by most New World peoples, who preferred roasted and grilled meats, which would lose much of their fat content during cooking. This technique of roasting and smoking, using fragrant ingredients such as allspice, became the foundation of the American "barbecue."

Many early Europeans used enslaved peoples to satisfy their subsistence needs by engaging them in the daily labors of food preparation. Even the first archbishop of Mexico (c. 1548) did not perform his own cooking, contrary to the laws of the Franciscan order. His two female cooks were slaves from India and Africa. From the sixteenth century, most cooks in the Caribbean were African-born or of African descent. On board ships the Africans, enslaved or noticeably underpaid, also eventually dominated the role of cooks. On land, they became the producers and consumers of the world's first global menus. Newly arriving cooks brought the foodways from their home experiences anchored halfway around the world. They augmented familiar diets, making necessary or preferred substitutions. This admixture of traditions was called Creole. What did it mean to become Creole? What flavors and tastes were mixed together in the new Caribbean cuisines? By the end of the eighteenth century, breakfasting in the Creole style meant a heavenly but elite table laden with both the familiar and the strangest of culinary delights: cassava cakes, chocolate, coffee, tea, fruits, pigeon pies, and meats—from sea turtle to "jerked" beef. Enslaved Africans constituted the largest percentage of ethnic populations brought to the Caribbean and two-thirds of the immigrants to the Western Hemisphere. Whether intentional or not, most of the nineteenth-century New World's inhabitants had become consumers along an unstoppable Creole continuum.

JERKED CHICKEN

1/4 cup allspice berries (or 2 to 3 tablespoons ground allspice); reserve a handful
1 2-inch cinnamon stick
1 teaspoon nutmeg
6 scallions
10 sprigs of thyme
1 pepper (Thai, jalapeño, or bird pepper)
1 tablespoon dark rum
4 pounds bone-in meat
salt and pepper

Using a hand mortar, crush the allspice, cinnamon, nutmeg, scallions, thyme, and pepper. Add rum to the paste. Use a little sugar with lemon or lime juice, or enough chopped mango fruit, to sweeten the marinade. Experiment by adding your own signature of citrus, bay leaves, or other creole spices to the paste. Rub the meat generously with the marinade and leave it in the refrigerator overnight or at least for a couple of hours. When ready to cook, salt and pepper the meat and wrap in banana or plantain leaves (or aluminum foil) to seal the flavors. Cook slowly in an oven (300°F) or grill (6 to 8 inches from an outdoor grill's fire). Place remaining allspice berries directly in the fire, stand back, and enjoy the aroma. Just before removing, unwrap and allow the outer surface of the meat to blacken slightly and smoke, while retaining the savory juices in the unwrapping process. Serves 6 to 8.

Jerked Meats

Many of the meats available to inhabitants of the Caribbean were wild or semiwild. The Spanish term *cimarron* was originally applied to wild or fierce runaway cattle and later to communities of escaped slaves or Maroons, the earliest freedom fighters of the African diaspora. "Jerk" is reportedly the English form of a Spanish word of indigenous South American (Quechua) origin. Since at least the 1700s, runaways and renegades called hog-hunters had hunted wild boar in the hills and sold the meat to passing ships. Bush meat quickly became associated with masculinity and all the "wildness" that culture on the margins of settled society implied. Smoked and salted meats were also part of the West and Central African culinary traditions. In 1688, Dr. Hans Sloane, while visiting Jamaica, noted the delicious flavors of smoked or "jerked" hog on the Worthy Park Estate in the Lluidas Vale, an idyllic agricultural area surrounded by wooded mountains. The estate's meats were sold to Spanish Town on the south coast. By 1802, the time of Lady Nugent, the jerked or barbecued and stewed wild hog or boar was an accepted part of elite banquets. Maroons provided the supply of hunted and prepared wild game. These escaped freedom fighters successfully maintained their African identity and relied on West and Central African hunting techniques in the inaccessible reaches of the island's interior. Some animals, like the agouti, also maintained wild populations long after they were domesticated. Even the domesticated chickens, goats, sheep, pigs, and cattle raised in European settlements were not fattened to the extent that they are today. These introduced species grazed on common lands and fed on scraps. As a consequence, fresh meats could be as tough as those dried or smoked and salted, and they required tenderizing with complex marinades.

Marinades

Early marinades most likely derived from the ones first common in the Spanish period and described by the early chroniclers. Using the newly introduced citrus fruit (initially limes and lemons), the Spanish created pickling marinades (*escabeche* or *ceveche*) for raw fish, shrimp, and scallops across Latin America and the Caribbean. In Barbados, grapefruit was known as "forbidden fruit," a new variety of citrus cultivated there by the mid-eighteenth century and also used in this manner. Vinegar and other pungent tastes from brined maritime foods were familiar to sailors and their passengers in the Atlantic world and beyond. They softened tough meat and helped preserve and homogenize flavors. Early Iberian arrivals in the Caribbean passed on the use of vinegar to preserve and flavor meat, sometimes adding thyme and garlic. Sometimes local peppers or fruits were added to a vinegar to achieve a peppery sauce served on the side of the plate to be mixed in with the gravy of a meal. The French Jesuit priest Jean Baptiste Labat, who traveled in the Caribbean between 1694 and 1705, describes just such a pepper sauce as the "gravy" for boiled manioc with lemon juice and crushed pepper and served with fish.

The most common early meat marinades of the Caribbean Creole kitchen were those made of rum, a widely available liquor distilled from sugar, in creative combination with Old World and New World spices. Labat described many local foods and culinary practices, including a marinade for roasted turtle made of lemon, chili, cloves, pepper, and salt. In Jamaica, allspice branches were placed in the fire pit, and their aromatic, smoky flavoring contributed to the high culinary status of "jerking." Fresh meats were rubbed down with spices that combined the best ingredients of Old World and New: allspice (in the form of pimento berries) and pepper from the Caribbean; thyme and garlic from Europe; ginger, nutmeg, and cinnamon imported from Asia; African guinea fowl or European chicken or pork wrapped in plantain or banana leaves, from plants brought over from Africa. Sometimes a bit of lime or mango juice or rum was added. Fish was also prepared in this way, as observed by Labat. Finally, after its spice bath, the seasoned meat was slow-cooked in pits—a technique combining the indigenous lattice-frame grill of the Arawaks and Caribs with African farm-style roasting. The jerk process was preserved and passed down by the freedom-fighting Maroons, escaped Africans who consorted with their indigenous brothers and sisters to resist slavery and seek freedom. One of the results of this partnership was the beginning of a truly global cuisine none could resist.

Tasting Modernity

The magic of the Caribbean was imparted to the early foods of global encounters. Indeed, food became one key cultural bridge connecting the disparate traditions specific to four continents and the island homes where they met. Foodways constituted a means by which the unseen worlds were linked to the familiar experiences of home and community. Despite the undeniable cruelty and deprivation of the early centuries, the Caribbean became a place of culinary encounters and ultimately transformation. This conceptual framing of change through food was reflected in three of the region's key dishes: salted codfish, pepper pot, and jerked meats. Eaten by the majority of people on land and at sea, salted cod symbolized the alchemical ability of the Caribbean cook to bring culture and foods alive again. Soaking removed the salt in which the dead fish slumbered. In this way, the salt of the sea gave way to delicate and fiery flavors of new lands, especially peppers. Like the continuous pepper pot, receiving change and conveying survival, each island cuisine's coded message signaled the Caribbean's most central historical theme: cultural endurance. Both pepper pot and jerked meats were powerful artifacts of the maritime world. They also represent the essential partnership between the indigenous inhabitants and enslaved Africans, an encounter common to many Caribbean islands and the regions along the shores of the Atlantic. These recipes combine the essential components of continuity and change in their creolized flavors. They produce tastes that preserve ancient and indigenous foodways. They reflect the Caribbean resistance against cultural imperialism amid the forces of globalization. They utilize the traditional, shared culinary techniques of preservation—from salting, brining, and soaking in citrus or cassava juice to simply smoking through slow cooking. And all three dishes are proof that white hands did not stir the Caribbean cauldron alone.

Notes

1. Olaudah Equiano, *The Interesting Narrative of the Life of Olaudah Equiano, Written by Himself* (1789), ed. Robert J. Allison (Boston: Bedford/St. Martin's Press, 2007), 68.

2. Caroline Walker Bynum, *Holy Feast and Holy Fast: The Religious Significance of Food to Medieval Women* (Berkeley: University of California Press Press, 1987), 61.

3. Excerpt from Sieur de la Borde, *An Account from the Jesuit Missions* (1674), in Peter Hulme and Neil L. Whitehead, *Wild Majesty: Encounters with Caribs from Columbus to the Present Day* (Oxford: Clarendon Press, 1992), 142.

4. Excerpt from Anthony Weller, *Still Conquering the Caribbean* (1983), in Hulme and Whitehead, *Wild Majesty*, 344.

5. Quoted in Henry John Drewal, *Mami Wata: Arts for Water Spirits in Africa and Its Diasporas* (Los Angeles: Fowler Museum, UCLA, 2008), 33.

6. See the discussion of the excavations of the ninth-century Viking settlement of Mosfell, Iceland, in Jesse Byock et al., "A Viking-Age Valley in Iceland: The Mosfell Archaeological Project," *Medieval Archaeology* 49 (2005): 194–218.

7. Suzanne Preston Blier discusses the Fon, Aja, Evhe, and related groups in *African Vodun: Art, Psychology, and Power* (Chicago: University of Chicago Press, 1995), 237–238. The mudfish and the tortoise are associated with longevity.

8. Quoted in Doran H. Ross, *Fighting with Art: Appliqued Flags of the Fante Asafo* (Museum of Cultural History, UCLA Pamphlet Series 1, no. 5, 1979), 17 n4.

9. Henry John Drewal, "Mami Wata Shrines: Exotica and the Construction of Self," *Proceedings of the May 1988 Conference and Workshop on African Material Culture* (Joint Committee on African Studies, American Council of Learned Societies and the Social Science Research Council, 1988), 69–71.

10. Henry John Drewal, *Sacred Waters: Arts for Mami Wata and Other Divinities in Africa and the Diaspora* (Bloomington: Indiana University Press, 2008). The association of divine kings in Benin with the mudfish likely predated the borrowed mermaid imagery. Conceptually mudfish and mermaid share qualities of liminality and longevity attached to watery realms.

11. Edward Ward, *The Wooden World Dissected in the Character of a Ship of War*, 2nd ed. (London: 1708), n.p.

12. Cited in Peter Linebaugh and Marcus Rediker, *The Many-Headed Hydra: Sailors, Slaves, Commoners, and the Hidden History of the Revolutionary Atlantic* (Boston: Beacon Press, 2000), 198.

13. Quoted in Osha Gray Davidson, *Fire in the Turtle House: The Green Sea Turtle and the Fate of the Ocean* (New York: PublicAffairs, 2001), 62.

14. Anne Grossman and Lisa Thomas Grossman, *Lobscouse and Spotted Dog* (New York: W.W. Norton, 1997), 102–103.

15. Richard Wilk, *Home Cooking in the Global Village: Caribbean Food from*

Buccaneers to Ecotourists (Oxford: Berg, 2006), 62–64; Lissa Roberts, "Geographies of Steam: Mapping the Entrepreneurial Activities of Steam Engineers in France during the Second Half of the Eighteenth Century," *History and Technology* 27, no. 4 (2011): 417–439; E.C. Spary, *Eating the Enlightenment: Food and the Sciences in Paris, 1670–1760* (Chicago: University of Chicago Press, 2012).

16. Wilk, *Home Cooking*, Table 3.1 and 33–35.

17. Rachel MacLean and Timothy Insoll, "The Social Context of Food Technology in Iron Age Gao, Mali," *World Archaeology* 31, no. 1 (1999): 78–92.

18. Willem Bosman, *A New and Accurate Description of the Coast of Guinea, Divided into the Gold, the Slave, and the Ivory Coasts* (London: J. Knapton et al., 1705), 280–283.

19. Bosman, *Description*, 123.

20. Mark Kurlansky, *Cod: A Biography of the Fish That Changed the World* (New York: Penguin Books, 1997).

21. The connection with travel may explain the later association with prostitution. In the Caribbean this shift in meaning moved to popular culture with the raucous calypso "Saltfish" by The Mighty Sparrow. For a further discussion of sexuality, see Chapter 5.

22. See, for example, the Mighty Sparrow's song "Saltfish," slang for a woman's genitalia.

23. Eric Kimball, "'The Meat of All the Slaves in All the West Indies': How Fishermen from Salem and Marblehead Sustained the Plantation Complex in the Eighteenth-Century Caribbean," paper presented at the World History Association annual meeting, Salem State College, Salem, Massachusetts, June 26, 2009.

24. Letter from Richard Vines to John Winthrop, July 19, 1647, *Winthrop Papers*, 6 vols. (Boston: Massachusetts Historical Society, 1929), V., 172.

25. Guido Pezzarossi, Ryan Kennedy, and Heather Law, "Hoe Cake and Pickerel: Cooking Traditions, Community, and Agency at a Nineteenth-Century Nipmuc Farmstead," in *The Menial Art of Cooking: Archaeological Studies of Cooking and Food*, ed. Sarah R. Graff and Enrique Rodriguez-Alegria (Boulder: Colorado University Press, 2012), 201–230.

26. Quoted in Jay Coughtry, *The Notorious Triangle: Rhode Island and the African Slave Trade, 1700–1807* (Philadelphia: Temple University Press, 1981), 51.

27. Elizabeth Donnan, *Documents Illustrative of the History of the Slave Trade to America*, vol. 3, *New England and the Middle Colonies* (Washington, DC: Carnegie Institution of Washington, 1932), 123.

28. Captain Daniel Cogeshall, March 19, 1726, Newport Historical Society, Abraham Redwood Papers, Book 2, MS #644, v. 1.

29. Edda L. Fields-Black, *Deep Roots: Rice Farmers in West Africa and the African Diaspora* (Bloomington: Indiana University Press, 2008), 64–65; Mark Kurlansky, *Salt: A World History* (New York: Walker, 2002); Paul E. Lovejoy, *Salt of the Desert Sun: A History of Salt Production and Trade in the Central Sudan* (Cambridge: Cambridge University Press, 1986).

30. R.E. Hughes, "Scurvy," in *The Cambridge World History of Food*, ed. Kenneth F. Kiple and Kriemhild Conee Ornelas, vol. 1, IV.D.8, 988–1000.

31. R.E. Hughes, "Scurvy," 988–1000.

32. Peter Linebaugh and Marcus Rediker, *The Many-Headed Hydra: Sailors, Slaves, Commoners, and the Hidden History of the Revolutionary Atlantic* (Boston: Beacon Press, 2000), 160–167 n38.

33. A.W. Crosby, *The Columbian Exchange: Biological and Cultural Consequences of 1492* (Westport, CT: Greenwood, 1972).

34. William F. Keegan, "The Caribbean, Including Northern South America and Lowland Central America: Early History," in *The Cambridge World History of Food*, ed. Kiple and Ornelas, vol. 2,V.D.3, 1260–1278. Keegan notes that pre-1492 diets and cuisines varied widely across the environments of the Caribbean islands and across time. One of the significant changes brought on by European contact was a shift from land resources to marine resources in the Antilles.

35. Robert H. Fuson, trans., *The Log of Christopher Columbus* (Camden, ME: International Marine Publishing, 1987), 134.

36. Lionel Cecil Jane, *Select Documents Illustrating the Four Voyages of Columbus* (originally published by the Hakluyt Society, 1930) (Nendeln, Liechtenstein; Kraus Reprint, 1967), vol. 1, 132.

37. Excerpt from Jean Baptiste Labat, *A Sojourn on Dominica* (1722), in Hulme and Whitehead, *Wild Majesty*, 158.

38. Excerpt from Hakluyt's *Principal Navigations*, in Hulme and Whitehead, *Wild Majesty*, 53.

39. Quoted in Hulme and Whitehead, *Wild Majesty*, 160.

40. Wilk, *Home Cooking*, 41–42.

41. Quoted in Sophie D. Coe, *America's First Cuisines* (Austin: University of Texas Press, 1994), 12.

42. Mary Frear Keeler, ed., *Sir Francis Drake's West Indian Voyage, 1585–86* (Hakluyt Society, 2nd ser., no. 148, 1975), 204.

43. Wilk, *Home Cooking*, 38.

44. Keeler, *Drake's West Indian Voyage*, 192.

45. The Europeans may have confused the cassia, a powerful laxative found in the Antilles, with cassia, the spice.

46. "Christopher Columbus: Extracts from Journal," quoted in *The Medieval Sourcebook*, Fordham University, www.fordham.edu/halsall/source/columbus1.asp.

47. Bryan Edwards, *The History, Civil and Commercial, of the British Colonies in the West Indies*, vol. 2 (London, 1793), 311–313. Edwards also claimed of allspice that there was not "a tree of greater beauty," and he brought seeds from Jamaica to England on his second voyage.

48. Cited in Eric Williams, *Documents of West Indian History: 1492–1655* (Port of Spain, Trinidad: PNM Publishing, 1963).

49. Thomas Brown, *The Works* . . . , vol. 2 (London: Benjamin Bragg, 1708), 474; Maria Nugent, *Lady Nugent's Journal of Her Residence in Jamaica, from 1801 to 1805* (Kingston: Institute of Jamaica, 1966), 64, 68, and 70.

50. M.G. Lewis, *Journal of a West Indian Proprietor* (London, 1834).

51. Washington's worries about the scarcity of meat and provisions are well documented; see for example, Edward G. Lengel, ed. *The Papers of George Washington: The Revolutionary War Series (December 1777–February 1778)*, vol. 13 (Charlottesville and London: University of Virginia Press, 2003); Karen Hess points out the apocryphal nature of this story in Mary Randolph, *The Virginia House-Wife, with Historical Notes and Commentaries by Karen Hess* (Columbia: University of South Carolina Press, 1984), xx, 283.

52. Richard Briggs, *The New Art of Cookery, According to the Present Practice* (Philadelphia: W. Spotswood, Campbell and Johnson, 1792).

53. Letter from Lovell to Redwood, June 27, 1735, Newport Historical Society, Abraham Redwood Papers, Book 2, MS #644, vol. 1.

54. G. Roy Horst, Donald B. Hoagland, and C. William Kilpatrick, "The Mongoose in the West Indies: The Biogeography and Population Biology of an Introduced Species," in *Biogeography of the West Indies: Patterns and Perspectives*, ed. Charles Arthur Woods et al., 2nd ed, 409–424 (Boca Raton, FL: CRC Press, 2001).

55. Quoted in Miguel León-Portilla, *The Broken Spears: The Aztec Account of the Conquest of Mexico* (Boston: Beacon Press, 2008), 146; see also Coe, *America's First Cuisines*, 233, who quotes the *Libro del cabildo*, n.d., 195.

56. The vinegary flavors are found in Spanish-speaking port cities, from Havana to the Philippines. Possibly the techniques of "cooking" fish in marinades and making an adobo sauce for cooking chicken were introduced simultaneously from the Pacific via the Spanish Philippines as part of the flow of people and goods accompanying the silver trade.

TWO

From African Kitchens
Food and the Atlantic Slave Trade

We thought by this we should be eaten by these ugly [white]
men, as they appeared to us; and, when soon after we were all
put down under the deck again, there was much dread
and trembling among us, and nothing but bitter cries
to be heard all the night.

—Olaudah Equiano, *The Interesting Narrative of the*
Life of Olaudah Equiano, Written by Himself[1]

Fate cannot harm me, I have dined to-day.

—Sydney Smith[2]

As the wooden ship weighed anchor in Luanda Harbor, a Portuguese chaplain dipped his hand into the animal feed trough and sprinkled holy water, thanking his God once again for safe delivery from the sea. African onlookers in this Central African port of call would later describe the scene on board the arriving ship.[3] They saw the copper cauldrons and the great barrels filled with red wine and cheese and believed them to be the preparations for a horrible feast of the white cannibals. The red wine they believed was the blood of slaves and the white man's cheese made from the brains of his enslaved victims. Pressed bodies supplied the oils of the soups. The bones of vanished slaves had been ground into gunpowder. Steaming kettles on board the ships were most certainly awaiting the fresh supply of purchased African slaves to be loaded on board. From the earliest days of the Atlantic slave trade, the haunting hunger for daily food formed the basis for both comprehending and surviving its horrors.

The Transatlantic Slave Trade

While the Atlantic remained a place of mystery, as it had been before 1508, when the first enslaved Africans arrived in the Americas, it also became the site of unquenchable desire and hunger during the slave trade. Both the path of hunger and the path of desire had led men and women across the Atlantic, and, for many participants, both led to death. The trade in human commodities lasted more than 300 years, continuing until the late nineteenth century in some parts of the circum-Caribbean and African interior. Tens of millions of enslaved victims suffered both social and physical death.

Novelist Barry Unsworth has described the era of slaving as one of "sacred hunger," in which money, not life, was sacred and the desire for profits moved men beyond the edges of humanity.[4] Abolitionists would later argue that the era constituted a kind of spiritual hunger because it violated Christian teachings and constituted a "domestic despotism."[5] Historian Joseph Miller similarly characterized the slave ships navigating between Africa and the Caribbean as floating tombs along the "way of death."[6] There is little doubt that the metaphors of hunger and death played an appropriately central role in the characterizations of the era. Yet the foods that were consumed by the enslaved peoples also reflect equally key relationships between enslaved and slave master, the obligations and mutual dependency of the living. Foodways thus played an ambiguous role in this era, sustaining both the continuity of life and the way of death.

Food was necessary to fuel the slave trade, and African foodways quickly became a measure of domination and acculturation along a continuum of responses. Despite the presence of chaplains and their holy water on board some slave ships, nothing about the consuming desires of mercantilist dreamers and their brutal operatives seemed remotely sacred during the deadly voyages. Greed and passion fed horror and fear in the Middle Passage, the term applied to the slave ships' crossings of the Atlantic from Africa to the plantations of the Western Hemisphere. The Middle Passage could last from weeks to months and was fraught with dangers for both the enslaved cargo and the ship's crew. One key to any individual's survival was the diet on board the creaking, groaning slave ships. Even as the Atlantic slave trade consumed its human cargoes, the seemingly contradictory association of food with both life and death lingered beyond this fearful passage.

African Foodways Remembered

Historians have long questioned, given the brutality, deprivation, and uncertainty inherent in the experience of slavery, whether and how any African foodways could have found their way to the Caribbean. Archaeological excavations and historical research in the past three decades have presented increasingly persuasive evidence for the complex story of survival, transformation, and destruction of African cultural traditions, simultaneously revealing that on both sides of the Atlantic, cuisine was at the heart of commerce and culture, difference and integration. African-derived cuisine has been discovered in the styles and techniques of preparation, in the foods themselves, and in the names and uses of specific ethnic dishes. It has become clear that continuities did exist in the African-American foodways of North America, in Latin American cuisines, and in the Caribbean. This chapter asks both why and how African continuities might have occurred and even persisted in the shadow of slavery, and it then examines their interplay with the dynamic economic, social, and political changes that characterize modernity.

Although the transatlantic trade has been characterized as a key event in the history of globalization and the rise of the West, the African contributions to this narrative often have been ignored. Our quest begins in Africa, where foodways presented unique markers of the distinctiveness of specific African ethnic identities as well as the commonality of group social and environmental behavior and interactions. In nearly every West and Central African society, food was used to regulate behavior and uphold values and traditions. As Jack Goody has written, foodways are above all else "the modes of feeling, thinking, and behaving about food that are common to a cultural group."[7] For the continent of Africa, this meant a staggering diversity.

In the Caribbean, African foodways also became vehicles for the uniquely hybridized or creolized identities that were forged from cultural encounters originating on four continents. A dizzying array of distinct cultures met and mingled. Yet the local island demographics had one thing in common: Africans from many distinct cultures dominated the integration of multiple populations. Why did cultural homogenization occur sometimes and why were differences at other times preserved? In the narrative of this past, we are witnessing the patterns and processes of the world's first experience of globalization. Foodways registered the era's dramatic historical changes, including the introduction of new foods, diets, material culture, and commercial markets. We tend to think of the premodern world as a witness to imperial desires and the imposition of modern tastes through colonialism writ large. Individuals also intimately consumed the forces of globalization on a daily basis. The economic architecture of globalization was put in place through the exercise of violence and the use of global markets to move labor and expand colonial control. Yet, on both sides of the Atlantic, African-derived cuisines, eating practices, and general knowledge of food and diet were also the essential vocabularies for communicating cultural advice and social instruction. At the group level, foodways provided opportunities for replicating or altering social relations. At the level of family and household, meals were teachable moments.

An Akan proverb emphasizes the African cooking hearth as the symbol of cultural and social reproduction. The proverb and its associated image might be used to admonish youth to hold on to their traditions by making reference to the cooking pot (either clay or cast iron) that sits balanced on three hearthstones: "The younger generation says they no longer rest in the same resting place. Then why don't they throw away one of the three hearthstones and use only two?"[8] Similar proverbs that extol the stability and centrality of the African cooking hearth form a continent-wide continuum from West and Central Africa to Eastern and Southern Africa. Food was the commonly held foundation for community life. Cuisines and the food practices maintained traditions and were key markers of shared identity. Food was central to the cultural expression and survival of African peoples and cultures long before the Atlantic era, and its continuities resonate even today.

Food was not only a cultural reference point or mnemonic device: it was also the means and substance of communication with seen and unseen realms. Conversely, hunger or lack of food may also have referred to spiritual matters, right and wrong. The Akan gesture of hand(s) on stomach or mouth is an image that is used to convey loss, agony, or spiritual hunger.[9] This gesture might communicate the idea that death leaves behind a survivor who must now work alone to provide food every day, a condition of traumatic departure from the communal life so widely valued. By contrast, the image of two crossed crocodiles (with two heads and two tails, but sharing a single stomach) spoke to the widely held African value of unity. The Akan proverb associated with the familiar image says, "Bellies mixed up, crocodiles mixed up."[10] This proverb has been interpreted to mean that it does not matter which mouth tastes the food; members of a community should cooperate harmoniously rather than fight for individual gain. Food sharing might go too far, however, as an Igbo folktale describes. In this tale, a giant named Anukuli becomes a nuisance because he eats too much. Whenever Anukuli sees a cooking fire, he joins the compound in order to share the food. As a result of his voracious appetites, the people come to know hunger. Although people try to eat secretly (and for a time, women have to cook silently), Anukuli eventually is tricked and killed.[11]

Some scholars argue that before the arrival of Europeans in Africa, hunger was rare and sharing was only one mitigating factor. They observe that the expansion of the slave trade in the era of imperialism exacerbated the effects of environmental stress, conflict, and disparities in resource access. Widespread evidence confirms that European colonization disrupted food systems and uprooted the patterns of interaction and response. These systems had operated for millennia, allowing vulnerable communities to survive any given food crisis. Other scholars suggest that hunger was not only familiar, but the constancy of scarcity meant that Africans could not develop an haute cuisine, since they had to worry about the quantity, rather than the quality of foods they prepared.[12] Since outsiders unfamiliar with the nuances of tastes and preparation have written many of the sources for African culinary history, the recognition of gastronomic artistry was thought to have been slow to occur. Clearly, the staggering antiquity and diversity of African cultural traditions have also impeded recognition of Africa's contribution to world cuisines in ancient and modern times.

Early Food Production in Africa

Two key events in human history occurred in Africa and both involved the mouth. Between 100,000 and 50,000 years ago, anatomical changes in the mouth, throat, and vocal cavity permitted the evolution of human speech, language, and communication. Following these, innovations flowed in technology and symbolic expression. Secondly, the production of food and the home-cooked meal are finally what made the human species uniquely able to form communities through daily interaction, transmitting cultural memories and preferred tastes across generations. Thanks to the research of archaeologists, paleontologists, and geneticists, we can now say the story of that human history began in Africa. As recently as about 50,000 years ago, the ancestors of all humans lived on the African continent. World history was African history. Successful communication and food procurement, especially the techniques of hunting, fishing, and collecting foods, enabled early African migrations to populate every environmental niche of the planet. Key to human survival on every continent was the adoption of agriculture, beginning about 13,000 years ago. On the African continent, modern humans made the transition from foraging and hunting wild foods to herding and planting. They used domesticated animals and intensively cultivated plants as their central foods in an increasingly diverse array of environmentally specific diets.

The deliberate manipulation of the plants and animals in their environments also enabled Africans to produce more predictable and larger quantities of food, which in turn increased the population size of communities. Wherever agriculture spread, Africans were settled into culturally rich communities, supporting urban systems, social stratification, and state building. Agricultural innovations occurred earliest in two parts of the continent: in the savannas and forests of West Africa and West Central Africa and in the homeland of northern Sudanians, a Nilo-Saharan people of the southern and eastern Sahara. The two megaregions forged two different approaches to early agriculture. In what today is Mali, the Ounjougou people (speakers of proto-Niger-Congo) began to intensively collect wild grains, among them the grain that Dogon folklore calls the "germ of the world," *fonio*. According to historian Christopher Ehret, who used changes in the vocabularies of early languages to document cultural innovations, Dogon ancestors made the transition to agricultural farming:

> Integral to their new subsistence system was their invention of the earliest ceramic technology in world history, between 10,000 and 9500 BCE. Rather than grinding whole grains into flour, the Ounjougou people apparently made the whole grains edible by cooking them in pots.[13]

Beginning in about the sixth millennium BCE, oil palm and yams were added the repertoire of West African cultivation systems. Black-eyed peas and groundnuts were eventually cultivated. Using polished stone axes that greatly aided in the clearance of rain forest, the Niger-Congo farmers with their crops and lifestyles spread toward the Congo Basin. The second wave of agricultural innovation involved a contrasting environmental setting, the tropical grassland and steppe regions that emerged in the middle Sahara, fielding different crops. The Saharan developments also included cultivated wild grains, but these Nilo-Saharan people ground their sorghum grain into flour. Between 8500 and 7200 BCE they had domesticated the wild cow brought from the Mediterranean and initiated the earliest herding of cattle in world history. Eventually the African farmers added melons, gourds, millet, and castor beans to their list of cultivated crops. By 3000 BCE, domesticated donkeys, sheep, and goats had spread from Cushitic-speaking peoples via Egypt to western Asia and also westward across the Sudan.

Trading Foods and Beliefs

The diversity of foodstuffs was embedded in broader cultural diversity and integrated into far-reaching commercial connections between North Africa and the Sudanic belt of ethnically distinct food producers. Yet the multiplicity of West and Central African cuisines shared some common characteristics. Shared genealogy belonging to language families, adaptation to similar environments, shared beliefs, common dietary restrictions, and the consequences of state building—all would help to unite hundreds of distinct African foodways, long before they entered the Atlantic world. These foodways emphasized a single starchy carbohydrate of rice, yams, sorghum, or millet served with complex, single-pot soups and stews of greens flavored with meat, dried or fresh fish, vegetables, seeds, or groundnuts. Pepper, onion, and salt were common seasonings. Palm oil formed an important base for most soups in forest regions. Elsewhere peanut or sesame oil or shea butter was produced.

Harvested millet, Banjeli, Togo
(Photograph by Candice Goucher)

Pounded yam, plantain, grain, or rice could be made into a starchy "implement" for dipping the starch into a central pot of stew, transferring its tastes to individual mouths.

Foods were consumed communally in West and Central African societies. The bowls for serving soups and stews were shared by all who ate together. Each person dipped his or her right hand or spoon into the pounded yam or rice and then deftly dipped it again into the soupy stew before placing the food in the mouth. The proper positioning of the hand was typically to hold the fingers and thumb together, palm side down. Not only hands were used for eating. Spoons were the most common utensils. Serving utensils, eating spoons, pestles, and dishes were sometimes elaborately decorated, serving aesthetic systems beyond their daily practical purposes. Food vessels eventually were made of pottery, basketry, shells, or calabash (gourds).

The spread of food production can be linked to the technologies that supported food cultivation and preparation, including stone axes, iron tools, weapons, implements, and pottery making. These technologies made possible the cycle of life. Following the distribution of pottery from living and burial sites across the African continent over thousands of years allows us to see the diversity and integration of African material life expressed symbolically in the consumption of foods. Robert Rattray, writing in the early twentieth century, documented the continued ritual role of kitchenware in Akan burials,

Pounding millet, Banjeli, Togo
(Photograph by Candice Goucher)

where it might be placed in ceremonies that occur six days after interment.[14] Similarly, among the Ibo and other groups, pottery for serving food was decorated and destined to display status and spiritual power in ritual contexts. In Central Africa, large pottery funerary urns were placed on grave sites, where they provided deceased BaKongo the possibility of posthumous consumption. Among the Fon, an elaborately beaded calabash referred to the pouring of libations but was never actually used for this purpose—it was purely an indicator of the high status of its owner. Sculptures of human figures on the lids of ceramic vessels might indicate that the food and the unseen spirits they contained were intended to be sources of healing intervention, as they were for the Benue River people called the Ga'anda. Their food pots are still fashioned in human forms with heads and arms, but they contain deities and ancestors. Documented by art historian Marla Berns, "these pots lead lives like people: their houses need repair, their bodies need washing, and their appetites need satiating."[15] Food animated objects just as it did people.

Eating was a sacred act in most of sub-Saharan Africa since food entered the mouth, and the head was nearly universally associated with spirituality. In fact, the head was generally believed to be the most spiritually significant part of the body. The Yoruba praise song for the powerful deity Shango, the god of the cooking fire, lightning, and thunder, echoes this emphasis. In the song the devotee offers his or her head:

Making pottery, Ghana
(Photograph by Candice Goucher)

Here is my head before you,
The head that is eating eba,
The head that is eating fish,
The head that is eating snails,
The head that is eating ram.[16]

Sacrificial food and drink were eaten and shared among the living, but also with ancestors and spirits. Shango and other deities were carried across the Atlantic to the Caribbean and remembered in ceremonies. In Africa, Yoruba mothers acknowledged the spirits of deceased twins, who were given food via the small sculptures carved in their honor. As observed by Richard Lander in the nineteenth century, "whenever the mothers stopped to take refreshment, a small part of their food was invariably presented to the lips of these inanimate memorials."[17] Not surprisingly, graves and shrines were (and still are) often littered with overturned food bowls, which were key markers of the remains of offerings to spirits and ancestors on both sides of the Atlantic.

Foods Making Meanings

Not only were objects associated with food, but also the foods themselves could have special meanings in their production, consumption, or use. This meaning making often used verbal or visual links. The names of foods, their origins, and their characteristics reflected the connections between individuals and groups. Towns and cities relied on agricultural imports from the hinterland. Excavations at the 2,000-year-old urban site of Jenne-jeno in the inland Niger delta have revealed that the city's growth was linked to the network of exchange and trade in foods and other items from the multiple ecological zones that Jenne-Jeno straddled. Some surplus foods were traded as necessities, such as salt, dried fish, oil, and grains. Elsewhere prestige accompanied imported foods, which became luxury items—such as the citrus fruit, wheat, spices, figs, and dates carried by camel caravans across the Sahara from North Africa and Eurasia via the Mediterranean. When domesticated plants and foodstuffs spread outward from Africa toward the trade routes of Eurasia by 2000 BCE, they did not travel alone.

Among the most important food products traded north across the Sahara were millet and sorghum and foods from the West African savanna and forests. Spiritual and social substances in the pre-Muslim world of West Africa, kola nuts also were required for every social and ceremonial occasion. Kola nuts grew only in the southern forest regions of West Africa, and their trade was linked historically to state-building efforts and to individual household etiquette. No mention of precolonial African cuisine would be complete without emphasizing the social nature of eating. The distribution of food could indicate social status, based on gender and age, as well as inherited membership in a clan. The generosity of a household was measured by one's ability to provide food for sharing. The generosity of a community was recorded in one of the most popular epic tales of West Africa, the story of Sundiata, the prince and rightful heir to the throne.

In this tale, Sundiata eventually grows up to battle and become the ruler of a powerful kingdom in the thirteenth century CE. Food is given to strangers and gourds are filled with rice to feed armies, sustaining the battle for power. Food intervenes at key moments in the tale, as when Sogolon, Sundiata's mother, recognizes the familiar scent of baobab leaves and a vegetable called *gnougou* associated with the city of Niani. These foods become a trail that leads messengers to the would-be king. The storyteller reminds us that Sogolon "took the baobab leaves and *gnougou* in her hand and put her nose to them as though to inhale all the scent. She opened her eyes wide and looked at her daughter . . . turning the precious condiments over and over in her hands."[18] Sundiata, his sister, and his mother are in exile until these Malian flavors in a foreign market bring news of home and tempt the exiled prince to return to his birthplace. Irresistible aromas and iconic flavors (such as the spice known as *datu*) lead to the capture of the hero.

Sundiata lives in a world where foods and their meanings mixed and mingled. The indigenous urban and commercial growth of West Africa had already intensified in the first millennium CE, bringing new flavors and food-ways through long-distance ties that stretched across the Sahara to Eurasia. In the ninth century CE, Islam arrived via the North African trade and altered the architecture, gendered spaces, and material culture of West Africa.

Archaeological research has revealed that the new faith was indigenously adapted to fit local needs and also served to unify the diversity of West Africa's communities. No doubt the legendary gold reserves of Sudanic empires like Ghana, Mali, and Songhai attracted foreign merchant-clerics. Gold was traded for salt in values, if not portions, of equal weights. In 1224, the Muslim geographer Yaqut boasted that "the king's treasures-houses [there] are spacious, his treasure consisting principally of salt." Salt, a dietary necessity rather than luxury trade item, was mined in the Sahara and traded in large blocks or cones in camel caravans. As Africans converted to Islam, they made the pilgrimage to Mecca and returned with new ideas, tastes, and commodities. These connections established the regularity of commercial exchange first on land and later via maritime routes. Among the most important trade items were aromatic spices described by the Moroccan traveler Ibn Battuta as useful in his own transactions and "commonplace" as a currency of exchange. Just as valuable were the imported books and manuscripts, providing the literate elite with connections to the cultures and cuisines of the wider Islamic world of cooking manuals and written recipes.

Both the Qur'an (the faith's written text containing the word of Allah) and *hadith* (sayings of the Prophet) provided dietary instructions by categorizing foods as *halal* (lawful) and *haram* (prohibited substances such as alcohol, pork, dog, milk, and carrion). A third category (known as *makruh*) included

Local mosque, Bondoukou, Côte d'Ivoire
(Photograph by Candice Goucher)

reprehensible, but not strictly forbidden foods, such as bottom-feeding fish or prawns for some Muslims. The dietary laws and other practices of Islam proved to be flexible and pragmatic. Excavations conducted by Rachel MacLean and Timothy Insoll at Gao, a medieval town on the Niger River, suggest that hippopotamus, elephant, and dogs were eaten, contrary to dietary practices elsewhere in the Islamic world.[19] The trade brought saffron, vinegar sauces, and new fruits, but patterns of culinary practices remained remarkably consistent as the new faith spread from city to countryside, perhaps since fish had been the traditional mainstay flavoring daily meals. Wet stews cooked in widemouthed pots, pounded grains steaming in couscousières, and bread baked in sand or on griddles remained the underlying foundations of local food preparation. Arab visitors discovered that individual meals were humble when eaten alone: in fourteenth-century Mali, the North African visitor Ibn Battuta scorned the food given to him by the Sultan Mansa Sulayman—loaves of bread with "a piece of beef fried in *gharti* (a local condiment) and a gourd containing yoghurt." Visitors emphasized the importance of formal and communal dining, when food was abundant and lavishly presented as a sign of status marking an important ritual occasion.

One of the common symbolic gestures of hospitality across the African Islamic world was the sharing of a kola nut, a reddish and bitter-tasting kernel or nut of the plant *Cola acuminata*, which was chewed as a stimulant and to ease hunger pangs. Taken to the Western Hemisphere, the nuts eventually would provide the mainstay ingredient for Coca-Cola drink's original recipe. Because African kola nuts grew only in certain regions, their trade supplied a lucrative network of merchants with a hardy, transportable product. Traditionally, guests in many West African homes were given a kola nut or some similar offering of drink or food upon entering.

Kola nuts or palm nuts also figured in many social and spiritual transactions—including divination, common to West and Central African religions. In divination, the practitioner seeks the assistance of deities by throwing the nuts onto a carved wooden board and interpreting their patterns. Anthropologist William Bascom described an Ifa divination scene among the Yoruba in the last century:

> Lodagba held up the calabash and prayed to Ifa. He then took the kola nuts out of the calabash, and poured a little water in front of Araba's odu. He broke one of the kola nuts into its four sections and removed the small bits (iseju obi, ise-oju obi) near the center and replaced them in the calabash. Holding the broken kola nut up to Ifa, he said, "Orunmila, this is yours. Eat it." He then divined by casting the four sections of kola nut on the ground.[20]

The receipt and consumption of a gift of food or drink—even water—also produced obligations on the part of the recipient. Such social transactions initiated what would become reciprocal relationships; they were the "gears" that ran society and mediated the relationships between the living and their ancestors. Although their serving dishes were simple, it was said that kola nuts were life.[21] In this way, these and many other African foods and their associated paraphernalia and meanings were a significant part of the full continuum of life and death.

African-European Coastal Encounters

European traders arrived in West and Central Africa in the middle of the fifteenth century. They came by sea and brought copper, brass, iron, textiles, beads, and new foods in exchange for local foodstuffs, slaves, ivory, and gold. European ships typically carried alcoholic drinks, wheat, and salted meat and fish. Some of the long-nosed merchants introduced imported foods, including maize, tomatoes, oranges, peanuts, guavas, papayas, sugar, avocados, breadfruit, mangoes, cassava, cashews, coffee, chili peppers, and pineapples, from Asia and the Americas. Not all of these foods were entirely new to the continent, but the Europeans facilitated the popularity of their cultivation in coastal regions. In return, they sought fresh water and local foods to remedy the notoriously monotonous ship's diet. Arriving in the Upper Guinea Coast in the fifteenth century, the Portuguese noted the manufacture of salt and its trade inland, a commerce that attracted people and goods over amazing distances.[22] Rice, yams, and millet were available as surplus staples and supported residents, including the local Portuguese and their slave ships. In the Kongo, the food and slave requirements of Atlantic commerce came together since the consolidation of the kingdom formed a great agricultural zone surrounding the capital.[23]

There were many indications that the early Europeans were treated like any other foreign traders and assigned to special quarters highly visible to the watchful eye of locals. The archaeological research of Kenneth Kelly has demonstrated that at Savi (in present-day Benin) the European presence was orchestrated and controlled by the African ruling elite.[24] Between 1670 and 1727, European trading establishments were built in the African style a half day's walk from the shore. With the expansion of Dahomey, the new capital at Ouidah assigned separate quarters to French and English, who in turn relied on African canoes to ferry goods to their ships in coastal harbors. While Ouidah became an increasingly multiethnic community, its merchants and cultures took on new Atlantic creolized forms, including the Afro-Brazilians, who brought their trade and culture back across the Atlantic. Foodstuffs (e.g., fish and grain) were exchanged along the African coast in precolonial times, but with a few exceptions (salt, kola, and alcohol) they were not major items of commerce and did not serve as important articles of payment in transactions.

Culinary Exchanges

Even where European commercial stations were successfully established, their households, churches, forts, and castles became points of culinary exchange. Between the fifteenth and seventeenth centuries, Luso-African culture in Central Africa revolved around Christianity, which shaped coastal tastes in music, food, and clothing. These Atlantic Creoles ate Brazilian beans, American corn, and European radishes and onions. The Kongolese processed cassava and baked bread called *mbolo* (cake) that was borrowed from the Portuguese. Gradually new preferences for food and drink spread inland. By the 1650s, Kasanje and Matamba coveted Spanish wine and "would even sell their domestics to get this wine."[25] In the Gambia River basin adjacent to two major sources of gold, slaves and foodstuffs became major exports in the fifteenth and sixteenth centuries. Soon Portuguese traders were carrying *Melegueta* pepper and kola nuts from one African community to another. Their African wives cooked for them and their Luso-African offspring negotiated multiple worlds. Historian Donald Wright notes their struggle:

> Newcomers naturally wanted to eat and drink what they were accustomed to, so some of the earliest short-term visitors from Portugal or the Cape Verdes attempted to grow things that grew back home. For one reason or another, many of their experiments ended in failure: European grains, grapes, peaches, olives, lettuce, cabbage, onions, and garlic failed test plantings.[26]

Other imports succeeded in taking hold: new strains of chickens and rice, melons, figs, pigs, eggplants, chickpeas, and eventually new plants from the Western Hemisphere.

At another source of gold production, Elmina (literally, "the mine") in present-day Ghana, the Portuguese relied on the success of local fishing in the fifteenth century even while importing flour, wine, livestock, fruit, and vegetables from Europe. By the time of its capture by the Dutch, the castle at Elmina boasted a kitchen and bakery as well as pigsties, and chicken coops had been added.[27] Yet for the most part, the early European diet in West Africa was much the same as that of the local African populations, who shopped the same food markets for fish, maize, cassava, yam, vegetables, and "dry lean Hen."[28] Butchering marks on the discarded bones of slaughtered animals and the patterns of food consumption belie the mutuality of relationships between host communities and their interlopers on the coast. The European dependence on local foods and local cooks meant that their diets as visitors, merchants, and colonizers would be largely influenced by African cuisines.

The transactions involving foods were highly gendered activities. It would be mostly African women who would introduce their cuisines to the daily lives of European merchants. In coastal Senegambia, merchants shrewdly married into local African families in order to position their trading operations within the networks of the local elites. Kinship ties offered new opportunities for the European men and African women alike and for their offspring, including the construction of creolized languages and complex, negotiated cultural identities. Permanent and semipermanent relationships provided the Europeans (*lancados*, as they were called) a more settled life and trading opportunities as early as the 1520s. Along the Pongo River, lineages of mixed heritage controlled local trade well into the nineteenth century. Creolized individuals and even some local African merchants could have a foot (and mouth) in multiple cultural worlds. An American ship captain described the African adoption of European customs visible in lifestyles along the Gold Coast in the 1820s:

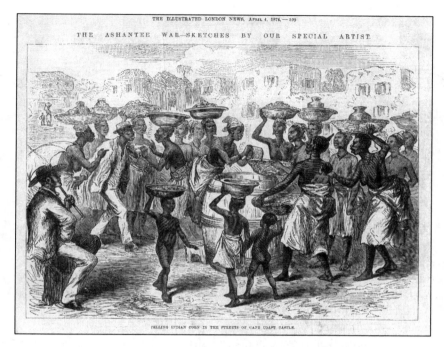

Selling Indian corn in the streets of Cape Coast Castle, Ghana
(*Illustrated London News*, 1874)

I, having to do all the business of trade ashore, was often invited to dine with them [the African merchants]. They live in good style, having rich chased silver plates and dishes and silver and gold handled knives and forks and spoons. Their dinners consist of several courses, soup, meats, chickens, fish &c, all well-cooked, and fruits, nuts, and sweet-meats for desserts, and choice wines, liquors, and porter, for drink.[29]

Individual dishes rather than the single-pot stew or soup would have been a fairly recent custom for African and European alike. It is highly likely that even these acculturated individuals negotiated their cultural identity according to the particular social setting or political advantage they faced.

The Cook Who Would Be King

The life of the African known as Assameni along the Gold Coast is an example of the breadth of social and political mobility in coastal exchanges. In the late seventeenth century, the local Danish garrison called Christiansborg Castle (at

Osu on the Gold Coast) employed a cook named Assameni.[30] As the garrison's cook, he would have supervised the purchase of foods and the preparation of meals inside the fort. The man's intimate proximity to the Europeans afforded him political advantage and access to wealth, and he eventually became a powerful trader and chief at Akwamu. In 1693, Assameni and a number of men disguised as merchants captured the fort. After royally entertaining and trading with private merchants and other foreigners for about a year, the former cook eventually sold the fort back to the Danes. His family kept the keys to the castle, which eventually became the seat of the government of the modern nation state of Ghana after independence from the British in 1957.

Slavery, Food, and Hunger

The serious laws of economics, of supply and demand, sustained the slavery that became part of a global system that moved people as human cargo. Enslavement within African societies had been historically produced by famines (rarely) and warfare (more commonly). The enslaved usually belonged to domestic households, where they could be adopted into new ethnic associations and identities, but even in those parts of the continent where slaves were traded, the enslaved were moved over shorter distances than were those during the transatlantic trade era. Civil strife and political instability were encouraged by European interlopers and by the increasing levels of violence attributed to guns. Wars frequently produced hunger, forcing migration and the abandonment of farming activities in exchange for protection in larger settlements. One result was that larger and larger numbers of enslaved Africans were available to wealthy chiefs and warlords for trade to the Europeans or for their own labor investments in farming, warfare, and raiding. The demand for trade goods fueled this long-distance exchange in humans.

Times of hunger and famine saw an increase in the chaos that created enemy captives and sometimes even led to the seizure of weaker family members for whom enslavement and their pledged labor meant access to food supplies and, ironically, the opportunity for survival. Before the transatlantic era, the food of slaves and the food of kings had differed little, except in the quantity available for consumption. One of the frequent obligations of the wealthy African elite was to provide food to the less fortunate, beginning with one's own household and continuing to distant relatives and neighbors. The generosity of kings or chiefs reflected the fact that the ruler was often synonymous with his people. A ruler's status could be measured by the labor of enslaved and free alike, who produced food and other goods for prestige and trade. Rulers such as Gidado dan Laima (the Waziri at Sokoto) were praised for their generosity to strangers, "making sure they had food and drink."[31]

Although some rulers like the Waziri continued to honor their obligations to their people, other elites attained firearms from European merchants. They expanded their territories and amassed great wealth by accumulating captives for sale in the Atlantic world.

The demand for slaves for shipment across the Atlantic had another significant link to food. Sugar and other plantation crops required labor on a larger scale than local populations in the Americas could provide. The trade in such goods as sugar, molasses, and rum paid for slave labor and financed the investments in European industry that would lead to a steady supply of cheap trade goods made available for African consumers. These foods were more than items in the Columbian Exchange. They were the basis for the growth of systems of forced labor and capitalism. The status and the security of many Africans soon depended on participation in the deadly Atlantic trade.

The enslaved Africans' daily existence was sustained by food and drink. Slaves constituted valuable commodities. Their feeding safeguarded the merchants' investments and ensured the trade's profits. Consequently, some effort was made to provide slaves with foods to their liking—the continent's staples of yam, rice, or cassava and sometimes even the familiar African cuisines based on palm oil and red pepper. On longer-than-anticipated journeys, food could become scarce. Still, the slaves were fed first. Crew members were expendable, but the ship's human cargo was not.

Drinking water was arguably the most critical provision needed for survival. Even though, by volume, fresh water occupied more space than any other item on board, there was never enough of it. Allotment was established at between 1.375 and 3 fluid liters per slave per day (175 casks of water for about 400 slaves), but actual consumption depended on whether slavers overpacked their ships and, ultimately, on the length of individual voyages. Good winds and fair weather meant that water and food supplies might be sufficient for human survival. Any deviation from optimal conditions, including storms and other delays, could lead to shortages. Drinking water was purchased locally in African port cities and stored in used rum casks or barrels. Not long into the voyage, the water supply became putrid with bacteria and so noxious that only extreme thirst could overcome the natural aversion to its horrible taste.

The enslaved languished in African coastal areas before being packed into the hot and humid ships that would carry them to the Caribbean. These inland captives were already malnourished, dehydrated, and sometimes diseased when they arrived on the African shores of the Atlantic. Members of inland trading caravans carried small bags of manioc (cassava) flour and dried meat. The African middlemen transported captives, who stumbled along paths chained together, destined for the coastal holding camps often adjacent to European-built forts and castles. For the most part, these captive communities ate little, but they ate like any other local African societies. Continuities in food culture—its procurement, preservation, preparation, and consumption—prevailed among captives when possible. The slave villages alongside slave castles had their own provision lands. Sometimes rations were provided by farmers in local communities, who also supplied the foreigners in castles and forts with rations of grains, vegetables, fish, and meat. African coastal merchants, such as the early entrepreneur John Kabes of Komenda, played a critical role in the coastal slaving activities at Komenda (c. 1680–1716) and other ports. One resident British merchant wrote that "if we lose him [Kabes] our interest here is all lost."[32] African coastal merchants planted, harvested, and stored crops of maize and other foods for sale to slave ships. They were cultural as well as economic middlemen. By contrast, the population of European merchants remained small and insignificant until the late nineteenth century. African continuities in food preparation persisted despite the many new foods the Europeans introduced.

The imported foods that traveled to African shores via the Atlantic trade routes included ones now common to contemporary cuisines: onion, tomato, peanut, cashew, guava, pineapple, papaya, avocado, wheat, maize, various beans, breadfruit, cocoa, lemon, lime, orange, coconut, cabbage, sweet potato, tobacco, sugarcane, sheep, pigs, cows, and geese. They were embraced by local cuisines. Some of these foods—like the lemon, observed by Diego Gomes, a fifteenth-century Portuguese traveler to the Senegambia region—were already known to West African cuisines because they had been introduced to the continent much earlier from North African and trans-Saharan trade. Other, unknown foods originated in the Americas. African domesticated crops, including local favorites such as yams, okra, and ackee, went in the other direction. The coastal material culture also reflected the large number of available imported metal wares, cast-iron pots, cutlery, and ceramics, imports that became markers of status and even the coveted decor in the homes of the African interior.

The enslaved Africans, once sold to the European agents, awaited their Middle Passage in coastal communities. The European-controlled holding places for slaves (such as the communities adjacent to Elmina and Cape Coast castles in what is modern-day Ghana) were often the sites of the first encounters between enslaved African and European cultures. While these communities registered the most devastating global economic impact on African shores, the cultural outcome was still weighted primarily toward continuity in foodways.[33] Enslaved and free Africans similarly ate the local foods prepared in traditional ways by African women. Markets offered new plants and products for culinary innovations and experimentation. By contrast, castle guests dined on some of the familiar dishes of their homeland, prepared by local

(African) cooks "instructed in Europe or, at least, in the different forts."[34] No doubt these cooks also took home some samples of the new plants and seeds, further spreading imported ideas for food preparation.

Other points of contact for the meeting of foods and cuisines in Africa were the coastal encounters between African and European merchants. Creoles and pidgins emerged as they were needed for commercial and social contact between speakers of different languages.[35] Foodstuffs were among the most important items of trade. And the trade went in both directions. European traders bought foods (meat, fish, yams, cocoyams, pepper, palm kernels, and palm oil) from African farmers. For example, when the pilot of the *Sao Joao* purchased food in Benin City in 1522, it was used both as victuals for the ship's crew and as provisions to feed purchased slaves. The prices fluctuated according to the seasons; yams at the end of the dry season, when supplies were scarce, could cost more than ten times the earlier harvest price.[36] The Portuguese also bought eating utensils, including ivory saltcellars and carved wooden food bowls and spoons, in the coastal markets. Africans sometimes bought or otherwise obtained foods—rice, maize, peas, and beans—from Europeans, but it was the Europeans' dependence on the African farming population for their provisions that often made their presence on the coast vulnerable to blockades and price-gouging tactics.

Subsistence on the coast also brought exposure to both European-introduced and tropical diseases. The ships' captains knew that the longer they stayed on shore, the less likely the survival of crew and slaves on board the ships. By the 1580s, English sailors on the coast were being warned against eating local fruits and drinking anything but "syder."[37] Such warnings were generally not heeded. Many visiting sailors drank palm wine and ate a variety of local foods, including honey, oranges, plantains, and yams. The latter were also recommended as a substitute for bread or biscuit and no doubt tasted much better than the ship's fare.

The ships soon became sites of intensive exchange of food cultures. The African (perhaps Fula) verb "to eat" (*nyam*) and noun for "food" found its way into Portuguese as *inhame* and hence to English as "yam" by the seventeenth century.[38] Fufu, ubiquitous in West and Central Africa as pounded yam, is listed in *The Sailor's Word Book* as "a well-known sea dish of barley and treacle," suggesting that the boiled porridges were interchangeable in the coastal encounters.[39] After the introduction of maize and plantain, the new foods were similarly treated by boiling and pounding into balls, a portable staple of the Atlantic world. European conventions also moved into African culinary traditions through the murky maritime connections. "Duff," a cloth bag of boiled flour mixed with seawater cooked in the ship's coppers, produced a steamed staple much like the African packets wrapped in leaves. Across the

Atlantic, the maritime technique was Africanized. The variety of selection (or rejection) can be seen in foods such as the sweet and savory "pastelles" and "blue drawers." They are called by many African names (see below), but the English term "duff" was given to the smallish, rolled flour and corn dumplings, vessels in the watery realms of African-Caribbean stews.[40]

Foods of the Middle Passage

Boiling cauldrons observed in the Luanda Harbor characterized the daily fare of the Middle Passage. Slave mortality rates were staggering even before ships left the harbor with their cargo. Soon after departure, the stench of diarrhea, bodily sweat, seasickness, and dysentery compounded the misery below deck. While the water supply and the foods were allotted to individuals, few had an appetite for the fare. Rations of rotted and wormy manioc meal were regularly augmented with beans, squash, dried fish, salt pork or beef, and perhaps some hot pepper or vinegar. In an attempt to make the food more palatable and appealing to despondent slaves, Africans, both enslaved and free, were sometimes employed to cook on shore and even on board the "floating tombs." Before 1820, more blacks than whites filled positions of mariner cooks and stewards on Atlantic voyages of all kinds.[41] Many of these workers joined the crews in order to obtain return passage in both directions across the Atlantic. This was a difficult occupation, with no documented compliments. In the words of one steward, he expected to find the crew behaving like "a pack of fault finding ignorant men."[42] It could not have been an easy or satisfying job in part because crew and cargo had much to criticize.

Meal breaks took place two or three times a day for slaves on board the early ships. During these spells, the enslaved would be brought to the deck, chained together in groups of about eight or ten. During early voyages, they would be fed from buckets or even troughs from which animals had been fed on the voyage from Europe, Brazil, or the Caribbean. By the nineteenth century, the individuality of food consumption had become the norm even for enslaved captives; about 1850, an American ship with captured slaves was supplied with 400 spoons.[43] All foods on the ships were either boiled in big iron pots or roasted. Dutch merchants furnished many of the ships with their cauldrons, pots, and cutlery. The meals were monotonous: boiled cassava and beans was typical in voyages originating in Central Africa. Rice, maize, plantains, yams, millet, or sorghum were the more likely staples from West African locations. Water was added to the dry meal to create stiff, starchy porridge, which would sometimes be augmented by fish or vegetables. Dried fish was usually the poorest grades of Atlantic codfish or the small shad, already rank-smelling by the time the voyage was under way.

Food at sea was barely tolerable, even to the crew. Not surprisingly, many slaves refused to eat and were punished accordingly. Shortages were as commonplace as complaints. Yet there are almost unbelievable examples of the kindness of slaves in sharing food with the crews on slave ships. The enslaved were fed first to protect merchants' profits, whereas sailors were considered expendable since they were to be paid rather than sold for a profit. Since wages were paid at the voyage's end, a dead sailor actually saved the captain the expenses of his upkeep. Rotten, worm-ridden foods were the rule. Boiled cassava, rice, yam, or plantain with beans was repeated day after day. This monotonous and salty diet brought life to the breaking point, and death at sea was the grisly result.

Approximately 35,000 slave voyages have now been recorded in the Trans-Atlantic Slave Database.[44] It is estimated that about four-fifths of the enslaved lives were documented. This amounts to more than 12 million slaves who survived the Middle Passage between 1508 and 1866. Most of the enslaved Africans (about 80 percent) were transported directly to Brazil. With the exception of the approximately 5 percent who reached North America, the rest went to various Caribbean islands. Losses ran high: on average, 20 to 30 percent mortality rates reigned. Sometimes nearly 50 percent of the enslaved perished at sea.[45] The culinary encounters brought about by the transatlantic slave trade would reflect this painful peopling of the African diaspora. The new Caribbean demography was to be principally African. Although the Caribbean experience was dominated by European desires and the hunger for profits, never would it be dominated completely by European tastes or cuisines.

Saltwater Slaves and Cannibals

The newly arrived Africans in the Caribbean were known as "saltwater" slaves. Fresh off ships from the transatlantic crossing, these slaves fetched a lower price than slaves born in the islands or even transplanted Africans, those who had already adjusted to the new environment. Once disembarked, the enslaved Africans found the greater variety of fresh food in Caribbean plantation communities an immediate relief. Salt came to have a double meaning. Diets were very salty and excessive salt intake became deadly insofar as it contributed to hypertension and multiple health problems. Beliefs about salt were commonly associated with losing the ability to fly back to Africa.[46] In tropical Africa, salt had been a highly valued commodity necessary for the body's replenishment in hot climates. Practices derived from African religions made important distinctions between freshwater and saltwater, between foods cooked with and without salt. In the Atlantic world, freedom from the lurching motion of the saltwater ship revived the appetites of both newly arrived slaves and the ships' crews. Salt would become a symbol of return.

At the core of the transatlantic horrors were tales of cannibalism carried out by all participants—Europeans, Native Americans, and Africans. Just as Central Africans thought the white man carried vats of red blood (wine) on board his ships, the indigenous peoples of the New World were regularly depicted in scenes of roasting human flesh. Human body parts were coveted as relics for empowerment rituals in several colonial cultures in Central Africa.[47] Since the time of Columbus, the inhabitants of the Caribbean were depicted as cannibals, and their supposed inhumanity was used to help justify their enslavement and eventual genocide. Spanish law permitted the capture and enslavement of those identified as cannibals. Dr. Diego Alvarez Chanca, the surgeon who, by order of the king and queen of Spain, accompanied Columbus on his second voyage, claimed his sailors had observed household cooking pots containing human body parts, and he described the logic of enslavement in terms of cannibalism:

> And since of all the islands, those of the cannibals are much more fully populated, it is thought here that to take some of the men and women and to send them home to Castile would not be anything but well, for they may one day be led to abandon that inhuman custom which they have of eating men.[48]

The belief among Europeans that cannibals made better slaves than any other captured people was widespread. Yet the practice of cannibalism was discouraged on Caribbean plantations. At least one case of cannibalism was tried in court in Antigua around 1770.[49] The present consensus among scholars is that if cannibalism existed in the Caribbean, it was practiced in ritual settings or as theatrical display and was not part of normal dietary practice.[50] The specter of African cannibalism was also a tale used first to justify the slave trade and later to grease the solicitation of money to support Christian missionaries. Food and taste, understood in both cultural and imaginative ways, quickly became the critical means of control and domination. When an Englishman "tasted" the sweat of the enslaved African to determine the relative health of his purchase, the act of commodity consumption was horribly enacted. Yet food and taste were also among the forces that fed resistance.

Domination and Resistance

How and why did the dietary preferences and the culinary styles of enslaved Africans come to determine the direction of Caribbean culture? The Yale

Serge Daget, *An Englishman Tastes the Sweat of an African*, Chambon, 1764
(Courtesy of the John Carter Brown Library, Brown University)

scholar Robert F. Thompson suggests the far-reaching implications of culinary patterns: "these were more than foods; they were writings in code. African systems of logic and belief followed unsuspected from the kitchen."[51] The manner of African food preparation and its formal, symbolic ordering of everyday experience constituted a body of knowledge and practice that could resist the dominant political cultures of imperialism. The forces of globalization tried to eliminate the humanity of those involved in the slave trade as its participants moved cargoes of people and homogenized and controlled access to food. The history of Caribbean food reflects the resistance to domination and death. Foodways played an essential role in maintaining African cultural beliefs and social cohesion. They were also the vehicles of ethnic distinction in the Atlantic world's complex heterogeneity.

A less celebrated feature of globalization was the increasingly complex interplay of new and old reflected in the creolization of food practices. While not all of the foods central to the African-Caribbean diet were African in origin, they were and still are procured and prepared in strikingly similar ways. Across a wide variety of Caribbean cuisines are found structures of meaning making whose origins are basically West and Central African in style and function. Sometimes the continuities of beliefs hold their meanings within the

William Berryman, *Woman Beating Cassava,* Jamaica, 1808–1816
(Courtesy of the Library of Congress)

vocabulary of recognized foods or similar preparation of borrowed items. For example, while cassava and corn are indigenous to the Americas and banana and plantain hail from Southeast Asia via Africa, they served as equally functional substitutes for their African counterparts (yam, sorghum, and millet) in the Caribbean. African-Caribbean women, who stand to wield long-handled pestles, pounded food like their African ancestors. They steamed provisions in folded packets of leaves. They constructed stews of greens, flavored with meats and ground seeds. The techniques transmitted orally across generations gave the flavors and rhythms of Africa to daily life in a faraway place.

Few possessions were carried across the Atlantic, yet aspects of material culture prevailed. Provisions were accorded a place in forming an African identity among runaway slaves. They offered communities a common language of daily life and thus were implicated in both the physical and cultural survival of peoples in the African diaspora. All manner of culinary utensils, from wooden pestles to carved spoons and calabash bowls, show great continuities with those used in African foodways. Found from one end of the Caribbean to the other, the basic Caribbean foods are commonly celebrated in the humble songs and games of rural communities, including the child's play of "One day, one day, Congotay" discussed below.[52] Familiar foods populate stories and proverbs, retaining their African meanings and sometimes called by their African names. However and for whomever these dishes were prepared, the Caribbean cuisine's distinctly African roots testify to the intentional physical and cultural survival of the enslaved.

Foodways of the African Homeland Arrive in the Caribbean

The cuisines of the African continent carried by the enslaved to the Caribbean were diverse, culturally complex, and numerous. The regions that provided steady supplies of slaves for the centuries of the Atlantic trade were vast and environmentally distinct, encompassing hundreds of unique cultural and linguistic groups. Important culinary distinctions were linked to geographical niches and based on the availability and choice of staples: rice, millet, sorghum, and yam. Without this familiar foundation for meals, the dining experience was considered incomplete. For example, among the Akan or Yoruba, a meal without yam was unthinkable. It was commonly believed that one had not yet eaten if one had not eaten yam during a given day.[53] Yam was the staple and centerpiece of many meals, its body to be "dressed" by accompanying foods. This elaboration of a staple food is also reflected in the Yoruba praise poem for the pure white yam, the body of which wears a "gown" of meat, a "cap" of vegetables, and "trousers" of fish.[54] Other regions were equally devoted to rice or millet. A unique type of Niger Delta riddle (really a series of questions with multiple answers) uses food to suggest both the distinctiveness and the interchangeability of foods, including the more recently introduced corn or maize:

Question: What is *kpai pai*, what is *kim kim*, what is an herbalist under a tree, what is a signal drum, what is *ekon play* (in which dancers move from house to house)?

Answer: Coconut, palm fruit, cocoyam, yam, maize.[55]

On both sides of the Atlantic, the practice of interchangeability was adopted. Functional substitutions were as common as outright embrace or rejection of a new food. The culturally distinct West and Central African regions that produced the bulk of slave populations also shared some common characteristics of cuisine through centuries of borrowing. Ancestral languages, migration histories, technologies, and collective belief systems related many of the groups. What people ate expressed their identity, to themselves and to others, and what people ate changed over time. The enslaved Africans arriving in the Caribbean in the sixteenth century brought vastly different cultural expectations from the nineteenth-century captives, whose foodways and cultural memory systems had been altered by centuries of coastal and riverine contact. Foods and preferences may have altered, but the manner of preparation, meaning, and use remained intact.

Not only the conceptual body but also the nutritive anchor for most sixteenth-century African diets was sorghum, pearl millet, African rice, or yam. The repertoire of techniques applied to the anchoring grain, grass, or root crop was expansive. These early domesticates were ground, mashed, and cooked as fritters by frying in palm oil, boiled as porridge, steamed in leaves, and mashed or pounded into the almost ubiquitous *fufu*, a dish commonly made from pounded yam meal. The rhythmic sound of women pounding food introduced every day in the village household. To this list of staples, other important foods were added to the diets of West and Central Africa before the Atlantic era, including bananas and plantains, indigenous to Southeast Asia. During the slave trade, new additions expanded the local repertoire of farmers and cooks—primarily with the introduction of corn and cassava. These crops imported from the Americas augmented local cuisines and, ironically, promoted population growth and supported slave communities during the era, since both crops could be grown in marginal areas and both could be grown successfully as intercropping between the established rotations of familiar grains.

Ancient Africans were aware of many of the slave trade era's most important legumes. Congo or *gunga* peas (*Cajanus cajan*), black-eyed peas, fava beans, and other vegetables were key sources of protein in diets that included little meat. Where the gungo beans (also called pigeon peas) were grown, essential nitrogen was added back to the soil. A mainstay of African diets for millennia, the wild cultigen was probably native to India, not Africa. But its journey was not finished. From West Africa, the gunga pea kept moving westward across the Atlantic. In the Caribbean, it became a staple of the island diet.

Anancy the Spider-Cook

Literate slave masters and colonizers rarely documented the food history of the African-Caribbean region beyond making lists of provisions. Not only people and goods moved across the Atlantic. The search for historical recipes must include the vast body of literature transmitted orally. Among the travelers aboard the earliest slave ships leaving West Africa was Anancy, the trickster spider-cook. An Anancy story in Jamaica records an early Africa-derived recipe. In the traditional trickster tale, the Jamaican Anancy (in Ghana, he is called Ananse) reports a scheme for going to market to buy food. Anancy is known for his voracious spider appetite, and in many tales he encourages gluttony by his selfishness. These actions come to no good, thus instructing the story's listeners to beware of such antisocial blunders. Food tasted by the social group exceeded that eaten alone. The Anancy character in this Jamaican tale recorded in the nineteenth century says,

> Me go buy me little salt fish an' me little hafoo yam,
> t'reepence a red peas fe make me soup, quatty 'kellion,
> gill a garlic to put with me little nick-snack, quatty ripe
> banana, bit fe Gungo peas, an' me see if me can get
> quatty beef bone.[56]

Anancy's meal includes salt fish and provisions of half of a yam and turning banana, together with a soup of red peas, flavored with a quarter bunch scallion, clove of garlic, and a soup bone. His meal could have been served on either side of the Atlantic. Meat was added to Caribbean stews mostly for flavoring, but only a modest amount of meat was consumed in the average African diet. Bones were key sources of flavoring and they were broken and chewed. Cattle and sheep had been introduced from North Africa across the Sahara in ancient times, but they survived with great difficulty in the tropical climates of West and Central Africa. In the Caribbean, freshly slaughtered meat would have been stolen from a plantation's great house. Such "theft" was widely reported.

As in Africa, the favored meats in the African-Caribbean region consisted of small mammals, which were hunted and trapped in forest and savanna woodland areas, together with gathered forest creatures such as snails and insects; fishing was a major occupation of coastal and riverine peoples. Trade in fish, salt, and other foodstuffs provided key linkages between the regions of the continent and ensured that most Africans were at least bilingual and more often spoke five or six languages. Their familiarity with multiple cultures extended to foodways and greatly aided the survival of African continuities across the Atlantic diaspora. Although knowledge of plants and animals was highly localized by geographical niches, foods were traded and borrowed constantly in the African past. Goat or beef would have been limited to special occasions, as in this transatlantic feast revealing Anancy's gluttonous desire and selfish ways.

Sauces, soups, and stews provided the variety and means of spicing the otherwise monotonous regime of rice, grains, and tubers. The mainstays of today's West and Central African spicy cuisines—notably tomatoes and hot chilis—also came on the scene after 1500 via the Atlantic trade. But many other peppers were indigenous or introduced in ancient times, including the peppers known as the "grains of paradise" (*Aframonum melegueta*), the Guinea or Ashanti pepper (*Piper guineense*), long pepper (*Piper longum*), Monk's pepper (*Agnus castus*), and those known as cubebs (*Piper cubeba*). Traditionally stews were made with pumpkins, okra, onions, garlic, eggplant, turnips, cabbage, and cucumbers. The seeds of melons and the baobab tree (*Adonsonia digitata*) were roasted and, when ground into a powder, added to thicken soups. Along with the use of sesame oil and palm oil, seeds gave West African cuisines their distinctively local character.

One Day, One Day, Congotay

Foods and food preparations that recalled the African homeland stood at the heart of the resistance to slavery, in part because the consumption of food cut across all other differences and established the interplay of commonalities. Foods consumed became the centerpiece of daily practice and their manipulation followed cultural rules and established norms of behavior and interaction. On the island of Tobago, Congotay is a simple tag-and-capture team game in which half the children are "chickens" and half are attackers. The attackers try to get past the female leader, the "greedy mama," to capture her chickens for their side.[57] First recorded by J.D. Elder in Tobago in 1936, the Congotay song and game are still remembered in several parts of the Caribbean, where children's laughter punctuates the lines of the song:

> One day, one day,
> Congotay!
> Ah meet ah ole lady,
> Congotay!
> With a box o' chicken,
> Congotay!
> Ah ask her fo' one,
> Congotay!
> She did not give me,
> Congotay!
> She's a greedy mama,
> Congotay!
> She's a greedy mama,
> Congotay![58]

The Congotay song has deeper meanings that relate to Caribbean food and history. Congotay is a thick, pasty gruel made from cassava (manioc), the plant native to the Americas. Cassava fed the enslaved Africans not only during the Middle Passage but also after they arrived on the plantations. Furthermore, cassava was an important plant used by African peoples and their descendants in the Caribbean during rituals, ceremonies, and celebrations. Chickens, introduced to the Caribbean from Europe, are known for protecting their young brood, but slavery had the potential to overturn this natural expectation of generosity and safety. The expectation inherited from African traditions would have recalled the Akan proverb "It is a bad fowl that sits by and watches its young being eaten up by an enemy."[59] The white slave master may have sometimes portrayed himself as patron or protector. But he was not. Rather, the enslaver was the unnatural "greedy mama." The proverb "One day, one day, Congotay" suggested that evil and greed would be discovered no matter where they hide. Justice would eventually prevail, in other words, and the day of reckoning would come. When it did arrive, it entered through the everyday kitchen of the Caribbean.

The Enslaved African's Kitchen

Cooking and eating under the conditions of slavery took on a twofold meaning. Meals were certainly among the few genuine moments of family social life in the Caribbean. The Dutch plantation owner John Stedman noted the social importance of sharing a meal among slaves in Suriname at the end of the eighteenth century. He wrote that "the poorest negro, having only an egg, scorns to eat it alone; but were a dozen present, and every one a stranger, [he] would cut or break it into just as many shares."[60] The persistence of such humanity in the face of oppression under slavery gave African peoples in the Caribbean a unique resiliency and survival advantage. Furthermore, the continuity of eating practices established the patterns of moral and ethical codes that bound together disparate individuals into a single community.

The enslaved African who managed to obtain something close to a nourishing diet stood a far better chance of survival under the harsh slave system, thus protecting the investments of the enslaver. Island assemblies enacted slave laws that prescribed the minimum amount of food an owner was to provide to the enslaved. Many soon realized that this allowance amounted to an unhealthy and poor diet, much too low in calories, vitamins, and minerals to sustain the work demands of the plantation. Rations were not always produced locally; they relied on shipments from Africa, North America, and Europe. Much of the food imported to the island colonies also was part of the enslaver's attempt to supplant the African-based diet and food customs.

Not only the enslaved suffered from want of basic food and water. In seventeenth-century Jamaica, shortages of water forced Europeans to gorge themselves on such strong drink as Madeira, canary, brandy, beer, and rum punch. Food could be abundant one decade and scarce the next.[61] Grocers imported foods that could survive storage during their months-long maritime voyages: sweetmeats, sauces, oils, anchovies, capers, olives, and other delicacies for the use of whites. On the St. Thomas-in-the-Vale estate in Jamaica, called Bybrook (c. 1687–1691), plantain was grown for slaves; meanwhile, white workers received a barrel of salt meat each week, as well as portions of fresh beef and pork.[62] Enslaved Africans received a fraction of this amount of meat from their owners. According to one Jamaican observer in 1789, "Every well-regulated Estate imports Herrings or Salt-Fish, or both; Flour and Pease. Twenty or Twenty five Barrels of Herrings [annually] to every One hundred Negroes (including all Ages) is the common Allowance."[63] In 1680s Barbados, slaves were given a monotonous diet supplemented by meat, often in the form of disease-weakened animals. Each slave house reportedly was furnished with a sleeping mat, calabashes, and a cooking pot.[64] Finding and growing provisions became the responsibility of the enslaved African.

Rice and Provisions

A variety of staples dominated the early diets of plantation slavery. Two of the ubiquitous dishes in the cuisines of the Caribbean were rice and peas (or sometimes rice and beans) and what were called "provisions," which were combinations of corn, yam, plantain, banana, coconut, and cassava. As dry provisions they might feed an individual while farming or hunting. Provisions referred to the food rations provided to the enslaved by their owners and sometimes grown by the enslaved Africans themselves on provision grounds. The rice dishes suggest more direct introduction from West African cultures and the later introduction of Asian and American rice in the nineteenth century. Rice and peas were prepared in dozens of different ways, from imitations (called gumbo and jumbalaya) of the Jollof rice dishes of the Senegambian region of West Africa (with meat and vegetable stew cooked together with the rice). Their artistry portrays the flexibility of meanings assigned to foods, especially as the dish called "Moros y Cristianos" in Cuba. Not only was this dish a subtle reference to the historical fighting of blacks and whites (Moors and Christians) on the Iberian Peninsula (the conflict that hurtled Columbus across the Atlantic, while first altering Iberian cuisines), but also it acted as an allegory for the racial conflicts of Caribbean life. Speaking in the African-derived languages of food, the dark, hard beans and soft, white rice "battled" in this savory dish.

Rice cultivation in the Americas owed much to African expertise and labor, as Judith Carney and other historians have pointed out.[65] Rice is an ancient African cultivar, domesticated on the inland Niger Delta more than 2,000 years before its appearance in the Americas. Other varieties of rice were domesticated in Asia. It seems certain that both Asian and African varieties of rice seeds were introduced to the Americas during the Atlantic era. Rice cultivation in the Americas was closely associated with the enslaved African's technology and culture, from the South Carolina rice fields to South America, where complex water-management systems were imported as surely as the Africans required to work them.[66] Importantly, the cultivation and preparation of rice were highly specialized and gendered activities, with African women initially dominating most, if not all, of the processes. Rice had been cultivated for centuries and prized by the cuisines of coastal and hinterland alike. Early Luso-Africans speaking Creole, practicing Catholicism, and intermarrying along the Senegambian "Rice Coast" described its rice varieties in the sixteenth century. Skillful winnowing to remove the husk and a clever parboiled version were the mainstays of coastal cooks. The slave trader Samuel Gamble subsequently wrote about the cultivation technology in 1793, when sowing of rice seed in nurseries before transplanting to the mounds and ridges of mangrove swamps, tidal floodplains, and estuaries supported large production schemes. The rice markets of African ports expanded to meet the provisioning needs of slave ships, which carried the rice, the growers, the processors, and the cooks to the New World. The transfer of crops implies both the environmental as well as the cultural dimensions of culinary practices. Judith Carney observed that this "rice culture embodied a sophisticated knowledge system that spanned field and kitchen."[67]

That rice was favored by some islands and not embraced by other populations was a consequence of its availability (through Portuguese, Spanish, French, and American merchant connections with the Senegambia, South Carolina, and Louisiana) and the culinary origins of enslaved Africans and indentured Asians. The availability of rice in the Caribbean increased dramatically after the 1830s, when Indian Ocean merchants brought indentured labor from South Asia to the circum-Caribbean region. Food practices of the East India Company following the Act V of 1837 were governed by dietary guidelines. This legal framework required that rice, lentils, ghee, salt, turmeric, onions, chilis, and tamarind must be provided to the laborers. In addition, on board the ships, *chura* (parched rice) was rationed. Rice cultivation in the Caribbean soon followed the paths of the new indentured immigrants.[68] Today the descendants of East Indian indentured laborers grow most of the lowland rice for export from Guyana and Trinidad.

Although laws supported the European colonizer's control over food markets of the maritime world, in reality control was much more difficult to accomplish on the ground. The terrain of the Caribbean could be forbiddingly resistant to the techniques and technologies of European farmers. Enslaved Africans frequently took the matter of diet into their own hands, supplementing the provisions they were given. Under the Jamaica Slave Act(s), local law actually prescribed the allocation of provision lands where slaves could grow their own foods. This soon became a common practice on the island, with successful results for slave populations:

> Their Owners set aside for each a small Parcel of Ground, and allow them the *Sundays* to manure it: In it they generally plant Maize, *Guiney* Corn, Plantanes, Yams, Cocoes, Potatoes, &c. This is the Food which supports them, unless some of them who are more industrious than others, happen to raise a Stock of Fowls, which they carry to Markets on the *Sundays* (which is the only Market-day in *Jamaica*) and sell for a little Money, with which they purchase Salt-Beef or Pork to make their *Oglios* or Pepper-Pot.[69]

The amount of food supplied by the slave owner never provided sufficient calories or nourishment on any island. Slaves reportedly begged at the door of wealthy plantation "great houses" for soup bones. Indeed, by the nineteenth century, some plantation slave owners believed that the slaves should be held entirely responsible for their own nourishment. Gilbert Mathison, writing about the provision system in 1808, declared that "it is the duty of the Negroe to feed himself; and it is his fault, it is said, if he does not take the necessary precautions against want."[70]

If slave diets were partly dependent upon the meager provisions received from slave owners, they were equally subject to the droughts, hurricanes, and wars that wrought havoc with the slaves' already tenuous subsistence. Endemic diseases followed from the poor diets and persistent periods of hunger. Famines sometimes occurred when food imports were disrupted and local supplies were exhausted. For example, Antigua was threatened by a famine in 1776–1777, a period coinciding with the American revolutionary war and subject to both the continual disruption of trade and generally depressed sugar prices. In the French Caribbean, settlements were isolated and the French navy was unable to maintain supply lines in the century between 1610 and 1717.[71] Similarly, between 1780 and 1786 multiple severe hurricanes and earthquakes hit the Caribbean, creating widespread food shortages, famine, and slave revolts.

The enslaved Africans typically found it necessary to supplement their own daily diets by maintaining kitchen gardens and the allocated provision fields, which they worked during their rare free time and days off. Archaeological evidence from a few slave habitation sites suggests that slaves also hunted and trapped small animals. In the eighteenth-century French West Indies village site of La Mahaudière, on Guadeloupe, slaves supplemented their diet by collecting wild shellfish. Their meals replicated those in Africa not only in the choice of recipes and the language by which they were named, but also in the patterns of meat cutting, the technology of food preparation and cooking, the use of a single communal pot, and the application of spices, fresh leaves, and other seasonings. The cultural role of food in the Caribbean continued to conform to patterns of meaning in African societies. The monotony of salted fish, pork, and beef provided by slave owners was tolerated by the enslaved only by the addition of tasty sauces made of fresh produce. The salt-laden provision diet was not limited to the poor and enslaved. It even plagued the elite black government troops of the West India Regiments, many of whom preferred to barter the salted provisions for fresh vegetables and fruits locally grown.[72]

Provisions—whether as yams, potatoes, corn, and cassava—were the mainstay of the slave diet during the voyage from Africa and after. The food shopping lists (*refacciones*) for slave provisions changed very little across the centuries. In 1832, the Cuban sugar plantation named Sta. Teresa El Agua, owned by Maria Loreto de Hechavarria, still included consignments of corn, yams, red beans, codfish, mackerel, herring, crackers, salt, and assorted spices. To these were added the provisions of the farm and field. The poorest of the enslaved, field workers, could not escape the basic monotonous anchor foods of their new plantation diet. Yet the descriptions of slave diets as "monotonous" and "boring" were labels given by Europeans, who probably never tasted the food given to enslaved Africans once it was cooked. Whites assumed that their own dietary preferences reflected their higher status and social class; similarly they sometimes encouraged Africans to emphasize their own distinctly ethnic diet and customs in order to sharpen those social differences, which they perceived as reinforcing a color line. Slave cooks added spices and herbs, augmenting the bland provisions with tasty and spicy sauces and stews, just as they had prepared single-pot meals dominated by collected greens in their African homeland.

Coconuts, Corn, "and Plantains Make It Good"

Provisions remained a significant legacy of the Atlantic slave trade diet. The boiled yams, *eddoes*, maize, potatoes, or cassava staples were widely considered "holding food," designed to keep away the hunger of a worker through the long and arduous workday. No matter how flavorful and tasty the foods consumed by the enslaved, they added up to an inadequate diet that could not replace the mineral losses and caloric expenditures from the slaves' extraordinarily demanding labor.

J.B. Kidd, *Plantain Trees*, c. 1840
(*West Indian Scenery* [London: Smith, Elder, 1834])

Slave provisions were elaborated on by subsequent generations, who enriched the basic food of African-derived cuisine by cooking the vegetables with coconut milk. Coconuts originated in the Indian Ocean, where early Spanish and Portuguese sailors noted the fruit's characteristic three holes and resemblance to a grinning face ("cocos"). The addition of coconut milk was the basis of a popular circum-Caribbean dish known variously as "run-down" (*rondon* in the Spanish Caribbean and *rending* in Indonesia), *sancoche* in Dominica, Grenada, Jamaica, and Trinidad, and the Guyanese *metagee*, a soup in which cooks could use the more traditional African flavors of dried and salted fish and/or okra as its foundation. The name "metagee" (also called *metemgee* and *metem*) comes from the Twi word for plantains or bananas, *metem,* and *gye*, "to delight."[73] Since the plantains cook more quickly than the cassava, they must be added last. The dish's name "metemgee" thus announced the meal's completion, literally adding "and plantains make it good." Provisions as part of the morning and evening meals continued to be served with the most complex, savory dishes characterizing Caribbean cuisine.

Corn or maize (from the Arawak word *mahiz*) was a central feature of the Columbian Exchange, new to both Africans and Europeans, since it originated as a domesticated plant in Mexico in about 8000 BCE.[74] Like the chili pepper, it would conquer the planet. According to Mayan legend, corn was created when the sun exploded and scattered tiny golden hailstones in the form of kernels across the earth. From Mexico, where nomadic peoples grew maize, its cultivation spread across North and South America and into the Caribbean. It is thought that the preparation of corn using alkali solutions and its combination with legumes improved the plant's meager nutritional value. The same corn was considered a poor substitution for the familiar wheat and thus was met by some early Europeans with dismay and fed at first only to animals and slaves. Eventually it made its way into the diets of the Atlantic world and beyond. The Kongo called it the "grain of Portugal." The English called it "loblolly" and eventually made it a garden vegetable.

Africans generally preferred plantain to corn, which they sometimes roasted and ate on the cob. Maize or "Guinea corn," as it came to be known, was associated with its use as an inexpensive means of provisioning the slave trade (on the Guinea coast of West Africa). Its spread in West and Central Africa mostly mirrored the spread of the Atlantic slave trade, although some kernels seem to have been traded from the Nile Valley across the Sahara along the *haj* routes as opposed to reaching villages via the coastal trade. African entrepreneurs invested in maize fields and provisioned villages of the enslaved and the ships that carried them to the Caribbean. Easily propagated and suited to an astounding variety of environments, corn became an important food crop in Africa by the end of the nineteenth century. Maize was even observed by the explorer Hugh Clapperton after he reached the inland town of Kano in northern Nigeria. To Clapperton's great surprise, after leaving the town walls, he found the rural countryside was planted with Indian corn. He also noted how "the food of the free and the slave is nearly the same."[75] Sometimes corn substituted for the pounded yam or plantain of African home cooks.

The West African-inspired cook in the Caribbean learned to lovingly prepare the New World vegetable as *kenke* or *dokono, funghi* or *coo-coo,* by boiling or steaming it in banana or local *soharee* leaves. Mande-speakers on the Gambia River had eaten it for breakfast, as a substitute for "a pleasant gruel [usually of millet or couscous] called fondi," according to Mungo Park, who traveled there in the 1790s.[76] Fondi became "funghi" in the Caribbean. Just as the Yoruba yam was "dressed" in trousers, the Jamaican version was sometimes known as "blue drawers" (meaning underwear), referring to the banana leaves that sometimes turned its contents blue in cooking.

Corn was also pounded and made into dough that could be substituted for the staple root crops traditionally prepared in Africa. De Marees described this substitution as early as the 1600s, when he observed the popular maize bread called "Kangues" that sold in local markets of coastal Guinea (the Gold Coast). The cornmeal dough was wrapped in a banana leaf and placed in the coals of the cooking hearth.[77] It was popular for long journeys because of the technique local women had developed to preserve the corn using the alkali of the hearth's ash. In both West African coastal regions and the Caribbean, the contents of the steamed dough packet were fermented sometimes. The *conkey* (sweetened) or *kankey* (savory) of the Caribbean and the *kenkey* of the Akan, Ga, and Ewe people of coastal West Africa hail from the same maritime routes. Steamed corn and other ingredients are constructed in tied packets just as pounded yam had been. Flour dumplings also were steamed directly in soups or stews. They were called "duff" in Guyana, descended from the dumplings or stiff flour pudding of the British Navy that became boiled pudding in the 1830s.[78] Its sweetened version was cooked in the stews of ship galleys; served as a dessert, it might contain currants and spices. When cooked with coconut milk in the tropics or with cow's milk, where available, corn had become an acceptable and familiar anchor of the New World diet of African descendants.

The most elaborate and most basic Caribbean versions of steamed provisions and porridge used the foundational recipe based on the African one-pot soup, with vinegary or salted meats from maritime diets and coconut milk that substituted for the more familiar tradition of a palm-oil base. Cooked in iron pots on both sides of the Atlantic, African corn (*pap* or *ugali*) could be prepared for breakfast, lunch, and dinner. Bananas or plantains might provide sweetness. By the nineteenth century, the standard fare on ships carrying freed Africans from Sierra Leone back to Jamaica looked very much the same: yams, cassava, pepper, vinegar, sugar, palm oil, and salted meats or salt fish.[79] The slightly sweet-sour-salty appeal of steamed provision was widespread, tracing the spread and expansion of the African diaspora, where African cooks like the celebrated John Jea took to the sea after their emancipation.

The African itinerant preacher John Jea was born in southeastern Nigeria and sold into slavery about 1780. He described the similar food of the enslaved Africans he encountered in New York: "Our food was what is called Indian corn pounded, or bruised and boiled with water, the same way burgo is made, and about a quart of sour butter-milk poured on it."[80] John Jea's meal retained both the whitened color of the coconut milk and the soured flavor of fermented grains. After obtaining his freedom, John Jea eventually became a steward and cook on a ship sailing regularly between North America and Liverpool. In about 1806, he described his first encounter with the confusing maritime world of food and food preparation in his autobiography, an account told in the slave narrative genre:

> After they had told me what to do, which was to clean the coppers, I went and looked all about the ship, but could not find them, not knowing what they were; at last I asked one of the sailors where the coppers were, for the captain had ordered me to clean them, so he showed me where they were. Those which they called coppers, were a couple of black iron things; and they told me I must make them very clean, and that I was to cook the victuals, being cook of the ship . . . I then began to rub the coppers as I was ordered, and the more I rubbed them, the more the rust came off and the blacker they looked. After two hours after I began cleaning them, the captain asked me if I had cleaned the coppers; I told him, I could not get them clean; but he told me I must be sure to clean them well.[81]

No doubt between Boston and Liverpool the newly minted cook used his personal memory of taste and aroma and applied his keen sense of observation, thus adding to his knowledge of the culinary craft. John Jea traveled, cooked, and ate in the globalized wake of an Atlantic revolution in culture and cuisine.

Excavating African Continuities

The enslaved Africans were once thought to have retained little of their original material culture and therefore none of their foodways. Excavations conducted inside the remains of the enslaved quarters on Caribbean plantations at first revealed negligible evidence of personal property and cultural items, especially as compared to the imported glass, porcelain, pottery, and ostentatious wealth of the plantation great houses. Finally, in the 1980s, archaeologists trained in African cultures began to explore slave habitation and work sites.[82] With experience excavating African house sites, they soon knew where to look and how to quantify what they found as they traced the African presence.[83] Like their ancestral African settlements, slave sites in the Caribbean were essentially outdoor, open-air sites. Settlements included small structures for sleeping and were built around a central courtyard area. Although the slave houses sometimes contained a cupboard that held cups, dishes, iron pots, and

CONKEY

2 cups yellow cornmeal
1/2 cup water
1 1/4 cups water for boiling
1 teaspoon salt
2 tablespoons sugar
2 tablespoons butter or oil
1/4 pound okra, sliced

Mix the cornmeal, salt and sugar with 1/2 cup water. Bring an additional 1 1/4 cups of water to boil in the top pan of a double boiler and add the cornmeal. Stir butter and okra into the cornmeal and continue boiling, stirring constantly, for 15 to 20 minutes, or until creamy. The mixture should pull away from the pan's sides. Form 4 or 5 small balls, or 2 or 3 larger ones. Serve with fish or chicken stew. While conkey (plural, conkies) is made with cornmeal in the Caribbean and a fermented and steamed version (kenkey) is made from maize in coastal Ghana, similar rice gruels (known as congee) originated in Asia.

DUNKANOO

6 ears of fresh corn, grated
1 cup brown sugar
2 cups coconut milk
2 cups raisins
2 teaspoons cinnamon, or 1 teaspoon each cinnamon and allspice
1/4 teaspoon ginger
1 teaspoon vanilla (optional)
2 dozen banana leaves, softened in boiling water for 3 or 4 minutes
raffia or string for tying

This Caribbean dish is similar to the one called dokono made by the Fante people of coastal Ghana. Mix ingredients (except banana leaves) into a paste. Place 2 or 3 tablespoons of the mixture on a banana leaf and fold all four sides into the center to make a thick packet. Tie with raffia or string. Place the packets in a pot of boiling water on top of the stove and cook for 45 minutes. Or put the packets into a microwave oven dish with about 1 inch of water and cook for 5 to 10 minutes in two batches in the microwave.

METAGEE

1 small onion, chopped
1 bell pepper, chopped
1 to 2 tablespoons oil
1 coconut (or substitute 2 to 4 cans of coconut milk)
4 cups water
1 pound each of yam, edo, cassava, and plantain
pinch of cayenne and black pepper
several cloves of garlic, minced
2 pounds of prepared salt fish, rinsed in vinegar or lime juice and
    flaked apart

Sauté the onion and pepper in 1 to 2 tablespoons of oil until slightly softened; drain and set aside. Use a hammer to break open the coconut. Cut the white meat away from the shell and break the coconut meat into small pieces. Add the coconut to 4 cups of water and blend in an electric blender. Let sit until it separates. While waiting for the coconut milk to separate, cut up the provisions into larger-than-bite-sized pieces and set aside. Strain liquid milk into a cooking pot. Add spices, garlic, and the sautéed onion and bell pepper to the coconut milk. In this order, layer half of the salt fish, the yam, and the edo into the coconut milk. Cook on high to bring to a boil; lower heat to medium and cook uncovered for 5 to 10 minutes. Add the cassava, plantain, and the remaining salt fish and continue to cook for about 15 minutes, covered, until all vegetables are soft and the coconut milk has thickened. Serves 4 to 6 as a main dish or 8 to 10 as a side dish.

tin pans for cooking, most objects were used communally and were shared in the courtyard "kitchen." Cooking, eating, craft activities, socializing—all took place in this open courtyard area.

By excavating these courtyard areas shared by slave houses, archaeologists have found that slaves cooked and ate in ways that most closely resembled those of West and Central African communities. Fruit trees and herb bushes grown for medicinal remedies ringed the slave settlement. The backside of the built structure contained a garbage pit. At a short walking distance from the houses were farms in which families grew yams and other crops. Enslaved African women called "higglers" eagerly traded surplus crops. With their owners' permission, the higglers traveled with goods (and news) to the periodic markets.[84] Foods were cooked over an open fire on roasting spits or in iron cauldrons set on three hearthstones. These scenes were identical to those of Central and West Africa, where "house corn milk and pudding [was] boiled in an earthen pot stirred with a large stick without salt or fat."[85] Such a meal was eaten with meat or leaves, just as boiled provisions were sometimes supplemented with stews to which salt fish, pork, beef, or the meat of hunted and trapped animals or birds might be added. Bones were chewed as they are widely in African societies today and were in the past.

Meals were eaten from communal pots. Lists of goods provided by slave owners record that each slave was supposed to be given one iron cooking pot and several small gourds or calabashes from which to carve utensils and small containers. The Ghanaian archaeologist Kofi Agorsah has found similar carving designs and food procurement strategies in Suriname and Jamaican maroon societies founded by African freedom fighters during the time of slavery.[86] Scholars have observed the common vocabulary of design elements on utensils. One early British traveler, Alexander Barclay, remarked on the use of calabashes in the Caribbean:

> The calabash tree produces a large fruit, not eatable, but nevertheless valuable, as the skin of it is a hard and solid substance, like the shell of a nut, and when scooped out, answers the purpose of holding water, or cut across the middle, makes two cups or dishes. Every negro has his calabash, and many have them carved with figures like those which are tattooed on the skins of the Africans.[87]

Food containers marked identity despite the superimposed status of enslavement. In some eighteenth-century communities, food was sold by the enslaved and served in small quantities out of gourds as "street food." In other communities, enslaved women worked as potters, producing local pots for trade. These have been known in Jamaica as "Yabba ware," a coarse hand-built pottery conforming to the familiar styles and patterns of Africa. This eighteenth-century earthenware was bought and sold by enslaved and free Africans in the island's informal markets. The enslaved ate from such dishes, but sometimes also from imported wares purchased from local merchants. Thus, the slave village pottery in eighteenth- and nineteenth-century Guadeloupe resembled French country wares (glazed cooking pots), and the excavated pottery of the Crève Cœur site in Martinique included a significant quantity of locally manufactured, hand-built earthenwares, known as Coco Neg.[88] According to archaeologists working in the Bahamas, slaves and slave owners there used the same patterns of imported ware, though the wealthier households owned a much greater quantity and variety of dinnerware patterns in porcelain and china.[89] Indeed, the dinnerware patterns they chose mirrored African preference for textiles that similarly revealed complex, syncopated patterns of local design and taste. These were not the only signs of the formal, symbolic ordering of African cultural practices in the shadow of European domination.

Meals in the Great House

Enslaved Africans also cooked in the kitchens of the plantation's great house, usually the owner's residence. The great house was exactly that—a grand, formal residence, usually two-storied and set high atop a hill overlooking the humble, single-room structures that housed slaves. Kitchens were commonly separate structures detached from the main house, owing to the possibility of fires in the wood- and charcoal-burning cooking hearth. These spatial arrangements continued as a legacy of the plantation system throughout much of the twentieth century. Cooking techniques were similar to those followed in slave kitchens. An African style was pervasive in the presence of seasonings—especially pepper—and in the combinations of staples, stews, and grilled meats. The quantity and variety of foods, dishes, cutlery, and utensils were sometimes enormous on the more prosperous estates.

From the European perspective, diet was looked upon as an opportunity to express, in hierarchical terms, the status and class of the individual. Whites permitted and even encouraged cultural and dietary differences in order to emphasize the inherent gulf they believed existed between blacks and whites.[90] In doing so, they supported the survival of the same African cultural patterns that would serve as the basis for resistance to slavery and oppression. And differences did exist, although by no means was the European diet transferred to the tropics unaltered. Lady Nugent, wife of the governor of Jamaica, kept a diary in 1802 describing her island host's second breakfast table, overloaded with food for twenty, followed by afternoon dinner tables that stretched the entire length of a piazza. When she breakfasted "in the Creole style," local

The Great House, Rose Hall, Jamaica
(Photograph by Candice Goucher)

cassava cakes, chocolate, coffee, tea, fruits, pigeon pies, and other meats were served.[91] An estate dinner at 6 p.m. was even more profuse and reflected African tastes, including a crab pepper pot or stew, together with multiple courses in the customary European style:

> The first course was entirely of fish, excepting jerked hog, in the centre, which is the way of dressing it by the Maroons [the runaway slaves who lived in African-derived communities]. . . . The second course was of turtle, mutton, beef, turkey, goose, ducks, chickens, capons, ham, tongue, crab patties, &c. &c. &c. The third course was composed of sweets and fruits of all kinds.[92]

Meals such as these were served on large estates to large parties of persons of all colors. Afterward, the gentlemen and sometimes some of the women would retire to smoke cigars and drink rum and brandy. On this particular occasion, Lady Nugent rejoiced to flee from the table of eatables and retreat to her own room. The food from the great house might also find its way to the plantation's enslaved residents as gifts for sexual labor or other acts of coerced indulgence.[93]

British garrison, Antigua
(Photograph by Candice Goucher)

Taverns, Punch Houses, and Garrisons

Not all meals were consumed in households. Taverns and punch houses were popular sites that welcomed the island merchant class and a motley crew of military personnel, sailors, buccaneers, and pirates. There were at least sixty taverns in eighteenth-century Jamaica. Free men met to exchange news, sell slaves and other goods, hold and adjourn courts, watch cockfights, play billiards, and purchase sex. Taverns and brothels in Bridgetown, Barbados, formed an essential part of the social organization of island garrisons.

Rachael Pringle, a Creole woman, owned one prominent tavern—the Royal Navy Hotel—in eighteenth-century Barbados. Pringle was born in the Caribbean a slave, the daughter of an African mother and a Scottish father. Eventually manumitted, she became wealthy through operating a prostitution business, which relied on at least nineteen slaves she owned. In the known portraits of Pringle, she wears a *tignon* (knotted headscarf worn like a turban or like the Senegambian *gélé*), the sign of Creole respectability, required dress for females of color (enforced by a 1785 law in Louisiana intended to protect class and color lines), and popular around the Caribbean. Most establishments of the sort Pringle ran were far from respectable. They housed travelers, prostitutes, and common thieves alike. In one of the lithographs of Pringle, she assumes a public pose as a market woman outside her shop on which reads a sign:

"Pawpaw Sweetmeats and Pickles of all Sorts."[94] Historian Marisa Fuentes points to the duality of this characterization of Pringle's business since the phallic imagery and language of consumption "worked to both masque and advertise the sexually overt activities within the tavern."[95]

Foods were an integral part of the exchanges in taverns and brothels. The New Street Tavern site in Port Royal, Jamaica (known as the wickedest city on earth a century earlier), served a variety of foods, including beef, lamb, tortoise, salad, sweet meats, fresh fish, chicken, capers, and custards. Foods were washed down with Madeira, brandy, beer, and rum punch.[96] The archaeological excavation of large numbers of individual drinking containers and cutlery, together with Chinoiserie porcelain, also suggests the replication of European dining styles of the time.

Ordinary sailors and soldiers did not often frequent such taverns, although officers and elite males did. Generally speaking, the military did not fare well on islands that offered little in the way of predictable or inexpensive food. Like the other local residents, they suffered through times of embargoes and devastating hurricanes. Expensive rations had to be imported when island assemblies failed to provide support. Although breakfast (coffee, bread) was usually served communally to British soldiers (who had to pay for the privilege of eating), the troops were left to sort their own evening fare as members of a "mess," a small group of five or six men. Issued a metal cooking pot, ladle, trenchers, platter, and spoons, each set of soldiers had to pool their resources to purchase fresh foods from African market women.[97] Rum was inexpensive and never far from the troops.

The African-Caribbean Continuum

In the end, European dietary patterns were greatly altered in the African-Atlantic world. Many people tried and failed to transfer directly the mainstays of European agriculture and cuisines, such as wheat, grapevines, and olive trees. The climate and local environments of the Caribbean did not sustain attempts to transfer food practices common to northern Europe or the Mediterranean. The significant early differences in degree of adaptation to newly available foodstuffs and the scarcity of familiar foods followed social, class, and ethnic lines. Enslaved Africans were underfed and forced to rely on skills and cultural traditions to survive. African ethnic identities were manufactured and Creole status displayed through the consumption of locally made and imported everyday and luxury items. Both were sustained through participation in an informal economy of African-style markets that mirrored the larger global movement of bodies and foods.

Indigenous people provided local foods to the conquerors through trade and tribute arrangements. Enslaved Africans brought skills in farming, fishing, and hunting of small game appropriate to the tropical environments of the islands. Enslaved and manumitted African women in particular found participation in island food markets to be a source of empowerment and one of the few alternatives to coerced sexual exploitation. African practices brought from the tropics proved to be locally suited and sustainable, lowering the costs of food and creating uniquely African-Caribbean cultural strategies. Some foods served in the great house (e.g., turtle, iguana, and tropical fruits) were thus strange to European eyes and unaccustomed palates. Other familiar foods were transformed by adopting entirely new spices and novel technologies and methods of cooking.

The logical outcome of the Caribbean's culinary history was the triumph of African influences, not only because the enslaved outnumbered their masters by ratios of four or thirteen to one. The reconfiguration and assembly of foods belie the architecture and agency of African cultural identity in the Caribbean. Enslaved status consigned by the slave owner was at odds with the independence of food procurement and preparation, profoundly African at every stage. The Caribbean recipes in this chapter are a few examples of the many that came directly from Africa: *conkey*, *dunkanoo*, and *metagee*. Foodways provided Africans the repeated opportunity to remember home. To have forgotten would have implied discontinuity and neglect of ancestors and spirits. Because African-Caribbean cooks associated food with memory and meaning, their cuisines became vehicles for negotiating and configuring identity. Speaking of the Bilumbu diviner's equipment, which is also stored in a calabash, Mary Nooter Roberts and Allen Roberts observed, "The contents of the gourd are a microcosm of memory, intention, and hope."[98] So, too, food containers held the magic of physical and spiritual survival. Whether prepared for the enslaved or enslaver, the foods from Caribbean kitchens would retain the memory of their distinctively African styles of preparation, practice, and meaning, along the Creole continuum they dominated.

Notes

1. Olaudah Equiano, *The Interesting Narrative of the Life of Olaudah Equiano, Written by Himself* [1789], ed. Robert J. Allison (Boston: Bedford/St. Martin's Press, 2007), 68.

2. Sydney Smith was a nineteenth-century British writer and Anglican cleric, known for clever social commentary. This quote is part of his rhyming recipe for salad dressing, reproduced in Sydney Smith, *Wit and Wisdom of the Rev. Sydney Smith* (New York: Redfield, 1856), 428.

3. Account based on Joseph C. Miller, *Way of Death: Merchant Capitalism and the Angolan Slave Trade, 1730–1830* (Madison: University of Wisconsin Press, 1988), 413–427; for further consideration of cannibalism, see also Kyla Tompkins,

"Everything 'Cept Eat Us: The Antebellum Black Body Portrayed as Edible Body," *Callaloo* 30, no. 1 (2007): 201–224.

4. Barry Unsworth, *Sacred Hunger* (New York: Norton, 1992).

5. Edwards, Jonathan, Jr., *Injustice and Impolicy of the Slave Trade and of the Slavery of Africans . . .* (New Haven, CT: Thomas & Samuel Green, 1791).

6. Miller, *Way of Death*, 314.

7. Jack Goody, *Cooking, Cuisine, and Class: A Study in Comparative Sociology* (Cambridge: Cambridge University Press, 1982), 68.

8. Herbert M. Cole and Doran H. Ross, *The Arts of Ghana* (Los Angeles: Museum of Cultural History, UCLA, 1977), 79.

9. Cole and Ross, *Arts of Ghana*, 59.

10. Literally, this is one translation of the Fante proverb *funtum frafu denkyen frafu.* The image is depicted in the graphics accompanying this book's chapter opening.

11. Herbert M. Cole and Chike C. Aniakor, *Igbo Arts: Community and Cosmos* (Los Angeles: Museum of Cultural History, UCLA, 1984), 139–140.

12. Reay Tannahill, in *Food in History* (New York: Stein and Day, 1973), 315–317, suggests that "cooking is an art only where food is consistently plentiful."

13. Christopher Ehret argues for the complex history of African innovations in "Africa in History," a presentation at the Conference on Understanding African Poverty over the Longue Durée, The Weatherhead Center for International Affairs (WCFIA, Harvard University) in Partnership with the International Institute for the Advanced Study of Cultures, Institutions and Economic Enterprise (IIAS), Hephzibah Christian Center, Peduase, Ghana, on July 15-17, 2010, www.wcfia.harvard.edu/sites/default/files/Ehret%20Africa%20in%20History%205-5-10.pdf.

14. Rattray (1927), quoted in Cole and Ross, *Arts of Ghana*, 63.

15. Lyn Avins and Betsy Quick, *Central Nigeria Unmasked: Arts of the Benue River Valley* (A Curriculum Resource for Teachers) (Los Angeles: Fowler Museum, UCLA, 2011), 71.

16. Henry John Drewal and John Pemberton III with Rowland Abiodun, *Yoruba: Nine Centuries of African Art and Thought* (New York: Center for African Art/Harry N. Abrams, 1989), 161–162. Cultural performances were one means by which hunger could be avoided; for New World versions, see also John Mason, *Orin Orisa* (New York: Yoruba Theological Archministry, 1992).

17. Richard Lander (1826), quoted in Drewal and Pemberton, *Yoruba: Nine Centuries*, 171. Special foods were prepared for twins on a weekly basis, including beans or cowpeas cooked with palm oil to "cool" their temperaments.

18. D.T. Niane, *Sundiata: An Epic of Old Mali* (New York: Longman, 2005), 44; Natalie Mettler, "Oily Sauce, Salty Sauce: Food, Cooking, and Identity in the Mandekan Region of West Africa," *African Studies Center Working Papers* (Boston: Boston University, 2008), cited by James C. McCann, *Maize and Grace: Africa's Encounter with a New World Crop* (Cambridge: Harvard University Press, 2005), 111.

19. Rachel MacLean and Timothy Insoll, "The Social Context of Food Technology in Iron Age Gao, Mali," *World Archaeology* 31, no. 1 (1999): 78–92; Rachel MacLean and Timothy Insoll, "Archaeology, Luxury, and the Exotic: The Examples of Islamic Gao (Mali) and Bahrain," *World Archaeology* 34, no. 3 (2003): 558–570.

20. William R. Bascom, *Ifa Divination: Communication Between Gods and Men in West Africa* (Bloomington: Indiana University Press, 1969), 101.

21. Cole and Aniakor, *Igbo Arts*, 62.

22. See Walter Rodney, *A History of the Upper Guinea Coast, 1545–1800* (New

York: Monthly Review Press, 1970), 18–24, for a discussion of salt and rice exchanges, as well as rice, yams, and millet made available to supply the slave ships.

23. This simplifies a much more complex narrative of state building and slavery as described by John Thornton in *Africa and Africans in the Making of the Atlantic World, 1400–1800* (London: Cambridge University Press, 1998), 95–97.

24. K.G. Kelly, "The Archaeology of African-European Interaction: Investigating the Social Roles of Trade, Traders, and the Use of Space in the Seventeenth and Eighteenth Century Hueda Kingdom, Republic of Benin," *World Archaeology* 28, no. 3 (1997): 77–95.

25. Linda M. Heywood and John K. Thornton, *Central Africans, Atlantic Creoles, and the Foundation of the Americas, 1585–1660* (Cambridge: Cambridge University Press, 2007), 168–169, 215–218.

26. Donald R. Wright, *The World and a Very Small Place in Africa: A History of Globalization in Niumi, The Gambia* (Armonk, NY: M.E. Sharpe, 2010), 80.

27. Albert van Dantzig, *Forts and Castles of Ghana* (Accra, Ghana: Sedco, 1980), 15, 20 n3.

28. Christopher R. DeCorse, *An Archaeology of Elmina: Africans and Europeans on the Gold Coast, 1400–1900* (Washington, DC: Smithsonian Institution Press, 1998), 115.

29. George Howland (1823), quoted in Norman R. Bennett and George E. Brooks, eds., *New England Merchants in Africa: A History Through Documents, 1802–1865* (Boston: Boston University Press, 1965), 118.

30. van Dantzig, *Forts and Castles*, 31–32.

31. Described by Hugh Clapperton, *Hugh Clapperton into the Interior of Africa: Records of the Second Expedition, 1825–1827*, edited by Jamie Bruce-Lockhart and Paul E. Lovejoy. (Leiden, Netherlands: Brill, 2005), 51.

32. Quoted in David Henige, "John Kabes, an Early African Entrepreneur and State Builder," *Journal of African History* 18, no. 1 (1977): 1.

33. Christopher DeCorse, *Archaeology of Elmina*, provides a persuasive case for continuity between West Africa and the Atlantic world based on archaeological evidence of the slave villages adjacent to Elmina and Cape Coast castles.

34. A. Dalzel, *History of Dahomey* (1793), opp. p. viii, pp. xiv–xv, quoted in Felipe Fernandez-Armesto, *Millennium: A History of the Last Thousand Years* (New York: Scribner, 1995), 271–272. Reportedly, guests dined using silver-handled forks amid a path of skulls.

35. An example of an English-based pidgin still spoken in Cameroon is *dis smol swain i bin go fo maket* (basically, "this little pig went to market").

36. See Alan Ryder, *Benin and the Europeans, 1485–1897* (New York: Humanities Press, 1969), 64, for a comparison of yam prices between 1522 and a later voyage.

37. Ryder, *Benin and the Europeans*, 81.

38. Merriam-Webster Online Dictionary cites earliest use in English as 1657 (www.merriam-webster.com/dictionary/yam); Columbus may have seen the yam in Guinea and applied the name.

39. Anne Grossman and Lisa Thomas Grossman, *Lobscouse and Spotted Dog* (New York: W.W. Norton, 1997), 82.

40. Grossman and Grossman, *Lobscouse*, 105–106. Doreen Simon remembers the recipe for "duff" from Berbice, Guyana, in the early twentieth century (personal communication, May 5, 1989).

41. W. Jeffrey Bolster, *Black Jacks: African American Seamen in the Age of Sail* (Cambridge, MA: Harvard University Press, 1997), 168.

42. The mulatto cook named Charles Benson, quoted in Bolster, *Black Jacks*, 168.

43. Andrew H. Foote, *Africa and the American Flag* (New York, 1854), 285ff., cited by http://gropius.lib.virginia.edu/Slave Trade.

44. The Trans-Atlantic Slave Database can be accessed at www.slavevoyages. org/tast/index.faces.

45. Eric Williams, *From Columbus to Castro: The History of the Caribbean, 1492–1969* (New York: Vintage Books, 1984), 139. Markus Vink notes 20 percent average mortality rates on slaving voyages (personal communication, September 23, 2002).

46. Okokon Essiet, personal communication, based on fieldwork in Tobago, 1997.

47. Florence Bernault, "Body, Power and Sacrifice in Equatorial Africa," *Journal of African History* 47 (2006): 207–239, traces the use of body fragments in empowerment rituals at least to the late nineteenth century.

48. Lionel Cecil Jane, *Select Documents Illustrating the Four Voyages of Columbus* (originally published by the Hakluyt Society, 1930) (Nendeln, Liechtenstein: Kraus Reprint, 1967), vol. 1, 88.

49. Reported by Bryan Edwards, *The History, Civil and Commercial, of the British Colonies in the West Indies* (Dublin, 1793), vol. 1, 56–77.

50. William F. Keegan, "The Caribbean, Including Northern South America and Lowland Central America: Early History," in *The Cambridge World History of Food*, ed. Kenneth F. Kiple and Kriemhild Conee Ornelas (Cambridge: Cambridge University Press, 2000), vol. 2 (V.D.3), 1273.

51. Robert F. Thompson, *Face of the Gods: Art and Altars of Africa and the African Americas* (New York: Museum for African Art/Prestel, 1993), 154.

52. Recorded by J.D. Elder in Tobago in 1936: J.D. Elder, *Song Games from Trinidad and Tobago* (Port of Spain, Trinidad: National Cultural Council, 1973), 52–54.

53. Kwaku Mensah, Portland, Oregon, personal communication, September 23, 2002, when he reminisced about Sunyani, Brong Ahafo, Gold Coast, in colonial times (c. 1930s).

54. Ulli Beier, *Yoruba Poetry: An Anthology of Traditional Poems* (Cambridge: Cambridge University Press, 1970), 96.

55. Simmons quoted in Jack Berry and Richard A. Spears, *West African Folk Tales* (Evanston, IL: Northwestern University Press, 1991), xiv. The answers are unrelated, except that all are beaten. *Kpa ka* also means to thrash corn and *kpa lo* to tell a riddle.

56. This version was collected by Walter Jekyll, *Jamaican Song and Story: Annancy Stories, Digging Sings, Ring Tunes, and Dancing Tunes* ([1907]; New York: Dover, 1966).

57. Elder, *Song Games*, 52–54.

58. Elder, *Song Games*, 65

59. Cole and Ross, *Arts of Ghana*, 79: "*akoko a onnye ba na otena ho ma aboa kyere ne mma.*"

60. John Stedman, *Narrative of a Five Years' Expedition against the Revolted Negroes of Surinam* (Amherst: University of Massachusetts Press, 1971 [1796]), 364–366.

61. Richard S. Dunn, *Sugar and Slaves: The Rise of the Planter Class in the English West Indies, 1624–1713* (Chapel Hill: University of North Carolina Press, 2000), 4, 185.

62. Dunn, *Sugar and Slaves*, 220.

63. *Report on the Slave Trade* (1789), no. 646a, pt. 3 Jamaica A. No.5, Parliamentary Papers XXVI, quoted in Richard B. Sheridan, "The Crisis of Slave Subsistence in the British West Indies during and after the American Revolution," *William and Mary Quarterly* 33 (1976): 615–641.

64. Dunn, *Sugar and Slaves*, 248.

65. Judith Carney, "Rice, Slaves, and Landscapes of Cultural Memory," in *Places of Cultural Memory: African Reflections on the American Landscape,* US Department of the Interior, National Park Service Conference Proceedings, Atlanta, Georgia, May 9–12, 2001.

66. Judith Carney, *Black Rice: The African Origins of Rice Cultivation in the Americas* (Cambridge, MA: Harvard University Press, 2001); Walter Rodney, *A History of the Guyanese Working People, 1881–1905* (Kingston, Jamaica: Heinemann, 1981), 84, 251 n85.

67. Carney, *Black Rice*, 117; see also Edda L. Fields-Black, *Deep Roots: Rice Farmers in West Africa and the African Diaspora* (Bloomington: Indiana University Press, 2008), for a discussion of local technology transfer based on linguistic evidence.

68. Act V of 1837 of the East India Company is discussed in Amitava Chowdhury, "Horizons of Memory: A Global Processual Study of Cultural Memory and Identity of the South Asian Indentured Labor Diaspora in the Indian Ocean and the Caribbean" (PhD diss., Washington State University, 2008).

69. Charles Leslie, *A New and Exact Account of Jamaica*, 3rd ed. (London, 1740), quoted in Roger D. Abrahams and John F. Szwed, eds., *After Africa* (New Haven: Yale University Press, 1983), 329.

70. Quoted in Sheridan, "Crisis of Slave Subsistence," 640.

71. Vincent Huyghues-Belrose, "Avant le fruit de pain: La cuisine martiniquaise au XVIIIᵉ siècle," in *Sur les chemins de l'histoire antillaise,* ed. Jean Bernabe and Serge Mam Lam Fouck (Paris: Ibis Rouge, 2006), 203.

72. Roger Norman Buckley, *Slaves in Red Coats: The British West India Regiments, 1795–1815* (New Haven: Yale University Press, 1979), 104–105.

73. Jeannette Allsopp, *The Caribbean Multilingual Dictionary of Flora, Fauna, and Foods in English, French, French Creole, and Spanish* (Kingston, Jamaica: Arawak, 2003), 132.

74. Kiple and Ornelas, *Cambridge World History of Food*, vol. 2, 1806.

75. Clapperton, *Hugh Clapperton into the Interior*, 231, 274.

76. Mungo Park, *Travels in the Interior Districts of Africa: Performed in the Years 1795, 1796, and 1797* (Reprinted New York: Dutton, 1960), 8, 75.

77. De Marees, quoted in deCorse, *Archaeology of Elmina*, p. 5.

78. Figgy duff was a steamed suet pudding in the maritime world.

79. Great Britain. House of Commons and Command. Parliamentary Papers. Correspondence Relative to Distress in the West India Colonies and Mauritius, PP 1847–1848, vol. 45, 72.

80. Graham Russell Hodges, ed., *Black Itinerants of the Gospel: The Narratives of John Jea and George White* (Madison, WI: Madison House, 1993), 89.

81. John Jea, "The Life, History, and Unparalleled Sufferings of John Jea, the Atlantic Preacher," in Hodges, *Black Itinerants*, 123–125.

82. See, for example, the work of Kofi Agorsah, Douglas Armstrong, Candice Goucher, Mark Hauser, Ken Kelly, and Merrick Posnansky.

83. See the work of archaeologist Mark Leone, cited by Thompson, *Face of the Gods*.

84. Sandra S. Awang, "Reinterpreting Afrocentric Resistance in the Diaspora: Slave Women Higglers in the Commonwealth Caribbean," paper presented at the African Studies Association annual meeting, Seattle, Washington, 1992.

85. Clapperton, *Hugh Clapperton into the Interior*, 274.

86. E. Kofi Agorsah, *Maroon Heritage: Archaeological, Ethnographic and Historical Perspectives* (Kingston, Jamaica: Canoe Press, 1994). Candice Goucher and E. Kofi Agorsah, "Excavating the Roots of Resistance: The Significance of Maroons in Jamaican Archaeology," in *Out of Many, One People: The Historical Archaeology of Colonial Jamaica*, ed. Delle, Hauser, and Armstrong, examine the Maroon experience in Jamaica within the context of broader Maroon studies. For more on archaeological perspectives on household material culture, see Kenneth Kelly, *Current Research in the French West Indies*, Department of Anthropology, University of South Carolina, 2008, www.cla.sc.edu/anth/faculty/KGKelly1/guadeloupe.html; see also Mark W. Hauser, "Routes and Roots of Empire: Pots, Power, and Slavery in the Eighteenth Century British Caribbean," *American Anthropologist* 113, no 3, 2011: 431–447.

87. Barclay, quoted in Robert Walsh, "Negro Slavery," *American Quarterly Review* 2 (1827): 245.

88. Kelly, *Current Research*.

89. Cindee and Paul Farnsworth, personal communication, Bahamas, 1998.

90. E.V. Goveia, *The West Indian Slave Laws of the Eighteenth Century* (*Chapters in Caribbean History 2*) (Aylesbury, UK: Caribbean Universities Press, 1970).

91. Maria Nugent, *Lady Nugent's Journal of Her Residence in Jamaica, from 1801 to 1805* (Kingston, Jamaica: Institute of Jamaica, 1966), 55.

92. Nugent, *Journal*, 70.

93. Trevor Burnard, *Mastery, Tyranny and Desire: Thomas Thistlewood and His Slaves in the Anglo-Jamaican World* (Chapel Hill: University of North Carolina Press, 2003).

94. Barbados Museum; Marisa J. Fuentes, "Power and Historical Figuring: Rachael Pringle Polgreen's Troubled Archive," *Gender & History* 22, no. 3 (2010): 564–584.

95. Fuentes, "Power and Historical Figuring," 571.

96. Maureen Brown, personal communication, World Archaeological Congress, Intersession, Kingston, Jamaica, May 21, 2007.

97. Roger Norman Buckley, *The British Army in the West Indies: Society and the Military in the Revolutionary Age* (Gainesville: University Press of Florida, 1998), 324–325.

98. Mary Nooter Roberts and Allen F. Roberts, *Memory: Luba Art and the Making of History* (New York: Museum for African Art/Prestel, 1996), 194.

THREE

Devil-King Sugar

Hierarchies of Caribbean Foodways

Sweat and profit
Cutlass profit
Islands ruled by sugar-cane.

—L. Edward ["Kamau"] Braithwaite[1]

Why did all-creating Nature
Make the plant for which we toil?
Sighs must fan it,
Tears must water,
Sweat of ours must dress the soil.
Think ye Masters, iron-hearted
Lolling at your jovial Boards,
Think how many Backs have smarted
For the Sweet your Cane afford!

—From a 1791 abolitionist pamphlet[2]

Sugar cane (ireke [in Yoruba]) is a sign of continuity.

—Robert Farris Thompson[3]

Trinidad Carnival masqueraders known as "Jab Molassies" swarm the streets in the final pre-Lenten days of revelry and mischief before Ash Wednesday. Their name comes from the French patois *diable* (devil) and *mélasse* (molasses) and so translates roughly to mean "Molasses Devil" locally. The revelers suggest the epitome of inversion at the heart of Carnival. Wearing short pants, a horned mask, a wire tail, and carrying a pitchfork and sometimes chains, lock, and key, dancers emerge from the darkness to threaten onlookers too slow to

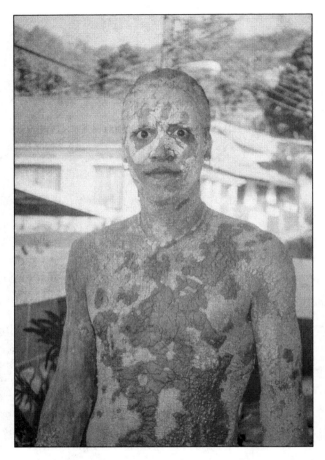

Member of a carnival mud band, Port of Spain, Trinidad
(Photograph by Candice Goucher)

run away. Nowadays the Jab Molassies wear mud, grease, tar, or sprayed body paint—sometimes blue or red or silver, but the nineteenth-century character's costume was not complete without a bath of stale molasses smeared from head to toe. In direct opposition to the island's sugar planters, who preferred to play masquerade dressed as garden slaves, the Jab Molassies were freed slaves now impersonating the devil himself and none other than the slave owner. A slightly later version of the masquerade "Jab Jab" was adopted by East Indian indentured cane workers, who dressed up the costume with brightly colored cloth pants and a horizontally paneled shirt punctuated by a fringe of fabric triangles decorated with bells. They carried whips, which they did not hesitate to crack in the air, imitating the threat of plantation brutality in the sugarcane fields. At the core of these inversions was also the deepest irony of every sugar island—something the scholar Sidney Mintz brilliantly terms the "sweetness of power."[4]

Devil-King Sugar

The term "King Sugar" has been used widely in Caribbean circles to refer to the central importance of sugarcane crops not only in the economy, but also in the food culture of the region. In the context of plantation slavery, such explicitly male terminology ("King") hints at the gendered pattern of hierarchy in the production of sugar and the patterns of empowered meanings sugar acquired in Caribbean food history. Sugar and its products (from molasses to rum) everywhere referred to exploitation. This chapter examines more closely the food and drink prepared with sugar, as well as specific foodways, whose arrival in the Caribbean were most closely associated with sugar's history.

As a world food, sugar has uniquely satisfied the human appetite for sweetness without greatly altering the flavor of foods it complements. Sugar in Europe and the Americas started as a luxury item and then became a food of the poor, bolstering exploited laborers with much-needed calories. Sugar was associated with the wealth and opulence of the Caribbean, but also with its debauchery. Sugar was brought to the Caribbean, where it entwined the cultures of the enslaved and indentured laborers; its myriad products together define the soul of Caribbean complexity.

According to Mintz, sugar's "imperial role" was relatively recent. Before the late eighteenth century, sugar was largely unavailable to Europeans.[5] Rare and valuable, sugar was used as a condiment and as a coveted medicinal ingredient. Access to this precious commodity provided pleasure beyond its taste. A medicinal substance in ancient Greece, sugar was more widely known in Europe by about 1100 CE, long before the plant's growth into a Caribbean industry.

The globalization of slavery changed the role of sugar in the modern diet. The expansion of production using slave labor in the seventeenth century fed a demand for the sweetness of sugar in Europe. This demand further fueled the slave trade and the global appetite for sugar, causing growth in the industrial production of sugar supplies. In turn, the resultant sharp drop in price meant that sugar would become more widely available. Mintz points out that "between 1750 and 1850, [sugar] ceased to be a luxury and became a necessity." He argues that sugar was used in Europe as an extraordinary ceremonial substance at the same time it became an ordinary—first for upper

Sugarcane fields, Barbados
(Photograph by Candice Goucher)

classes, then lower classes—daily consumable. What of the Caribbean, where sugar was not only ubiquitous in all its forms (liquid and crystal), but was charged with meanings associated with the direct experience of brutality and the bitter sorrows of plantation slavery and indentured labor?

Sugar's History

More than any other food, sugar represented the ironic role of the Caribbean in world history. Because of its roots in slavery, sugar altered the world's diets in significant ways. The history of sugar marked the commoditization of labor and food, both tied to imperial control over markets and food systems. King Sugar, although not native to the region, came to epitomize the history of the Caribbean. The commodity's global history connects Asia, Europe, and Africa to the Americas.

Sugarcanes (*Saccharum* spp.) are perennial grasses, probably first domesticated in New Guinea about 10,000 years ago.[6] By 800 BCE, the first written evidence (in preclassical Sanskrit) confirms that sugarcane was consumed in India in a whole range of products, in combination with foods such as milk, rice, and barley, as sugar crystals, and fermented from cane juice as a drink flavored with ginger. The tropical crop then spread across Eurasia, first east to China and west via Arab trade to Persia and the Mediterranean. Chinese imperial delegations attempted to learn the technique of producing crystals. Sugar technology in the Mediterranean eventually was able to extract the cane juice more efficiently. J.H. Galloway describes the processes of crystallization as an intensive labor of machines, animals, and men until, finally, the "juice was then clarified, reduced to the point of crystallization in open pans over furnaces, and the resulting syrup was placed in conical pots from which the molasses drained, leaving a loaf of sugar in each pot."[7]

In the fifteenth century, the Spanish and Portuguese, seeking tropical tracts of land for the cultivation of sugar, brought the crop to islands off the coast of Africa. There African labor was first applied to plantation experiments around the 1470s. Workers added the juice of local plant extracts from okra (*Hibiscus esculentus*, known as *gombo*) to improve sedimentation at the clarification stage.[8] Columbus himself had trained in the Madeira sugar trade. His second voyage of 1493 carried sugarcane to the island of Hispaniola in the Caribbean, where sugar plantations would become the "favored child of capitalism." Triangular trading connections were constructed: European goods to Africa, enslaved Africans to the Caribbean, sugar back to Europe; manufactured rum from North America to Africa, enslaved Africans to the Caribbean, West Indian sugar back to America, where it was also made into rum. These threads came together to make up the Atlantic world's global networks in a mighty combination of "sweetness and power."

Expanding Caribbean Sugar Production

The Portuguese were instrumental in expanding the Atlantic slave trade. They supplied the sugar islands in Africa, their colony in Brazil, and the Spanish Caribbean. While the Spanish first cultivated sugar on Hispaniola in the early 1500s and began commercial production by 1520, the later success of the Portuguese in their Brazilian operations attracted global interest. After the 1650s, when the Dutch captured and came to control the territories of northern Brazil, they helped spread sugar technology and profits across the Caribbean and into North America.

Copper Cauldrons

The Dutch were pioneers in the technology and trade of the Atlantic. Their reach was truly global. The Dutch East India Company controlled exports from Japanese copper mining and held a near monopoly on non-Chinese trade in copper in Asia and Africa. The enormous rise in the prices of copper after

1606 witnessed the flow of capital into the hands of Dutch merchants who traded in copper. At almost the same time, the Dutch West India Company seized and controlled the richest sugar-producing area in Brazil (around Recife) from 1630 to 1654. Dutch sugar enterprises in Brazil served as models for other large-scale Caribbean ventures. The two directions of investment soon came together. Dutch merchants controlled the copper trade, supplying the plantation's boiling houses with their enormous pots used to boil the cane juices. Typically up to seven large copper kettles of various sizes were required for each sugar operation. Household items, including kitchen kettles and utensils, were also made from copper.

Copper cauldrons consumed the economic interests that were integral to the rise of a capitalist economy. Entrepreneurs relied on the systems of credit, insurance, and finance that Dutch trading companies experimented with and that were necessary to risky overseas enterprise. Corporate financing and state support jointly promoted the development of sugar plantations and, along with them, slavery. Creditors in Amsterdam, London, and other cities, who accumulated capital from the sale of both goods and people, financed shipping concerns involved in the transfer of these goods and people, investing the profits in manufacturing.

By the eighteenth century, British manufacturing industries also had become involved in the copper trade to the West Indies. The marketing and movement of copper cauldrons reflects the shifting balance between the Dutch East India Company (Vereenigde Oostindische Compagnie or VOC) and the British East India Company (EIC). Historian Ryuto Shimada has examined the rise in British copper exports, which began to replace Dutch-carried copper. Copper was the first item of British manufacture to be produced in a capital-intensive system. Shimada makes the case that copper, not textiles, "acted as the harbinger of the Industrial Revolution to the world economy."[9] In the 1740s, 60 percent of all British exports of wrought copper went to the West Indies.

Copper technology was not the only prerequisite for successful sugar production ventures. By the first decades of the seventeenth century, African captives were landed in Bermuda, Veracruz, and North American and Caribbean ports in between. French, English, and Dutch privateers and smugglers also spread the forced migration of agricultural laborers from West Central Africa (Kongo and Ndongo) to western ports of the African Atlantic, where they worked fields of tobacco and foodstuffs. Around the 1640s, sugar plants began to be introduced to other islands. John Ogilvy's map of Barbados in the mid-seventeenth century shows crops of sugar, pawpaw, and pineapple there. On this island, slave artisans constructed a

Sugar production on Antigua: *A Mill Yard*, London, c. 1833
(Courtesy of the John Carter Brown Library, Brown University)

new kind of mill with vertically mounted rollers. Some evidence points to the global origins of this technology in China.[10] In any case, other Caribbean islands soon followed the lead of Barbados, producing sugar crystals for export. Dutch settlers may have introduced the crop to Martinique. In 1685, the French King Louis XIV issued "La Traite des Noirs," authorizing the capture and transport of enslaved Africans to work French sugar plantations in the Caribbean.

Jean Baptiste Labat, a Jesuit priest in the French Antilles (1694–1705), described a plantation owner's gift of sugarcane syrup to visiting Carib Indians for the making of their local drink from cassava.[11] The keen interest in liquid derivatives of sugar spread rapidly. These processes also employed copper kettles for boiling water and adding molasses and various combinations of spices, fruit, cassava, or potatoes, utilizing the principles of fermentation. Distillation into rum did not appear until the eighteenth century (see below). Growing cane sugar became so lucrative that the British tried to trade all of Canada for the French Caribbean islands of Guadeloupe, Martinique, and St. Lucia after the Seven Years' War. The French refused the offer.

Sugar and Labor

The production of sugar was a particularly labor-intensive enterprise. Even as new technology increased their production and efficiency, sugar plantations continued to rely on enslaved labor. Dutch merchants were also involved in the early slave business, moving captives from Central Africa to the Netherlands' Brazil plantations and, beginning in 1605, to islands spread from Trinidad, South America, to Bermuda and the Atlantic seaboard.

Enslaved Africans worked together in cooperative groups. They planted fields, weeded, cut and hauled cane, and participated in the industrialized processes of boiling and refining the sugar. Nothing was wasted—even the cane trash became fuel for the boiling house. After working the fields and factories, they cooked and ate together. These team endeavors encouraged the growth of community from a disparate number of ethnic groups, and sometimes the innovation of work songs followed.[12] The chorus of one such song was recorded in the nineteenth-century West Indies by Wentworth—"Aw boil my pot, aw boil um sweet/Chaun [open?] fine my deary hunney"—in a lyrical reference to sugar manufacture and use. The enslaved sang the chorus, so he claims, while "transporting the canes to the mill . . . [amid] the confused clamor of voices in dialogue and song."[13] This harvest celebration continued for centuries after slavery's end. In Barbados, the festivities marking the final cane cutting were called "Crop-Over," described in the following nineteenth-century account:

> A kind of harvest-home generally takes place at the end of the crop-gathering upon each estate. A cart laden with the last canes is drawn by mules decorated with ribbons, and attended by a crowd of laborers: the principal woman being attired in white muslin. The mill and other estate buildings are gay with coloured kerchiefs which do duty as flags. Some ancient negro is put forward to make a speech to the planter, which he often does with considerable humour and address. Then the planter replies, and a glass of "falernum"—a beverage compounded of rum, lime-juice, and syrup—is handed round to each. Then the dancing begins, and is carried on to a late hour to the sound of fiddles and a tambourine. Sometimes the proceedings are varied by the introduction of a "trash man," a figure, i.e., stuffed with cane trash and tied upon the back of the mule, which, being finally let loose, gallops about with his incongruous burden, to the great delight of the spectators.[14]

Each phase of operations was distinct and sometimes marked by celebration. Particularly notable was the romanticized observation that "the day on which the last of the canes are cut down upon a sugar plantation, flags are displayed in the field, and all is merriment."[15]

In fact, the grueling heat and intensive labor involved in sugar production took its toll on daily life. Violence and coercion were at the heart of plantation life. Sugarcane field laborers were a miserable lot, working from sunrise to sundown under the watchful eye of white slave masters, their overseers, and drivers with whips. John Luffman described a late eighteenth-century plantation in Antigua:

> The negroes are turned out at sun rise, and employed in gangs from twenty to sixty, or upwards under the inspection of white overseers . . . subordinate to these overseers, are drivers, commonly called dog-drivers, who are mostly black or mulatto fellows, of the worst dispositions; these men are furnished with whips, which, while on duty, they are obliged, on pain of severe punishment, to have with them, and are authorized to flog wherever they see the least relaxation from labor.[16]

Planting, cutting, and hauling cane to the mill was only the beginning of the brutal process that brought sugar to the tables of the rich and opulent of Europe.

The setting for sugar manufacture was much like that of industrial organizations of subsequent centuries. The mill was a large mechanical apparatus used to extract juices. It was powered by animal, slave, water, wind, and, later, steam power. The sugar mill crushed the cane, and what followed was the cleaning and reduction of the juices via boiling. This process could be likened to the fires of an industrial hell, as a description from Barbados (c. 1700) vividly suggests:

> In short, 'tis to live in a perpetual Noise and Hurry, and the only way to render a person Angry, and Tyrannical, too; since the Climate is so hot, and the labor so constant, that the servants night and day stand in great Boyling Houses, where there are Six or Seven large Coppers or Furnaces kept perpetually Boyling; and from which with heavy Ladles and Scummers they Skim off the escrementitious parts of the Canes, till it comes to its perfection and cleanness, while others as Stoakers, Broil as it were, alive, in managing the Fires; and one part is constantly at the Mill, to supply it with Canes, night and day, during the whole Season of making Sugar, which is about six Months of the year.[17]

Once the boiled liquid was finished, it was time for the "striking," or transfer, of the hot liquid into molds to drain and dry while cooling. This transfer had to occur at just the right moment for the once liquid and now semicrystalline sugar to crystallize completely into cones. In the transfer, temperature, timing, and the manipulation of the sugar were everything. Sugar boilers were true artisans who worked under brutal, dangerous conditions.

The demands of the sugar industry encouraged specialization in the technology and techniques of handling large copper kettles. These were skills that would later transfer to maritime cookery. Some colonies became famous for the innovations of enslaved experts in sugar refinement. By carefully controlling the temperature and other conditions, sugar refiners produced a fine brown sugar known as demerara, after the river in Guyana where the technology evolved. While it behaved like finely granulated white sugars, demerara's yellow-brown color enabled the Guyanese producers to avoid the refined white sugar's higher customs duties in American markets. Other global sugar producers followed suit. The island of Mauritius, in the Indian Ocean, produced and marketed a version of the prized brown sugar that was also called demerara. Another version, known as London demerara, was actually refined sugar with added molasses, rather than raw sugar. The monopoly over the boiling pans likewise gave Dutch entrepreneurs an advantage. In seventeenth-century Barbados, sugar became a currency against which the value of other goods was measured. For example, when Henry Willoughby recaptured Suriname territory in 1668, he returned to Barbados with 67,412 slaves, 160 head of cattle, and 150,000 pounds of sugar, besides plants, speckled wood, and dry wares worth another 150,000 pounds of sugar.[18] Even fines were sometimes paid in sugar, as laws in the early colony reveal.

Sugar was everywhere an export crop, and its viability depended greatly on large-scale production and low shipping costs and customs duties. The sharp increase in British import duties on *muscovado* sugar (a moist and dark brown sugar made with cane juice, sometimes referred to as Barbados sugar) at the end of the eighteenth century proved painful to the manufacturers across the West Indies. Especially hard-hit was the Jamaican sugar industry, which already had two refineries in Kingston. John Reeder, a local iron and brass foundry owner in Morant Bay, relied on nearly 300 African craftsmen to develop innovative, watertight copper vessels for the sugar industry.[19] Other experimental projects focused on the fuel shortage. In the end, British import duties on sugar proved to be prohibitive, and the local refining industry died out.[20] Thus, refined sugar tended to remain expensive and unavailable to all but the wealthy Caribbean islanders. Sugar in its raw and unrefined forms nonetheless played a significant role in the cultures and cuisines of its Caribbean workers.

Sugar and Caribbean Cultural Innovations

African-derived forms of cultural expression used sugar as a key element in their conceptualization and practice. Public processions were moving monuments to the historical experience of the enslaved. That sugar products were viewed as synonymous with oppression is suggested by the use of dark molasses smeared all over the bodies of participants during the J'Ouvert (*Jour Ouvert*, opening morning of) celebrations of Trinidad Carnival described at the beginning of this chapter. Today the local "mud bands" still assemble on Sunday night and early Monday morning, using paint and mud in place of molasses. Some participants still carry slave chains symbolic of their ancestors' history on sugar plantations.

Cannes Brûlées: Performing the History of Sugar

Trinidadian historian Hollis Liverpool sees other associations between sugar and this carnival ritual. According to Liverpool, in these rituals "the enslaved created their own hidden transcript, their own secret cultural code."[21] Setting fire to cane fields in controlled burns was a regular occurrence, for purposes of clearing the fields and ridding the area of deadly snakes. As in parts of West Africa, the practice also served to drive small game into the hands and traps of hunters. But burning cane also provided an opportunity for rebellion and destruction of the enslaver's property, and a lighted cane was routinely used as a torch in slave processions. In 1820, Alison Carmichael heard the lyrics associated with burning cane, "Fire in da mountain/Nobody for out him [will put it out]," sung by the enslaved on her Trinidad plantation.[22] She explained the song as a satirical reference to the deliberate setting of fires to the canes. According to historian Lionel Fraser, the estates held a kind of "Cannes Brûlées" (or Canbouley, French for "burning canes") fire drill, anticipating the ritual that became Cannes Brûlées on J'Ouvert, Carnival Monday.[23] In the drill, gangs of enslaved Africans from surrounding properties were called by blowing conch shells, a call to fight employed by Africans (especially Maroons or escaped slaves) on some islands. The enslaved were marched in processions led by drivers with whips, just as described during the previous century in Antigua. After emancipation, freed slaves may have mimicked their slave masters, adding songs of their own resistance.

Eventually harvest and emancipation celebrations were transferred from August to the time of Carnival and the pre-Lenten calendar of the colonizers. The popular traditional character from the early days of harvest procession, the Jab Molassie, shifted to the pre-Lenten season of masquerades. Charles Day, an observer of Carnivals in the 1840s, suspected that the performance was a reenactment of the condition of enslavement in an atmosphere of inversion or satire. He saw "that whenever a black mask appeared, it was sure to be a white man."[24] Errol Hill found remarkable that "molasses, a product of the sugarcane, whose cultivation might have been hateful to the plantation slaves, could be yet another of the freedom symbols used in the masquerade."[25] From at least the 1830s, the cane field workers swarmed onto city streets to deliver their message about "King Sugar" at Carnival time. Their performance became a political statement about the true source of devilry in the Caribbean; that bad-smelling sugar was smeared on the messenger only sweetened their message of resistance.

Cooking with Sugar

There is little doubt that the use of burnt sugar in Caribbean cooking is a metaphor suggesting the region's deep historical roots in the pain and suffering of slavery. Using refined white sugar in cooking quickly blackened it, a transformation that gave depth and character to sweet and savory foods. Sugar and molasses were frequently added to hot oil at the time of cooking or employed in marinades prior to cooking meat, providing a rich, smoky flavor as they caramelized. Too much heat produced actual burning and a bitter flavor. The participation of Africans in all stages of sugar production provided instruction in the handling of sugar in the kitchen. Burnt sugar was perhaps best known for its prominent role in the most specialized of island desserts, including the Caribbean's "Black Cake," aptly named for the black, chocolate-like color of the finished steamed or baked fruitcake. The cake was an English or European tradition that was Africanized. The black cake gained its dark color from a dose of burnt sugar and water in equal parts as a coloring agent. Reflecting sugar's bitter role in the islands' history, burnt sugar also found its way into snacks that were peculiar to the festival days celebrated by the nineteenth-century descendants of slaves and indentured laborers who worked in the cane fields. Burnt sugar mimicked the indigenous and African use of the thick, black cassareep, enveloping ingredients in its darkened glaze of enzymes released in processing the cassava. The gumbos of New Orleans and French islands similarly relied on slow, patient darkening of butter and flour into a racialized and color-coded roux.[26]

Creole recipes used burnt sugar to enhance the smoky flavor of meats, especially fowl. In the Caribbean, chickens were scarce and their substitution by other meats was commonplace. In Jamaica about 1804, Lady Maria Nugent's husband played "rather a naughty trick" on a visiting Colonel Irvine by passing off an iguana as chicken. In early Catholic communities, the iguana had been declared a "fish," allowing it to be consumed on holy

STEWED BROWN CHICKEN

1 small chicken, cut up (or 2 pounds bone-in, skinless thighs)
3 tablespoons demerara, muscovado, or dark brown sugar
1 teaspoon cayenne flakes
1 teaspoon cumin
2 teaspoons ginger, finely minced
1/4 teaspoon each of cinnamon, nutmeg, cloves, salt, black pepper
1 tablespoon coriander
1 bell pepper, chopped
1 onion, chopped
1 to 2 tablespoons cooking oil
18-ounce can diced tomatoes
1 bay leaf
1 curry leaf (available from Caribbean or Asian food stores)
2 tablespoons cooking oil
1 tablespoon balsamic vinegar
2 cups water or chicken broth

Cover the chicken with sugar and spices; set aside. In a separate pan, brown onion and bell pepper in 1 to 2 tablespoons of cooking oil. When softened, blend in tomatoes, add bay leaf and curry leaf, and cook for about 20 minutes. Meanwhile, add the seasoned chicken to 2 tablespoons of hot oil in a separate pot and brown thoroughly. Add tomatoes, vinegar, and enough water or broth to cover. Simmer uncovered for about 20 minutes or until chicken is done, adding more water or broth if necessary to avoid burning. Salt and pepper to taste. Remove the leaves. Serve with saffron rice.

days. According to Nugent, iguana was thought to be a "great delicacy, by many Creoles; but the sight of it, while living, is disgusting, as it is covered with scales, and looks frightful altogether."[27] Although iguana may not have suited Maria Nugent's tastes, it was one of several popular alternatives to chicken. Consequently, the iguana went extinct on some islands and became desirable and expensive bush meat on others. Mountain chicken, a large frog

(*Leptodactylus fallax*) in Dominica and Montserrat, was similarly hunted in large numbers for its tasty legs.

Indentured Labor: Asian Contributions to Caribbean Culture and Cuisine

The desire for sweetness and profit also drove the flow of labor from Asia to the Caribbean after emancipation. After the gradual abolition of slavery came into full force with the British Slavery Abolition Act (1834), plantation labor became scarce on the sugar-producing islands. One means of expanding production on the large sugar-producing islands was the importation of East Indian and Chinese workers as indentured laborers. Recruited in Calcutta, the laborers entered into contracts with British companies for a set number of years. It was reported that these contracted laborers often did not understand where they were going, having been told they would be sent to "Chini-dad" (literally, land of sugar).[28] Unlike early African populations, the indentured laborers were at first recruited in equal proportions of male and female workers. This practice was later altered to recruit more men. Indeed, more than a million laborers were sent to Mauritius (in the Indian Ocean) and Natal (South Africa), as well as Trinidad, Jamaica, Guyana, Surinam, Grenada, St. Lucia, St. Vincent, St. Kitts, Martinique, and Guadeloupe. Immigrants came mostly from central and eastern Indian provinces, but also some migrated from southern India. They represented a variety of South Asian regions, languages, cultures, and castes; most were not "Hindoos," as the British officers thought, but Muslims or those who practiced the foodways affiliated with other local religions.

The experience of indentured Indians in the mid-nineteenth century mirrored that of the earlier enslaved Africans, in part because merchants employed the same successful tactics they considered would improve survival on the ocean journey. Important among the multiplicity of identity components were regional differences that manifested in mutually unintelligible languages, religious practices, caste prejudices, and culinary folkways. The historian Amitava Chowdhury has studied this multiplicity and argued that the process of identity erosion toward the creation of a singularity of Indianness began at the Indian emigration depot, where emigrants awaited their departure.

Transporting Cuisines

The transport of laborers was protected by a legal framework initiated by the Act V of 1837 of the East India Company. The guidelines governed the emigrant diet by defining the foods to be provided in the depot and on board ship. Foremost were provisions of rice, lentils, ghee, salt, turmeric, onions, and tobacco. These were augmented with the addition of chilis, tamarind, and *chura* (parched rice) in 1843, in the wake of laborers' complaints about not being given "curry" powder. The ingredients did little to soothe Brahmin displeasure at being made to cook and eat together with lower castes. The term "curry" likely comes from the south Indian Tamil word *kari*, meaning "sauce." "Curry" was in many ways a seventeenth-century British invention derived from colonial encounters with an amalgam of ethnic cuisines. The British definition of a curry resided in any wet stew mixture of onion, ginger, turmeric, garlic, pepper, chilis, coriander, cumin, and other spices cooked with vegetables or meat. No singular Indian identity had yet formed. An erasure of differences and their embrace under the umbrella of national identity anticipated the processes of colonization and decolonization under way in the subcontinent's homelands. Nor was there a single "East Indian" culinary tradition, born as a new Creole in the Caribbean. Just as "curry" emerged from multiple strands of culinary encounters registering the variety of sauces and gravies unique to individual regions, both "Indo-Caribbean" and "Caribbean curry" were more simply associated with the arrival and array of exotic spices of East, South, and Southeast Asia.

Ancient Foodways, New Borrowings

Early overland trade and maritime connections had brought ingredients for the Tamil wet sauces from afar. Archaeologists have documented a more ancient protocurry that was cooked and eaten 4,500 years ago by inhabitants of the Indus civilization.[29] Analyzing cooking pots, the researchers have identified the oldest known record of ginger and turmeric using the unique genetic signatures of molecular structures left behind as starch grain residues. No doubt trading voyages and caravans added to the complexity by bringing new ingredients, including nutmeg and peppers, to the curry pot. Other borrowed influences in the South Asian foodways came from Portuguese settlements on the west coast of India in the sixteenth century; the subsequent coastal trading encounters became global nodes. For example, "Vindaloo" derived from the Portuguese terms for the spicy dish that contained wine (*vin*) and garlic (*ail*). The chilis from Africa and the Americas produced the variety of much sought-after flavors and heat.

The maritime cauldron again played a key role in emphasizing and even imposing similarities. Caste, religion, and language were irrelevant. Hindu ate with Muslim; Brahman ate with non-Brahman. Some of the dry goods served on board—*chura* (from flattened rice), gram (from ground chickpeas), and sugar—were used when cooking was impossible owing to rough seas.

Clearly, the addition of "curry" was a culturally specific preference made by the East Indian laborers, and company officials had learned in the slave trade to heed the culinary demands of their passengers in order to ensure successful transport of laborers to the Caribbean. At nearly the same time, Sierra Leone departures from West Africa to the British Caribbean were regulated by a different set of provisions. The seven-week voyage provided biscuit, rice or yam, palm oil, vinegar, salted beef, pork, or fish, and African pepper. Once the East Indian workers reached their island home, newly emancipated Africans resented the recent arrivals; and the colonial governments created binary distinctions between the African-descended and Indian-descended workers, emphasizing unnatural historical categories of African Creole (native-born) or African-Caribbean and Indo-Caribbean identification. The emancipated foodways present samples of both homogenizing narratives and hybridity, revealing that the Indo-Caribbean immigrants were also participants in the Creole continuum.

Finding East Indian Identity

Between 1838 and 1917, these immigrants brought new cuisines and some new foods to the Caribbean, but they often lacked the sufficient numbers needed to maintain a separate cultural identity on many islands. On nineteenth-century sugar plantations like the Danks Estate in Clarendon Parish, Jamaica, the new immigrants ate alongside the African arrivals, sometimes even arriving on the same ship. Island governments had concerns about the relations between the two groups and mounted investigations. Danks Estate owner Edward Ewbank confirmed in his 1845 testimony that the two groups ("Coolies" and "natives") ate together and sometimes "[the Indians] partake of some of the foods of the natives."[30]

By 1847, most of the East Indians had their own provision grounds.[31] These they supplemented with periodic thefts of hogs and goats, which were commonly acquired for nights of feasting. Even with the financial drain from constant thievery, the Danks Estate was successful by any count; in 1848, the owner was presented with a silver vessel to commemorate having produced the largest amount of sugar from the smallest field (178 hogsheads from 82 acres of cane). By the end of the indenture system in the early twentieth century, some 150,000 Indians lived in the larger colonies of Trinidad and Tobago, Jamaica, and British Guyana alone. Ironically, the bitterest complaints against East Indian laborers were those of recently freed slaves, whose labor the indentured immigrants replaced. African descendants felt they were being taxed to prop up the sugar industry.[32] The Indian community was by no means homogeneous and the workers were not all situated on rural estates.

Madras jobbing gangs and workers with Calcutta and Bengal origins were identifiable, and the differences created conflict on some estates. Regardless of any intergroup strife, eating together aptly characterized the commonalities of the laborer's experience.

Asian foods had arrived long before the South Asian indentured workers, however. Rice, the staple of Asian diets, had already been brought from Asia to the Caribbean in the seventeenth century.[33] It is likely that African varieties and production techniques were imported even earlier, perhaps in the sixteenth century, when they also reached Brazil (Bahia), possibly the tidal waterways of the Guianas, and certainly the American South. African rice was native to the Senegambia and also known to West Central Africans, before the Europeans arrived. Portuguese, Dutch, and New England sailing ships eventually carried tons of American-produced rice either to Africa or to the Caribbean. Sir Hans Sloane, the founder of the British Museum, observed Africans in Jamaica planting rice in 1687 (he also identified hundreds of new botanical species in Jamaica).

As early as 1700, small quantities of rice were brought from the Indian Ocean to the Caribbean. By the end of the eighteenth century, rice was carried as provisions aboard ships crossing the Atlantic, moving in both directions. Africans on the continent liked the Carolina gold rice that originated in Asia. The nineteenth-century Chinese and South Asian immigrants popularized rice in Caribbean cuisines. In larger numbers than on most other islands, they labored in Trinidad and Guyanese rice fields and developed new technologies for husking the grains. East Indian immigrants also went to the French Caribbean, where they grew rice in exchange for housing, food, medicine, clothing, minimal wages, and their passage. In Trinidad, they made *khichari*, using rice and lentils, and *channa* (garbanzo beans) became widely adopted as the term from Indic origins. Even in the lowlands of Jamaica and Cuba, enslaved Africans found opportunities to grow rice as provisions against hunger.

Not every food was so successfully transplanted and willingly incorporated into the kitchen lexicon. A 1793 voyage of the HMS *Bounty* from Tahiti is credited with the arrival of breadfruit brought by Captain William Bligh. The enslaved reportedly refused to eat the vegetable, and it only became part of the Caribbean diet (roasted, boiled, baked, fried, and dried to make flour) with the influx of Asians after slavery. It was just as well since the breadfruit added little nutritionally to the plate. By this time, many American food crops were also making inroads into the food cultures of the South Asian subcontinent. The American tomato and potato were especially welcomed additions to the Hindu diet on days when grains were forbidden. In Kerala, an area from which many South Asian immigrants originated, cassava was promoted in the 1880s. Elsewhere maize was prepared alongside traditional native plants such as roasted barley, as poor people's food, or eaten with spring greens as ceremonial food.[34] Once successfully introduced, both peanuts and corn became cash crops in India.[35]

In this way the food ingredients encountered by East Indian arrivals in the Caribbean differed little from the foods they left behind. These "cross-over" foods sometimes were the most difficult to trace in the Atlantic world. The globalization of foods was well along in the Indian Ocean by the time of the indenture system. Europeans moved between the Indian Ocean and the Caribbean, carrying tastes for the foods they encountered. The Mughal emperor Akbar, like his royal European counterparts, was responsible for increasing the variety of available flavors and foods carried by Iberian merchants to South Asian elite households. Akbar added Caribbean pineapples (1590), whereas guavas were probably introduced later by the Dutch rather than contemporary Portuguese traders. The chili pepper provides another example of this complex food history linking the Indian Ocean and the Caribbean, and its story suggests that multiple paths of introduction were likely. The chili pepper was identified in South Asia in the sixteenth century and was known as "Pernambuco pepper," recalling its Brazilian slave-trade connections. The Carib term for chilis (*axi* or *achi*) adopted by the Portuguese also may have persisted as a borrowing in Indian vocabulary as *achar* or pickles.[36] This is turn was later carried back to the Caribbean by the nineteenth-century immigrants, who described their pickled condiment of unripe mangoes and peppers with vinegar, salt, and spices as *achar* in Guyana and *kuchela* in Trinidad. Mangoes (and peppers) are known in Indian cuisines as "hot" foods, which, according to the ancient Vedic medical theory of humors, were required by the body to balance the cooling impact of other foods.[37] East India Company merchants also played a role in the spread of culinary tastes: jars of achar were taken on long voyages.[38]

East Indians brought few possessions with them, but some carried seeds, food knowledge, and techniques for grinding spices. Wet curry pastes were ground on a stone called a *sill*. New spices, including coriander (*dhannia*), cumin seed (*geera*), turmeric, and fenugreek, were introduced. As Trinidadian cook Wendy Rahamut argues:

> The East Indians brought not only ingredients, but also their own specific methods of cooking. When they first arrived they began to cook on a *chulla*, or mud stove, made with a combination of river mud, leaves and sticks, and cow dung. Water was used to smooth the mud to get a finished look, a process called *leepay*. The fire burned from the base of the *chulla*.[39]

In addition to iron griddles called *tawah* for baking bread, the East Indians also imported water buffalo and humped cattle for producing the yoghurt and ghee they knew back home. The Indo-Caribbean impact was most enduring in places where the East Indians sustained a large community and continued immigration into the twentieth century.

Chinese Immigration

Chinese immigration to the Caribbean began in the early nineteenth century with the arrival in Trinidad of nearly 200 Chinese men recruited in Macao, Penang, and Calcutta, and transported on the ship *Fortitude*.[40] Few if any of these survived to meet the next wave of immigrants. Between 1853 and 1866, the British contracted thousands more Chinese as indentured labor and transported them from territories in Asia. In Guyana a bounty was offered to planters able to recruit and land Chinese laborers. Although late in arriving and small in numbers, the Chinese immigrants contributed their labor and their cuisines to the Caribbean cauldron. Initially they were settled in Trinidad, Guyana, Cuba, and Jamaica. Most of the mid-nineteenth-century Chinese immigrants to the Caribbean spoke Cantonese and came from the southern port city of Guangzhou in Guangdong. Guangzhou's nickname "Goat City" comes from the legend of having been founded by five immortals whose rams planted stalks of rice. The inhabitants of the city and its environs offered a complex cuisine for which many key ingredients—such as sesame oil, soy sauce, and rice wine—were unavailable in the Caribbean. The lack of appropriate condiments may have spurred their entry into entrepreneurial activities. By the 1850s, Chinese contract laborers were staying beyond the three years of field labor to open small grocery stores and other commercial businesses. The Chinese Exclusion Act of 1882 resulted in widespread migration of Chinese from the United States to Puerto Rico, Dominican Republic, and Cuba, where they worked in sugarcane fields, built the railroad, and opened restaurants on Havana's outskirts.

In Jamaica, Cuba, Trinidad, and Guyana, the widespread use of combinations of sugar, salt, ginger, spring onion, and pepper reflected a significant Chinese influence on Creole cooking. The immigrants cooked with cashews (native to Brazil and brought to Asia by the Portuguese), made noodles when wheat flour was available, and concocted sugary (sweet and sour) sauces for pork and duck. Their recipes were preserved in homes and restaurant venues, which promoted their duck dishes. Caribs had captured native ducks by whistling. As a consequence, the species became known as the West Indian black-billed whistling duck (*Dendrocygna arborea*). After the arrival of Asian immigrants, the birds became a threatened species in the mangrove and wetland areas of rice cultivation; curried duck wrapped in roti skins reflected an embrace of Chinese culinary traditions and became a favorite dish of the region's evolving Asian-Creole cuisines.

Caribbean Curry and Roti

The most important contributions of Asians to Caribbean kitchens came from their complex use of hand-ground spices, especially "curry," and in their unleavened, grilled breads called "roti," regardless of ingredients or preparation. Since curry was a term used by the English and other Europeans in the eighteenth century to describe any spiced relish or seasoned dish they encountered, it came to mean a generic blend characteristic of no particular region of South Asia. Hannah Glasse's *The Art of Cookery* was published in London in 1747. It contained Indian recipes for curry and "Indian pickle." In the hands of nineteenth-century British colonizers, Indian curry had become familiar gravy used to disguise an otherwise monotonous diet. Its preparation became standardized after the series of world's fairs and exhibitions, including the 1895–1896 Empire of India Exhibition in Earl's Court, where a Curry House offered visitors "Eastern dishes."[41] This Orientalist version of Asian foods curried popularity, and the British carried curry wherever they went in their imperial world, including the Caribbean. The arrival of East Indian indentured laborers reinvigorated and creolized the flavors of Caribbean curries. Curry in the Caribbean became a category of complex mixtures of spices, distinctive from either Indian or British curry because of its primary use of Jamaican allspice (*Pimenta dioica*).

Allspice was first observed during Columbus's voyage and named by Europeans around 1621, because they thought its taste resembled a mixture of cinnamon, nutmeg, and cloves. Allspice was a prized flavor on its own. Native to the Caribbean (it still grows wild in Jamaica) and to Central America, it was carried from the Caribbean by birds and merchants, who found that the unripe fruits of the plant, when dried in the sun, resembled large, brown peppercorns and traveled well. Allspice eventually joined the prized spices of European bakers and West Asian cooks, German sausage-makers and distillers of Sardinian liqueur.[42]

There are as many curry recipes as there are Caribbean cooks. The prepared curries commonly have salt and pepper to taste and roughly equal parts of spices: cardamom, cumin, nutmeg, cinnamon, turmeric, ginger, fenugreek (*methi*), clove, basil (*tulsi*), and allspice. In the French West Indies, the spicy wet stew was known as *colombo*, after the former capital of Sri Lanka. It relied on toasted coriander, allspice, cumin, and pepper ground together. It was a reminder that the sources of global currents circulated on the seas, often to return and further alter the Caribbean, in wave after wave of influence lapping on its shores.

Curry powder in the Caribbean usually includes allspice, making its flavor distinctive from Indian or English combinations of spices. Adjusting the

CARIBBEAN CURRY GOAT

2 to 3 tablespoons commercial curry powder
1 teaspoon ground allspice
2 onions, minced
6 cloves of garlic
3 pounds bone-in goat meat
4 cups chicken or vegetable broth, tomatoes, water, or coconut milk
1 teaspoon lemon juice
2 tablespoons chopped cilantro
1 Scotch bonnet pepper (or milder pepper)

Combine curry powder, allspice, onions, and garlic, and cook in oil. Add meat. Some cooks will add sugar at this point to burn a smoky essence into the meat. Sear the meat and then add enough liquid (broth, tomatoes, water, or coconut milk) to cover the meat and make thicker gravy at the end. Simmer slowly until the meat and vegetables are cooked and flavors are blended. At the very end, add lemon juice and cilantro, if desired. Serve over rice and/or with roti.

Personally ground mixtures of spices are favored by Caribbean cooks for use in their curries. They are sold in the region's informal economy. Commercial brands are also available. Some are made in the Caribbean (with and without garam masala) and some are British-owned relics of the colonial era and sold as "hot" or not. Commercial curries will require the addition of allspice. This curry recipe uses goat, which can be replaced by large shrimp or a vegetarian version comprised of 2 cans of garbanzo beans and 4 large potatoes, diced and substituted for the meat. Fresh chives, parsley, and thyme (a nod to the British influence) can also be added. The distinctive hot pepper used in the Caribbean is aji, the Scotch bonnet, native to the Caribbean.

turmeric and pepper will have an impact on the hotness or relative mildness of the curry. Some curries, if they become too hot during cooking, can be cooled down with coconut milk. Shrimp is often prepared in this manner. Part of the essential West Indian cooking process is to use freshly ground spices

NISHA'S ROTI

2 cups flour (unbleached white or pastry)
1 1/2 teaspoons baking powder
pinch of salt
1 cup water

Combine ingredients and mix with your hand. Pinch dough together first, then knead it. Form into 8 to 10 balls about the size of tennis balls (smaller if you want smaller roti). Leave for about 10 to 15 minutes, covered with a cloth. Then roll out each ball, flattening with a rolling pin to 1/8 to 1/16th inch thickness. The edges should be slightly thinner than the middle. Place on a heated, greased griddle and cook until slightly brown in spots, turning as bubbles form. Brush the top with a little oil before turning.

ROTI WITH "PEAS"

3 cups flour (unbleached white or pastry)
1 1/2 teaspoons baking powder
pinch of salt
2 cups water
2 tablespoons soybean oil
1/4 dry ground, cooked peas
1/4 teaspoon each of salt and pepper
1 tablespoon cilantro
1 tablespoon oil
1 tablespoon flour

Combine flour, baking powder, salt, water, and oil, and form balls of dough as described above. Combine peas, salt and pepper, and cilantro. Punch a hole into each ball and fill with 1 teaspoon of the peas mixture, covering it so that, when rolled, it will be an inner layer of the roti disk. Roll out the balls of dough. Sprinkle with oil and flour. Fry on a griddle as directed above.

as much as possible and to heat the spices in a dry pan or in oil to bring out their flavors fully. Some cooks marinate the meat beforehand in a papaya-lime juice solution, adding garlic, onion, and greens with a small amount of curry to improve the taste and tenderness. Other popular vegetables can be curried: pumpkin, squash, potatoes, okra, chestnuts, and garbanzo beans are Caribbean favorites.

Caribbean curry was seldom served without rice or bread, particularly roti. Indian roti is bread now made from corn, a Punjabi staple that reflected the arrival of Columbian Exchange foods from the Americas. In the Caribbean, roti is made from wheat flour and sometimes has a dal (cooked chickpea or lentil) layer added to the thin dough disk. It is eaten as a wrapper around food and also broken in pieces. In Trinidad, these pieces are known as "buss-up shot," literally a burst-open shirt, since the bread resembled torn cloth.

By the twentieth century, curry had joined the early African-derived stews like callaloo and pepper pot as essential markers of identity. The indispensable ingredients in the Indo-Creole Caribbean foodways were signifiers of the wider cultural and political struggle to become one people while maintaining inherited diversity. In a multiracial society, foods expressed the cultural meaning of difference and the opportunities to select contradictory elements of identity. When calypsonian Hollis "Chalkdust" Liverpool sang, "you cyan [cannot] put curry in callaloo," he was questioning the social and cultural difficulty in contesting race and ethnicity, not just mixing or creolizing foods and flavors. Much of the cultural separation and distinctiveness of African- and Asian-derived cuisines has been blurred by their common culinary experience in the shadow of the sugar plantation and European imperialism.[43]

Gifts of Sugar

Since slavery and the indenture system emphasized values of avarice and greed in their most obvious embrace of violent coercion for individual profit, it may seem impossible to imagine the opposite expression. Yet generosity and reciprocity were also defined through food's production, preparation, and consumption. In both South Asia and in the Caribbean, sugar figured in gifts to deities and people. Nineteenth-century Caribbean cuisines had become a thoroughly complex cultural blend of indigenous, Spanish, French, African, British, Portuguese, Chinese, and East Indian customs. Yet the taste and desire for sugar was shared in common. Sugar was boiled with water and juice for drink. Sugar was given to the spirits and ancestors as drink. Cones of sugar loaves, the solidified cane syrup, wrapped in banana leaves and decorated with a flourish of rosette carved into the top, became gifts of dark luxury. Called "papelons" or "jaggery," they were given by the sugar estate owner to pregnant laborers. Sugar was also provided to workers as "gifts" that would add energy to field labors. By the time of emancipation, sugar was also part of the required dietary rations and "medical comforts" aboard British ships bound for the Caribbean from African ports after 1848.

Arrival in the Caribbean only increased the culinary desire and taste for sweetness. Marking holidays were the specially prepared customary sweet dishes, like *parsad*, in which sugar, milk, cardamom, and raisins were mixed with flour to form dough and then fried. Tamarind and sugar conjured numerous sweets for Diwali or Phagwa celebrations. Sweets were produced on every island, from Jamaica to Cuba, and sold door-to-door or at corner shops and taverns. Sugar-cake was a sweet that was made by boiling coconut in heavy syrup. Tamarind seeds, native to Africa, were peeled, pulped, rolled in a ball with brown sugar, and finally dipped in white refined sugar (with pepper sometimes added) to become a confection sold by street vendors. Food was called "sweet" as a compliment to the cook, and that had little to do with sucrose content. Sweetness was rather employed as appreciative commentary that food tasted delicious.

Drinking Sugar

Sometime in the sixteenth century, rum was first produced from the fresh cane-juice water and later from the brownish-black liquid called molasses, the leftovers of sugar-crystal manufacture. The road to rum was not an easy one. Distillery techniques were a recent European technological innovation and their underlying science was complex. Yet, against these odds, the distilled drink known as "rum" became part of what greased the machinery of global food cultures, captivating the coastal African societies, motivating the North American and Liverpool sea captains, and lubricating the social life of nearly every strata of Caribbean society.

Distilled Spirits

By September 1647, when Richard Ligon arrived in Barbados hoping to make his fortune on a sugar estate, rum was being distilled on the island. Ligon was a keen observer of the seventeenth-century processes involved in making sugar more and more profitable. Not all sugars were equal. They required critical stages of curing and storage, the conditions for which could vary widely:

> At the time of our arrival there, we found many Sugar-works set up, and at work; but yet the Sugars they made were but bare Muscavadoes [brown, less refined sugar], and few of them Merchantable commodities; so moist,

and full of molasses, and so ill cured, as they were hardly worth the bringing home for England. But about the time I left the Island, which was in 1650, they were much bettered; for then they had the skill to know when the Canes were ripe, which was not, till they were fifteen months old; and before, they gathered them at twelve, which was a main disadvantage to the making of good Sugar.

According to Ligon's account of molasses making in Barbados, working with high temperatures was dangerous: "Firemen made the fires in the furnaces . . . [and sometimes] to such part of the boyling-house, as they were sure would fire the rest, and so burn all" in acts of resistance.[44]

The next step was fermentation, when yeast and water were added to produce the actual alcohol content (between 5 and 9 percent) of "dunder" or "burned ale." The first boiling captured the cane juice. A second boiling process produced dark, thick treacle. A third and final boiling created blackstrap molasses, sticky and even bitterer in taste. These activities took place in boiling houses on the sugar estates. They were hot, unpleasant, and dangerous places in which to work. Large copper cauldrons served as containers for the thickening sugar products in the factories, and they sometimes afforded opportunities for murder, suicide, and general destruction. Water was evaporated out of the product to create a crystalline structure.

During distillation, the water was separated again by heating the liquid molasses and removing the alcohol's vapors, or "spirits." Early rum producers transferred the raw spirit directly into bottles. According to Leblond, in late eighteenth-century Martinique, *tafia* was a "cane brandy" drunk in the evening in the island's inns. Eventually, when the excess rum was stored in oak barrels, it was observed that the clear spirit also absorbed the flavors and colors of the wood, just as it collects the flavored chemistry of the distillation over time. Today, the finest, most expensive rums are those distilled twice and aged like brandies.[45] In the days of the slave trade, rum was an essential part of the rituals of gift-giving and exchange on both sides of the Atlantic and a most necessary cargo on the slave ship. One trader on the West African coast, John Barbot, called it an "inviolable custom."[46] Across the Atlantic, rum was given to the recently arrived Africans as part of their "seasoning," and it also found its way into the hands of sailors and soldiers.

Kill-Devil

There is some debate about the origins of the name of the Caribbean drink "rum." Thomas Ligon had remarked that the islanders were particularly fond of "Rumbullion" or "Kill Devil," and about the same time, the term was associated with a drink made of sugarcane. From its inception, the evils of rum were debated by European society. Rum was thought to intoxicate Africans at higher rates than for Europeans (as opposed to their just drinking excessively). Rum became known as a distilled drink, described as a "hot," "hellish and terrible liquor."[47] Rum was not nearly as popular in England, where early seventeenth-century imports reached only a little more than 200 gallons per year (but leaped to 2 million gallons by the last quarter of the eighteenth century). The reputation for excessive rum drinking that many West Indian planters lived up to was furthered by the lampooning cartoonists in the London newspaper *Punch*. One visitor noted that alcohol consumption was so high that the local West Indians had "bodies like Egyptian mummies."[48] Lady Nugent mentioned that the drinks of a first or second Jamaican breakfast included claret and coffee, Madeira and tea. Rum punch was often kept for guests. A certain sign of wealth and opulence, excessive drinks were accompanied by plentiful, elite banquets of foods, such as those described by Lady Nugent at the beginning of the nineteenth century. To her amazement, the scene of overabundance and intoxication was repeated over and over again: "I don't wonder now at the fever the people suffer from here—such eating and drinking I never saw! Such loads of all sorts of high, rich, and seasoned things, and really gallons of wine and mixed liquors as they drink!"[49]

Only the wealthy upper classes had the means to drink excessively. Richard Ligon described the drinks of slaves, noting they had only "water or Mobbie for drink."[50] "Mobbie" originally referred to a traditional Carib alcoholic drink made from sweet potatoes (later with sugar added). A completely different term, "mauby," came to mean a local sweetened drink made from the bark of a tree. Its bitter taste after brewing was offset by adding huge amounts of sugar. Similar sugared drinks were made from hibiscus flowers and various fruits or berries. In one Jamaican folktale, Anancy the trickster spider is credited with inventing the brewing of a sorrel drink. When someone tastes it too soon before it is completely brewed, Anancy sings the recipe: "It want some sugar,/a little piece a ginger/A little cinnamon/And then you stir so/And then you stir so."[51] Slaves also drank a colorless raw alcohol made from sugarcane juice and known variously as "high wine" (Guyana), *clairin* (Haiti), *aguardiente* (Cuba), and *cachaca* (Brazil). In potency, it approached the firewater of women's home-distilled drinks in West Africa and tasted much like the *akpateshi* of Ghana. *Chicha*, a brew of corn fermented in sugar, and *sambumbia*, a mixture of water and molasses, were also consumed in Cuba in the 1860s and probably much earlier.[52] The popular *falernum* was a concoction with rum, sugar, and lime juice that tasted a bit like the Cuban drink "mojito," made famous by Ernest Hemingway. Falernum, usually mixed with cloves and/or ginger, was drunk in Barbados during the nineteenth century. Sometimes almonds were added for flavoring. It has been proposed that the name originated with a Creole response to a request for the drink's recipe: "Yo go' fa learn'um."[53] The mixture of lime juice, rum, and brown sugar-water was also called "swank," probably derived from the eighteenth-century Dutch term meaning "supple" or "swagger." To the basic limeade was added a flourish of crushed mint leaves, imitating a mint julep, the infusion that arrived with Southerners fleeing the aftermath of the American Civil War with their slaves in late nineteenth-century Cuba.

Most Africans had come from social cultures and religions that used alcohol prior to the expansion of the slave trade. Alcoholic beverages supplied to African societies altered and expanded their use. Central Africans drank imported Spanish wines, and peoples on the Gold Coast sought Dutch gin and brandy. With the important exception of devout Muslims, Africans on both sides of the Atlantic continued to manufacture their own brews, fermented drinks, and infusions, made from potato peelings, cassava, plantain, and grains. Palm wine was also tapped.

Despite the misconception that the Asian immigrants were all "Hindoos," whose ascetic philosophy of dharma restricted alcohol use, East Indians in the Caribbean did consume rum. Those of higher castes eschewed alcohol as an interference to spiritual growth. Lower castes made up for this temperance by consuming more, leaving the impression that East Indians indulged in "all sorts of liquors without repugnance or restraint" on their days off and during festivals and ceremonies.[54]

Drinking took place in the Caribbean's community spaces, from the open courtyards of slave villages and the dining rooms of great houses to the port town taverns. Among the earliest taverns in the Caribbean were the ones at Port Royal, Jamaica, frequented by all manner of travelers, merchants, sailors, buccaneers, and pirates. Until it was destroyed in the earthquake and tsunamis of 1694, Port Royal was known as "the wickedest city on Earth." Since about two-thirds of the town's structure and 4,000 inhabitants were submerged, much of the evidence of historical consumption of food and drink comes from underwater archaeology. More than sixty punch houses and taverns have been recorded on the island of Jamaica. According to archaeologists Marianne Franklin and Maureen Brown, taverns became the bellwethers for the new consumer culture. At the tavern, the drinking traditions of three continents merged.

Caribbean rum joined the bottles of many other alcoholic drinks made around the world and served on ship tables and at port taverns. After passage of the Molasses Act in 1733 provided the cornerstone for British mercantilism, rum became even more profitable for English planters. Distilled grain and cane spirits were quickly favored over ale, beer, and wine in the Caribbean,

PLANTER'S PUNCH

1/2 ounce lime juice
1 ounce cane sugar syrup
1 1/2 ounce white rum
2 ounces fruit juices

Add ingredients to a glass half-filled with crushed ice and stir. Garnish with fresh fruit.

MOJITO

2 sprigs mint
crushed ice
2 ounces rum
2 tablespoons fresh lime juice
soda water
lime slices

Grind several mint leaves with a small pestle, bruising the greens in order to infuse the drink with their flavors. Place one crushed mint leaf in the bottom of each glass and cover with crushed ice. Add rum and lime juice. Fill with soda water. Garnish with a slice of lime and another mint leaf.

DARK AND STORMY

2 ounces dark rum
8 ounces ginger beer

Add rum and then ginger beer to a glass of ice. The ginger beer available in the Caribbean is often homemade and has a strong, pungent flavor of ginger. Add freshly pulverized and strained liquid ginger to taste, if the stronger "beer" is unavailable.

Rum shop, Barbados
(Photograph by Candice Goucher)

whereas imports came to be associated with the whiskey-drinking elites. Other imported drinks did not disappear from early Caribbean shopping lists. Sailing from Demerara to England on the ship *Reliance* in 1830 was Captain Luckie, whose journal listed the following bottles boarded for the three-month voyage: "two doz Madeira wine, 3 doz, Old port, 3 doz. Beer and 2 doz. Porter, 1 doz claret, 1 doz champagne, 2 doz old [unreadable], 1 doz. Brandy, 1 old rum and falarnum, 1 doz of rum."[55]

Not only in the taverns, but also in the colonizer's armies and navies, rum defined the sociable realm in which a distinctive multiracial Caribbean male culture formed. Rum was a necessary ration on ships, in garrisons, and on plantations. Rum was used medicinally, for ceremonial oaths, and in excess by almost all categories of laborers and overseers. As with food, African traditions eventually dominated when the widespread practice of acknowledging the spirit world culminated in libations being poured on the ground "to absent friends."

Ligon was right about the role of rum in creating profits from sugar production. In the seventeenth century, Barbados alone exported more than half a million barrels around the world. A century later, rum ruled the Caribbean seas. It continued to be blamed for everything devilish, from debauchery to prostitution. The hit song in North America during the Second World

War, "Rum and Coca Cola," was actually stolen from the lines of a calypso protesting the rise of prostitution accompanying the arrival of American sailors on the island of Trinidad. Sung originally by Lord Invader, the lyrics criticized the bad behavior of foreign (American) sailors who "buy rum and Coca-Cola / Go down Point Cumana / Both mother and daughter / Working for the Yankee dollar."[56] High profits continued after the abolition of slavery. Finally, the competition from beet sugar in the second half of the nineteenth century ruined the industry on many islands. By this time, Brazil and Cuba had become the leading producers of rum, with sugar from Guyana shipped to North America and Britain for manufacture, as it still is.

Hot and Cold

Sugar was the basis for the fermentation of other kinds of spirits in the circum-Caribbean region, including coffee-flavored drinks in Mexico and Jamaica and orange-flavored drinks in Curaçao. The eventual arrival of ice was related more to food preservation than to cocktails. Evaporative cooling techniques were recorded in India and were in common use across Africa from ancient times. In the Caribbean, ice arrived before electricity. American ships carried blocks of northern lake ice to the Caribbean as ballast in the nineteenth century, when massive exports were stored in ice houses and sold door to door in cities and small towns. One ice merchant, Frederic Tudor, described an interesting application for ice in the West Indies in 1810, using milk, cream, and fruit juices to create "a beverage . . . or tepid water . . . palatable [in a hot climate]."[57]

Once sugar became widely available, it appeared prominently in other drinks of the New World, notably, coffee, tea, and chocolate. Again, the changing cuisines of several continents intersected as they responded to the new libations. Sugar in English tea, for example, represented the meeting of West Indian and East Indian colonial cash crops. As one abolitionist pamphlet noted, their combination expressed the bitter taste of human suffering: "As [the Englishman] sweetens his tea, let him reflect on the bitterness at the bottom of the cup."[58] Together, sugar and tea fueled the long hours and hard labor of the global industrial revolution. Since imported tea was not widely available to the majority of the population in the Caribbean, the enslaved laborers and indentured workers substituted other drinks under the generic term "tea," which mimicked the teatime of the great house. Bush tea was made with herbs such as lemongrass, which was steeped in boiling water, but so were coffee and cocoa, whipped to a frothy texture. In the French Caribbean, Charles de L'Yver observed a wooden tool for mixing chocolate, water, egg whites, and fruits in season, including oranges, around 1767, when the hot drink's continental origins were recognized.[59]

In former British colonies, these hot drinks are still called "coffee tea" or "cocoa tea," as they were earlier (or as Van Sertima referred to "cawfee wata" in nineteenth-century Guyana).[60] Coffee was native to Africa, where it was domesticated and later taken by Arabs to western Asia and eastern Europe. Coffee plants were carried by Europeans to Brazil, Jamaica, Haiti, Guyana, and eventually elsewhere in the French and Spanish West Indies, as well as to the tropical South American highlands in the eighteenth century. People drank coffee largely for its medicinal effects; social uses evolved later. In the 1720s, Gabriel Mathieu de Clieu, a French naval officer, introduced coffee to the French West Indies islands of Martinique and Guadeloupe.[61] The beans, called "bonifieur" (from the French *bonifier*, to make better or improve), were seeds of the *Coffea arabica* plant obtained from the Dutch and thought to be the ancestor of what would become famously known as "Blue Mountain" coffee, when they reached Jamaica. By the end of the eighteenth century, coffee was the preferred morning drink of Jamaica, but it was served alongside cocoa and tea in the wealthy Creole houses.[62] From these global intersections of coffee and sugar, the coffeehouse of Europe was also born. Among its early fans were sleep-deprived students in Oxford and the patrons of Café Procope in Paris (founded in 1686), where comrades of the philosopher Jean-Jacques Rousseau joined the philosopher for conversation and debate. Sugar and coffee consumption were thus closely linked in drinks and the sweet dessert courses associated with the drinks.

Spiced Drinks

While indigenous peoples of the Americas had used chilis to enliven their ritually important cacao beverage, Europeans added sugar instead (Spanish nuns were possibly the first to do this). And "chocolate tea" was born. Cortez had learned from the indigenous peoples how to mix the cacao beans with vanilla beans (*Vanilla planifora*, from the climbing orchid). He called cocoa the "divine drink which builds up resistance and fights fatigue. A cup of this precious drink enables a man to walk for a whole day without food."[63] Once mixed with sugar, cinnamon, vanilla, musk, and anatto, the hot cocoa drink and other chocolate-flavored foods became very popular in Europe. Although before the nineteenth century chocolate was consumed for medicinal purposes as much as for the enjoyment of its taste, chocolate houses soon joined coffeehouses and teahouses as locations where drinks were consumed for social pleasure. The new global drink, despite its origins, was identified with the Caribbean. Indeed, chocolate was "an excellent West India drink, sold in Queen's-Head Alley, in Bishopsgate Street, by a Frenchman," read a London advertisement in the truly global world of 1659.[64]

Kumina ceremony, Morant Bay, Jamaica
(Photograph by Candice Goucher)

Sugar and the Caribbean Body

Sugar had many uses in the dynamic cultural waters of the Caribbean. The recipes in this chapter extol the wide-ranging uses of sugar and its by-products, as well as the key Caribbean foodways brought to the region in response to the demands of sugar production. Sugar was consumed as food and drink, even as its production consumed human lives. Applied to the body, rum became more than an intimate libation. Its essence as "spirit" activated the link between humans and nonhuman realms. The human body thus altered became a container for spirits during trance or ritual performances in African-derived religions, Africanized Christianity, and Indo-Caribbean ceremonies. Similarly, a stone placed in a basin of (cane liquor) rum was duly activated when the liquid was ignited, becoming a vehicle for mystical powers during certain Rada ceremonies in Haiti.[65]

Practitioners of numerous Africa-derived religions, including Kumina in Jamaica and Shango in Trinidad, believed that the rum rubbed on the body in a ceremony or dance enhanced the communicants' abilities to see far and receive the presence of spirits and ancestors. Rum bottles were shared with the ancestors by opening new bottles and dropping a "drink" to the invisible world. The empty rum bottles decorated with sequins and beading functioned in the sacred realms of Vodun shrines in Haiti. Singing and drinking were often intertwined as social and religious actions, making the use of rum on occasion complex and nuanced. Rum and other foods or drinks became intricate, coded expressions in the cultural contexts of African systems of belief.

Richard Ligon recognized how unstoppable the continuum of the Caribbean cauldron could be when he wrote of a would-be sojourner from Europe:

> If it be such a one as loves the pleasures of *Europe*, (or particularly of *England*) and the great varieties of those, let him never come there, for they are things he shall be sure to miss. But, if he can find in himself a willingness to change the pleasures, which he enjoyed in a Temperate, for such as he shall find in a Torrid Zone, he may light upon some that will give him an exchange, with some advantage.[66]

Inherent in Ligon's vision was a hierarchy of taste determined by profits. Caribbean foodways were also systems of bodily practice and identity construction. Understood against the background of political resistance, "King Sugar" and "Devil Sugar" acquired darker and decidedly ironic shades of meaning.

Notes

1. From the poem "Caribbean Theme: A Calypso," published in *Trinidad Carnival* (Port of Spain: Paria, 1988), a republication of *Caribbean Quarterly* 4, nos. 3/4 (1956).

2. *Cowper's Negro Complaint* (1791), quoted in Julie Arkell, *Classic Rum* (London: Prion, 1999), 14.

3. Robert Farris Thompson, *Face of the Gods: Art and Altars of Africa and the African Americas* (New York: Museum for African Arts/Prestel, 1993), 255; Thompson further explains the proverb's logic, since sugarcane, once planted, easily spreads.

4. Sidney Mintz, *Sweetness and Power: The Place of Sugar in Modern History* (New York: Elisabeth Sifton/Viking, 1985), xviii; Mintz writes of his time in Puerto Rico as "floating on a sea of [sugar] cane."

5. Mintz, *Sweetness and Power*, 156.

6. J. Redhead, *Utilization of Local Tropical Foods: Sugars, Spices and Stimulants*, FAO Food and Nutrition Paper 47/6 (1989): 1–3; K.T. Achaya, *Indian Food: A Historical Companion* (Delhi: Oxford University Press, 1998), 37.

7. J.H. Galloway, "Sugar," in *The Cambridge World History of Food*, ed. Kenneth F. Kiple and Kriemhild Conee Ornelas, (Cambridge: Cambridge University Press, 2000), 1:443.

8. Redhead, *Tropical Foods*, 7.

9. Ryuto Shimada, *The Intra-Asian Trade in Japanese Copper by the Dutch East India Company* (Leiden, Netherlands: Brill, 2005), 79.

10. John Daniels and Christian Daniels, "The Origin of the Sugarcane Roller Mill," *Technology and Culture* 29 (1988): 483–535.

11. Labat, *A Sojourn on Dominica* (1722), in *Wild Majesty: Encounters with Caribs from Columbus to the Present Day*, ed. Peter Hulme and Neil L. Whitehead (Oxford: Clarendon Press, 1992), 158.

12. Roger D. Abrahams, *Singing the Master: The Emergence of African-American Culture in the Plantation South* (New York: Penguin Books, 1992), 85.

13. Trelawny Wentworth, *The West India Sketch Book* (London, 1834), 1:65–67, quoted in *After Africa*, ed. Roger D. Abrahams and John F. Szwed (New Haven: Yale University Press, 1983), 308–309.

14. John Chester Grenville, *Transatlantic Sketches* . . . (London, 1869), 81–82, quoted in Abrahams and Szwed, *After Africa*, 318.

15. Alexander Barclay, *A Practical View of the Present State of Slavery in the West Indies* (London, 1826), 10, quoted in Abrahams and Szwed, *After Africa*, 83.

16. John Luffman, Letter XXII, Oct. 3, 1787, in Abrahams and Szwed, *After Africa*, 332.

17. Thomas Tryon, *Friendly Advice to Gentleman-Planters of the East and West Indies* (London, 1700), 201–202, quoted in Mintz, *Sweetness and Power*, 47–48.

18. Quoted from a letter from Willoughby to the Privy Council, dated December 16, 1667, Cal. St. Pap. 1661–1668, no. 48, cited by L.L.E. Rends, "Analysis of Annals Relating to Early Jewish Settlement in Surinam," in *The Jewish Nation in Surinam*, ed. R. Cohen, (Amsterdam: S. Emmering, 1982), p. 37.

19. For a discussion of Reeder, see Candice Goucher, "African Metallurgy in the Atlantic World," in *Archaeology of Atlantic Africa and the Atlantic Diaspora*, ed. Toyin Falola and Akin Ogundiran (Bloomington: Indiana University Press, 2007).

20. L. Edward Brathwaite, *The Development of Creole Society in Jamaica: 1770–1820* (Oxford: Clarendon Press, 1978), pp. 82–89.

21. Hollis "Chalkdust" Liverpool, *Rituals of Power and Rebellion: The Carnival Tradition in Trinidad and Tobago, 1763–1962* (Chicago: Research Associates School Times Publications, 2001), 165.

22. Mrs. (Alison) Carmichael, *Domestic Manners and Social Customs of the White, Coloured, and Negro Population of the West Indies* (London, 1833), vol. 2, 301–302.

23. Lionel Fraser, quoted in Liverpool, *Rituals of Power*, 161.

24. Charles Day, *Five Years Residence in the West Indies*, vol. 1 (London, 1852), 315–316.

25. Quoted in Liverpool, *Rituals of Power*, 239.

26. Lafcadio Hearn, in *La Cuisine Creole: A Collection of Culinary Recipes from Leading Chefs and Noted Housewives, Who Have Made New Orleans Famous for Its*

Cuisine (Carlisle, MA: Applewood Books, 2008), records that gumbo holds a place next to the use of codfish in the African-Creole cuisine of 1880s New Orleans.

27. Lady Maria Nugent, *Lady Nugent's Journal of Her Residence in Jamaica, from 1801 to 1805*, ed. Philip Wright (Kingston: Institute of Jamaica, 1966), 203–204.

28. This deception was reported by Brinsley Samaroo, "Two Abolitions: African Slavery and East Indian Indentureship," in *India in the Caribbean*, ed. Dabydeen and Brinsley Samaroo (London: Hansib/University of Warwick, Center for Caribbean Studies, 1987), 28. See also the PhD dissertation by Amitava Chowdhury, "Horizons of Memory: A Global Processual Study of Cultural Memory and Identity of the South Asian Indentured Labor Diaspora in the Indian Ocean and the Caribbean" (Washington State University, 2008), which explores Indian identity in the African diaspora. The following paragraphs rely heavily on his insights. Anita Mansur, *Culinary Fictions: Food in South Asian Diasporic Culture* (Philadelphia: Temple University Press, 2010), 81–82, also explores the implications of sweetness and power.

29. See the recent work by Arunima Kashyap and Steve Weber, "Harappan Plant Use Revealed by Starch Grains from Farmana, India," *Antiquity* 84, no. 326 (2010).

30. Thomas Heath to Richard Hill, House of Commons Papers no. 4, 1847.

31. Heath, 31.

32. John H. Parry, "Plantation and Provision Ground: An Historical Sketch of the Introduction of Food Crops into Jamaica," *Revista de Historia de America* 39 (1955): 1–22.

33. Kiple and Ornelas, *Cambridge World History of Food*, 2: 1737.

34. Suchea Mazumdar, "The Impact of New World Food Crops on the Diet and Economy of China and India, 1600–1900," in *Food in Global History*, ed. Raymond Grew (Boulder, CO: Westview, 1999), 71–72.

35. Mazumdar, "Impact of New World Food Crops," 73–74.

36. Mazumdar, "Impact of New World Food Crops," 61.

37. See Chapter 4 for a discussion of similar European and Yoruba ideas. Marsha B. Quinlan and Robert J. Quinlan describe the system in another Caribbean (Dominica) context in "Balancing the System: Humoral Medicine and Food in the Commonwealth of Dominica," in *Eating and Healing: Exploration of Wild and Domesticated Plants and Animals as Food and Medicine*, ed. A. Pieroni and L. Price (Binghamton: Haworth Press, 2005). In the Dominican system of hot/cold humoral theory, all fruits are "cold."

38. Lizzie Collingham, *Curry: A Tale of Cooks and Conquerors* (Oxford: Oxford University Press, 2006), 147.

39. Wendy Rahamut, *Curry, Callaloo, and Calypso: The Real Taste of Trinidad and Tobago* (Oxford: Macmillan, 2011), 16.

40. Kim Johnson, *Descendants of the Dragon: The Chinese in Trinidad, 1806–2006* (Kingston, Jamaica: Ian Randle, 2006); Walton Look Lai, *The Chinese in the West Indies: A Documentary History, 1806–1995* (Kingston, Jamaica: University of West Indies, 1998).

41. Collingham, *Curry*, 152.

42. "Allspice," in *Cambridge World History of Food*, ed. Kiple and Ornelas, 2: 1716–1717.

43. Viranjini Munasinghe, *Callaloo or Tossed Salad? East Indians and the Cultural Politics of Identity in Trinidad* (Ithaca: Cornell University Press, 2002), uses food as metaphor to debate the processes of assimilation and separateness of the East Indians

in Trinidad, represented by stewing into the African-derived cultural matrix (callaloo) or maintaining their distinctiveness (tossed salad); see also Lizzie Collingham, *Curry*, 250. This history of curry fails to identify much of a Caribbean role in the evolution and dispersal of the global cuisine.

44. Richard Ligon (1673), quoted in Abrahams and Szwed, *After Africa*, 63.

45. See Arkell, *Classic Rum*, and Frederick H. Smith, *Caribbean Rum: A Social and Economic History* (Gainesville: University of Florida Press, 2005).

46. John Barbot, *A description of the Coasts of North and South Guinea* (London, 1746), 260.

47. Richard Ligon, *A True and Exact History of the Island of Barbadoes* (London, 1673), and Carson Ritchie, *Food in Civilization* (1981), quoted in Kiple and Ornelas, *Cambridge World History of Food*, 1: 659–660; Smith, *Caribbean Rum*, 16–17.

48. Kiple and Ornelas, *Cambridge World History of Food*, 1: 659–660.

49. Nugent, *Lady Nugent's Journal*, 57.

50. Ligon, *True and Exact History*, 52.

51. "Anancy an Sorrel," in *Anansesem: A Collection of Folk Tales, Legends and Poems for Juniors*, ed. Velma Pollard, (Kingston, Jamaica: Carlong, 1985), 52.

52. Natalia Bolivar Arostegui and Carmen Gonzalez Diaz de Villegas, *Afro-Cuban Cuisine: Its Myths and Legends* (Havana, Cuba: Editorial Jose Marti, 1998), 14.

53. Jeannette Allsopp, *The Caribbean Multilingual Dictionary of Flora, Fauna and Foods* (Kingston, Jamaica: Arawak, 2003), 126.

54. Great Britain. House of Commons, vol. 45, encl. 1 (5), 9; see also Smith, *Caribbean Rum*.

55. JOD/77 n.a. *Journal of Two Voyages, April-June, 1830, on Reliance (British Guiana)*, National Maritime Museum, Greenwich, London, UK; the ship sailed on April 28 and arrived in the English Channel on June 14.

56. Liverpool, *Rituals of Power and Rebellion*, 435.

57. Tudor, quoted in Achaya, *Indian Food*, 115–116.

58. Anthropous, *The Rights of Man . . . (*1824), quoted in Jenny Sharpe, "The Rise of Women in an Age of Progress," in *Allegories of Empire: The Figure of Woman in the Colonial Text* (Minneapolis: University of Minnesota Press, 1987), 27.

59. Vincent Huyghues-Belrose, "Avant le fruit a pain: La cuisine martiniquaise au XVIIIᵉ siècle," in *Sur les chemins de l'histoire antillaise*, ed. Jean Bernabe and Serge Mam Lam Fouck (Paris: Ibis Rouge, 2006), 211–212.

60. J. Van Sertima, *Scenes and Sketches of Demerara Life* (Georgetown, Demerara [Guyana], 1899), 99–102, in Abrahams and Szwed, *After Africa*, 326.

61. Mark Pendergrast, *Uncommon Grounds: The History of Coffee and How It Transformed Our World* (New York: Basic Books, 1999), 15–16.

62. Nugent, *Lady Nugent's Journal*, 55, 168.

63. "Vanilla," in *Cambridge World History of Food*, ed. Kiple and Ornelas, 2: 1874–1875.

64. Christine McFadden and Christine France, *The Cook's Guide to Chocolate* (Oxford: Sebastian Kelly, 1997), 22.

65. Elizabeth McAlister, *Rara! Vodou, Power, and Performance in Haiti and Its Diaspora* (Berkeley: University of California Press, 2002), 95–96.

66. Ligon, *A True and Exact History,* 1657; also see Keith A. Sandiford, *The Cultural Politics of Sugar* (Cambridge: Cambridge University Press, 2000), Chapter 1, for a literary and social analysis of Ligon's language and narrative.

FOUR

From Poisoned Roots

Feeding Power and Resistance

> *Ogun is not like pounded yam:*
> *Do you think you can knead him in your hand*
> *And eat of him until you are satisfied?*

—Yoruba praise poetry[1]

> *The self consists of food. Of breath, of mind,*
> *of understanding, of bliss.*

—Taittiriya Upanishad[2]

In 1795, the Maroons of Trelawney Town, Jamaica, were engaged in a second war of resistance against the British. The Treaty of 1738–1739 signed by the Maroon leader Captain Cudjoe, secured lands for Maroon hunters and the added right to hunt wild hogs outside the bounds of their territory as long as the "Hogs [were] to be equally divided between both Parties." The Maroons sold jerked pork, a spicy delicacy made from salted and smoked meat, in the island's public markets to supplement the community's income. Ironically, the provisions and meats sold by Maroons were also a critical supplemental food source for the plantation system, especially during the embargoes of the American revolutionary era, when the enslaved and slave masters endured food scarcity and widespread hunger. The British had begun to realize that "so long as the Maroon holds out the charm of Food and Freedom," the slaves would be tempted to join the ranks of freedom fighters.[3] Early in 1795, two Maroons had been accused of stealing pigs from a nearby plantation. Their humiliating punishment at the hands of white planters led to armed conflict. Differing views of rum were also at war. After defeating British troops in one uprising, Maroons "returned to their town to recruit their spirits [deities] by the aid of rum," thus resorting to African cultural practices as a means of empowerment. Meanwhile, the British thought that the Maroons should be resettled near towns and given access to liquor. They plotted that the access to alcohol would "soon decrease their numbers, and destroy [their] hardy constitution."[4]

Resistance was a life-and-death matter in the Caribbean, and, needless to say, food and drink were involved in fighting. The region's complex cuisine emerged from the bitter and poisonous roots of plantation slavery and oppression. Yet Caribbean foods and foodways came to express not only a past of pain and sorrow but also a path of resistance and survival. This chapter looks at the role of food in the resistance to oppression in Caribbean history. Not only did the changeable control over food supplies alter relationships of power. Both poisoning and herbal healing relied on the extensive knowledge that enslaved Africans had acquired of New World plants and environments. Foods were integral to the well-being of the enslaved and the enslaver, the exploited and the exploiter. Foods provided a means of connecting to the world of spirits and ancestors, thus maintaining African identities. African cuisines fed and empowered the Caribbean spirit of resistance.

Food as Domination and Resistance

The experience of slavery shaped the cultural life and foodways of the Caribbean region. Consumption of food was closely linked to survival, domination, and resistance. This is perhaps best illustrated through the intimate and meaningful experience of taste. Enslavers "tasted" the sweat of the enslaved in the marketplace, believing that the flavor would reveal aspects of the human commodity's quality, potential diseases, or sickness.[5] Africans interpreted these acts more ominously: as portending a cannibalized end, or, perhaps worse, the threat of ultimate domination.

The mouth was widely considered a locus of supernatural power in Africa. For example, among the Bamana people, the mouth was a symbol of the oracular powers to neutralize evil.[6] Across the continent, speech was widely considered to be spiritually charged, and the mouth's (and saliva's) association with these sacred realms carried over to food. Saliva was widely regarded as a form of activation, the container of magical forces that carried the innermost essence to the outer material realm. This notion of ritual transfer carried over to all foods; it was potently a part of the act of preparing objects of empowerment or protection (called *bo* or *bocio* in Haitian vodun). Some of the most significant ritual acts included the spraying of sacrificial drink from the mouth of a practitioner or performer, an added layer of empowerment inherent in feeding spiritual forces. Whereas the open mouth was associated with eating and life, the closed mouth was a symbol of silence and death.

**Selling bottled cassareep and pickled foods, Bourda Market,
Georgetown, Guyana, c. 1985**
(Photograph by Candice Goucher)

Poisons and Power

Eating food implied survival, and survival of the enslaved Africans relied on
borrowed indigenous knowledge. Pepper pot was one of a number of Native
American dishes adopted by the enslaved. Pepper pot started with cassareep,
the syrup produced by removing poisonous juices from bitter cassava. The
pot then receives every kind of meat into its dark and peppery flavors, leading
one observer to call the African version "oglios" (a medley or hotchpotch).

Ackee
(Photograph courtesy of Heidi Savery)

A pepper pot epitomized survival since the pot might last a cook's lifetime, thanks to the practice of reusing the seasoned cassareep stock, adding more, and augmenting the dark contents with new bush meat. From the poisonous beginnings of oppression came a resilience and resistance that flavored a distinctively Caribbean attitude. By the end of the eighteenth century, African cuisines dominated local tastes. One of the earliest Jamaican ("creole" or local) foods that Lady Nugent, wife of the governor, tasted was pepper pot and she came to enjoy it, even requesting the recipe for a version (although without cassareep) that was prepared with crab.[7]

Pepper pot spread across the Atlantic world. A woodcut of a black pepper pot street vendor serving her customers appeared in *The Cries of Philadelphia* (1810). The 1811 painting by artist John Lewis Krimmel shows a barefoot black woman street vendor ladling soup into the containers of white customers.[8] By serving food from food stands in cities, descendants of enslaved Africans invented new livelihoods. This American pepper pot was a thick, spicy soup made of vegetables and tripe, ox feet, or other cheap meats. However, by the time it reached city streets on American shores, it had lost some of its dark and distinctive tropical flavoring of the Caribbean and its association with poisonous beginnings.

The pepper pot of Amerindian origin transformed a potentially deadly

---

ACKEE AND SALT FISH

1 onion, finely chopped
1 mild chili pepper, minced
1 cup red, yellow, and/or green sweet peppers, chopped
1 to 2 tablespoons light oil
2 cloves garlic, minced
1/2 teaspoon dried thyme
1 tablespoon fresh chives
1/4 teaspoon allspice
2 medium tomatoes, chopped
2 pounds salt fish, soaked and prepared
1 can ackee, drained
1 tablespoon rum
salt and pepper to taste

In a deep frying pan, cook onion and peppers in light oil until soft. Add garlic, thyme, chives, and allspice. Simmer about 10 minutes, until blended. Add tomatoes, fish, ackee, and rum. Cook about 30 minutes. Add salt (remembering that even the cleaned salt fish retains a salty flavor) and black pepper to taste.

---

poison (bitter cassava's prussic acid) into a tasty and beloved meal. There were also other poisons whose powers and pleasures the Caribbean cook harnessed. Ackee (*Blighia sapida*) was a fruit brought from Africa to the British West Indies by the late eighteenth century.[9] When perfectly ripe, it was served as a delicious food. From the insides of the red outer shell, experienced cooks scooped a delicate fruit, resembling scrambled eggs, pale and whitish to yellow in color. Its texture and mild flavor complemented the popular salt fish, with the combination so beloved that it eventually became Jamaica's national dish. If picked unripe, however, or if the wrong part of the fruit's tissue were used, the ackee tree's fruit was toxic and even deadly. One bite was enough to kill a strong man instantly. But as one plantation owner wisely observed, suspicions [of poisoning] were "frequent, but detections rare."[10]

The power of the enslaved cook to nurture or kill with local foods did not go unnoticed on the plantation, whose slave masters lived in constant fear of death by poisoning. Poisonings were commonplace in societies with great disparities in power and wealth. In the Caribbean, the source of most suspected poisonings was not the cook but rather the obeah practitioner in the slave community.

Obeah and War: Planting Resistance

Traditional African religious practice—"obeah," as it came to be known on some Caribbean islands—relied on knowledge of spiritual and medicinal powers. The planter John Stewart claimed that "an Obeah man or woman (for it is practiced by both sexes) is a very wicked and dangerous person on a plantation." Regardless of the term's derivation (perhaps from the Twi word *obeye*, a minor god), it is clear that obeah played a role in resistance and rebellion. The whites feared obeah because it was associated with secrecy and the manipulation of poisons. Many West and Central African religions embraced a belief in hidden energies and forces that could be harnessed for both destructive and beneficial purposes. Poisons themselves, while known, were not thought to be necessary for working the spirits. Either actual substances or their invisible energies could be activated by ritual means for carrying out good or harmful intentions.

Enslaved women, especially elders, were feared and held in awe for their knowledge of medicinal and other herbs and plants. Planters were concerned that the enslaved would target their masters, other slaves, and animals with painful poisoning administered via food and drink. Increasing death rates and a number of suspicious deaths in eighteenth-century Guadeloupe, Martinique, and Saint Domingue led French authorities to concoct a series of ordinances to curb the poisonings. As a consequence, many cooks were accused of wrongdoing.

According to Richard Madden, a physician and observer in Jamaica in the 1830s, a number of poisonous plants were "better known to the Africans than to the whites."[11] Because the symptoms were not unlike those of the common virulent diseases of the time, such as plague, cholera, and yellow fever, intentional poisonings often went undetected. Given the poor medical care available to the enslaved, it is not surprising that Africans became masters of the herbal medicine cabinet. Edward Long observed this Jamaican medicine chest, which included lime juice; cardamom; the roots, branches, leaves, bark, and gums of various trees; and about thirty different herbs.[12]

Poisons also played an important role in the rituals of vodun, an African-derived religion in Haiti. Best known are the paralytic poisons like tetrodotoxin, derived from the pufferfish, that gave rise to the tales of zombies, persons believed to return from the dead and be under the command of a ritual specialist.[13] Legal codes suggest that charges of sorcery were taken very seriously in Haiti, where Makandal, a famous ritual leader active during the Haitian revolution, was convicted of poisoning more than 6,000 whites. A decree passed in 1758 prohibited the use of medicines called variously *pwen*, *bocio*, *garde-corps*, or *makandals*. The small packets of medicines that protected and empowered their owner contained various objects, such as bits of hair, bone, wood, plants, and food. Herskovits reported charred grains such as corn, millet, and beans given as gifts in vodun.[14] It is significant that these were cooked or transformed foods, rather than raw, since cooked foods were considered further empowered. The class of objects called *bo* also may serve as sources of protection against poisonings.[15] These sometimes contain substances believed to be poisonous (duck's blood, frog's stomach), as an antidote (apotropaic) to poison and an emblem of empowerment.[16] The ancestral Fon of West Africa have a proverb—"the duck cannot flap its wings and say cock-a-doodle-doo"—suggesting that someone who wishes to harm you will not be able to do so to your face, since their true nature would be known. The invisible will be made visible, rather than remain hidden. Karen McCarthy Brown has described the religious practices of Alourdes, a vodun priestess, who used small, cloth-covered dolls to influence human behavior: "For restive, 'hungry' spirits, she prescribes a meal of their favorite foods. To treat a violent marriage, Alourdes makes a charm for the wife by filling a jar with ice ('to cool him down') and molasses ('to make him sweet')."[17] In today's Haiti, specialists use ritually cooked food, infusions, and baths to help them direct the spiritual course of events. Some of their most powerful mystical work is undertaken at cemeteries. A Haitian proverb warns that "if the crossroads doesn't give, the cemetery doesn't eat."[18] One interpretation of this proverb recalls the importance of making sacrifices (pouring libations, leaving a medicine packet or *pwen*) at a crossroads before entering a cemetery, the core site for purposes of empowerment. This type of crossroads "feeding" occurred in processions in both Cuba and Guadeloupe. West and Central African warfare also began with processions that carried food and ritual preparations.

The enslaved Africans may have learned of many Caribbean plants alongside native peoples with whom they shared a history of resistance against white tyranny. Kofi Agorsah, an archaeologist of the Maroons, the early African freedom fighters in the Caribbean, has studied surviving medicinal systems in Jamaica and Surinam. According to Agorsah, the key plants used by Maroon groups consisted of both native plants indigenous to the islands and plants imported from Africa during the slave trade. A Maroon leader,

Colonel Harris, described the ability to prepare foods that could be cooked in the ground or left hidden:

> The *kakoon* (cocoon) soup and dish are made from a nut born on a vine of the same name. This nut after falling naturally from the dried pod is collected, thrown into the fire, taken out after giving off a popping sound, and pounded to extract the kernal which . . . is sliced into quarter-inch-wide strips and placed in a bundle made from the fronds of a giant fern known as *ferril macca;* the bundle is placed in the river where it remains for three days. The *kakoon* is then removed and salted. At this stage it can be eaten without being cooked. In combination with *black junga*—a kind of shrimp found in the springs but never in the rivers—it makes both a soup and a stew that are most highly favoured by the connoisseurs in the culinary art.[19]

The Maroons sometimes raided plantations and eventually developed highly portable cuisines; these included wild meats they hunted, cooked, and smoked underground as "jerked" meat, *bammie* (dried cassava bread that could be reconstituted by soaking in coconut milk), and *dokonu* (cornmeal wrapped and cooked in banana leaves). Within a generation of the treaties, British officials recorded regular visits to the Maroon mountain communities in Accompong and Moore Town, Jamaica, where local ceremonies reenacted the Maroons' resistance. Maroon-prepared foods found their way to the table of the governor, according to his wife, Lady Nugent. The 1802 version of this "jerked" hog meat was spiced with the smoky flavor of Scotch bonnet peppers, pimento, and nutmeg. In contemporary communities on the island of Jamaica, the *dokonu* is still prepared in the West African (*dokono* among the Fanti) style on Nanny Day to commemorate the signing of the 1739 Peace Treaty with the British after the First Maroon War.

Not all of the Maroons remained free. Some were recaptured and punished in violation of the treaties described above. Some troublesome and rebellious enslaved, including some of the Trelawny Town Maroons, who had been led by Cudjoe and engaged in a war of resistance, were sent to Nova Scotia by the British and eventually transported back to Africa. According to George Ross, an employee of the Sierra Leone Company, which transported these Maroons back to Freetown, Sierra Leone, in 1800, food became the centerpiece for understanding Maroon culture. Leaders ate first and never in the company of women. Rum was required for the acknowledgment of ancestors at births and deaths. Although the British had anticipated the transport of acculturated Africans from the Caribbean to play a leading role in "civilizing" the West African colony, the opposite seemed to occur, especially when food was the measure of change. The foods and meals of Europeans were Africanized. The

Caribbean's "salt pork and cold rice" continued to be "pleasant dishes" on board the ship returning to Africa. On the Gambia River, Ross ate "an excellent dinner" of goat, rice "well pressed," and "Kus-kus" (couscous) made of Indian corn and eaten from a calabash.[20]

One of the great Maroon leaders was a woman named Nanny, also an obeah practitioner. Today, in the still-independent Jamaican and Surinamese Maroon societies, potions and poisons are produced in liquid form from recipes passed down through generations. Historical poisoning cases were recorded not only in Jamaica, but also in the island courts from Trinidad to St. Lucia to Barbados. In the famous Antiguan revolt of 1737, one of the first examples of collective resistance in the Caribbean, obeah and food were involved. The plot, which would have blown up guests at the annual ball and feast commemorating King George II's coronation ten years earlier, occurred during a period of worsening scarcity. Conspirators were initiated at a feast with food and drink, after which they took an oath. Testifying to an island meeting, the slave Quamina described Quawcoo's role:

> I saw this Obey [obeah] Man at Secundi's House after I waked at Midnight. I found him and Hunts Cuffy there. Secundi gave him a Chequeen [gold coin], a Bottle of Rum and a Dominque Cock and Quawcoo put Obey made of Sheeps Skin upon the ground, upon and about the bottle of Rum, and the Chequeen upon the Bottle, Then took the Cock, cut open his Mouth, and one of his Toes, and so poured the Cocks blood Over all the Obey, and then Rub'd Secundi's forehead with the Cocks bloody Toe, Then took the Bottle and poured Some Rum upon the Obey, Drank a Dram, and gave it to Secundi and made Secundi Sware not to Discover his name to any body.[21]

Quawcoo was banished from the island. The crimes were punishable by public torture and transport to convict colonies, but the punishments did not deter the continuum of resistance.

The Marketplace

The Yoruba have a proverb, "The world is a market, [and] the otherworld is home."[22] The proverb suggests the transitory nature of existence and offers up the notion that the market should be associated with the temporary and with ideas of change. Most foods grown by the enslaved ended up at market, rather than being consumed by their growers. Indeed, the marketplace in the era of plantation slavery was an important site of resistance, one of the rare places where ideas and news could be exchanged by the enslaved. The role of higglers was crucial. Usually women, higglers bargained in the exchange of goods and services on behalf of slave masters. Their bargaining skills were essential to the transfer of foodstuffs between plantations and to the successful feeding of the plantations' communities. Plantation owners considered stealing food one of the worst crimes. It was sometimes punishable by applying an apparatus made of iron that covered the enslaved person's mouth and prevented all eating, speaking, and sometimes even swallowing.

Enslaved Africans relied on provision grounds and the collection of wild plants and animals to supply essential foods. Provision grounds were situated near their habitations. A number of other food-growing sites occupied the island landscape. These included kitchen gardens, with vegetables and fruit trees familiar to the European enslavers but also containing unfamiliar plants such as African yam (*Diascorea* spp.) or Asian cassava.[23] The word "yam" originated from one of several West African words (perhaps the Fula verb) meaning "to eat": *njam, nyami, or djambi.* The verb carried through to Jamaican English. In Africa, yams were associated with fertility and wealth. They were also traded widely and sometimes even served as currency.

The higglers did more than transfer yams, tomatoes, okra, and onions from provision grounds to marketplace. Behind their market roles, the women were also resistance fighters and spies. By passing along secrets, gossip, news, and information critical to the survival of escaped slaves, Maroons, and others, higglers played a key role in large-scale uprisings that linked distant plantations. These market women were essential nodes in a network that even connected islands in times of rebellion and resistance.

Many Caribbean markets today resemble their African counterparts. They are bustling, colorful stages for dramatic interactions between people and food. In Grenada, for example, the market square has operated continuously since 1791, when slaves and vegetables were sold side by side. In all but a few islands, the provision grounds were more important to slaves than the master's storeroom on the plantation.[24] Enslaved Africans produced a variety of crops and also kept medicinal plants on their provision grounds or on pathways leading from the slave houses. This produce made its way to the marketplace and the cooking pot and provided a key means for expanding the diet beyond the limited supplies of salt and pickled fish, vegetables, and fruit. Sometimes the revenues gained from selling surplus provisions provided the savings needed to purchase one's freedom. At times in the history of Jamaica, the accumulation of small coinage by slaves through transactions in the marketplace resulted in a shortage of small coins. As in Africa, this informal marketing sector of the island economy was almost entirely in the hands of women and consequently enhanced their autonomy.[25]

Visiting the Caribbean island market was an occasion for social transactions as well. While the mobility of slaves was severely restricted, markets

BITTER MELON ROOT (CORILLA OR CARAILLEE)

1 pound bitter melon, finely chopped
1 onion, sliced
1 clove garlic, minced
4 ounces ground meat or fried shrimp, for flavoring
1 tablespoon lard
salt and pepper to taste (heavy salting will cut the bitterness)

Prepare the corilla by splitting the fruit lengthwise and cleaning out the seeds. Slice thinly into 1- or 2-inch strips. Boil the corilla in salted water for about 5 minutes, or season by sprinkling with a 1/2 teaspoon of salt and 1 tablespoon of vinegar. Then fry with onion, garlic, ground meat, and lard. Season with salt and pepper.

Heavily salted and smothered in onions or stuffed, the bitter corilla is transformed into a coveted vegetable side dish. Thinly sliced corilla can also be used in pepper sauces. The corilla leaves are dried and brewed to treat various stomach ailments. When ripe, the bright red seeds are actually quite sweet. The bitter gourd karele was an important Hindu religious food, imported to the Caribbean from Asia.

provided an exception to the rule. For example, in the Laws of Jamaica (1826), a clause suggested that "no slave *except when going to the market* [emphasis added] shall travel without a ticket, specially worded and signed by his [*sic*] owner."[26] Markets benefited both slave and master, providing independence and a source of added income. Skilled higglers could earn additional income for their slave masters.

Markets were commonplace on Sundays, the only day of leisure for the enslaved. After emancipation, many women used their culinary arts to become entrepreneurs. They made pickles, pepper sauces, jams, jellies, breads, and sweets. Fresh produce also traveled to some islands (e.g., the Netherlands Antilles) in floating markets, schooners, small boats, and canoes. This spread the availability of favorite foods otherwise not readily available, like certain varieties of plantain or the Asian caraillee (*karele*), a Hindu religious food.

Travel accounts and journals describe the noises, smells, and sights of the markets and their wares. The street cries of women in British Guyana, recorded by Scoles in 1885, suggest the women's outspoken independence with sexual innuendo:

Nice cassava bread ladies
Nice cassava bread;
He who want me call me,
He who no want me no call me,
He who shame to call me, give me
The wink, wink, wink.[27]

Among the foods sold in the markets were cassava cakes. Cassava cakes and cornbread were substitutes for the familiar bread of Europe, which was scarce because of the lack of wheat flour in the Caribbean. Both the French and the British scorned corn and cassava, which they found dry and tasteless. Said one English clergyman in Barbados, "Casada is a bread I approve not of." Richard Ligon and others eventually learned to enjoy cassava pie crusts and cakes from the ground flour.[28] Cassava flour, called *farinha* in Bahia, Brazil, was mixed with onion, oil, and pepper and also toasted and used as a topping on beans and other dishes. It is called *gari* in coastal West Africa, where it is beloved as a steamed porridge that thickens to a certain firmness and can be eaten with one's fingers like the ubiquitous *fufu*.

Cornmeal was eventually substituted for use in steamed leaf packets and other dishes, prepared similarly in the Old World, including coastal Africa. On the other hand, corn was considered animal food and rejected by most upper-class Europeans in Europe, the Americas, and the Caribbean, although Thomas Jefferson, who spent four years in France in the eighteenth century, grew corn in his Paris garden and was fond of serving guests corn on the cob and spoon bread (cornmeal porridge).[29] Africans preferred cassava to corn, but even the deities eventually did not agree and food preferences shifted. A bottle tree outside the Yoruba-derived shrine to Ogun in the town of Chaguanas, Trinidad, holds corn offerings to ward off thieves, and a portable altar of corn wrapped in a knotted red cloth is given to an overseas traveler to protect her during the long journey home.

Feeding the Ancestors and Spirits

The enslaved Africans inhabited a world they shared with deities, spirits, and ancestors. At the core of many acts of slave resistance were empowering beliefs derived from the multiple religions of West and Central Africa. Integral to most African religious systems carried across the Atlantic was a profound, shared belief in the transmutability of the divide between the

Bottle tree, Kenny Cyrus Shrine, Chaguanas, Trinidad
(Photograph by Candice Goucher)

world of the living and the unseen world of ancestors and spirits. Food and drink formed one significant bridge between realms. Spirits and ancestors could be called upon to act on behalf of and strengthen an individual or group. Pouring libations was both acknowledgment of the spiritual realm and the means by which its powers and energies might be invoked. Feeding the ancestors and spirits reflected both the changes and continuities in Caribbean foodways.

CASSAVA CAKES

1 pound sweet cassava
salt to taste
1 tablespoon cooking oil
optional: 2 tablespoons butter and 2 cloves of garlic, minced and
   heated separately

Wash and peel the cassava; finely grate into a cheesecloth to drain excess liquid. Shape into 4 thin cakes. Fry on a preheated cast iron skillet or griddle with cooking oil. Optional step: Add the cakes to the butter and garlic mixture until they are heated through and have absorbed the garlic flavor.

SWEET CASSAVA PONE

2 cups grated cassava, strained in cheesecloth to remove liquid
1 cup dry, unsweetened coconut
1 cup sugar
1 teaspoon cinnamon
2 teaspoons nutmeg
4 tablespoons butter, melted
2 cups evaporated milk
1 teaspoon vanilla essence

Combine all ingredients in a bowl; pour into a greased 8-inch-square baking dish. Bake at 350°F for about 45 minutes or until browned. Cut in small squares and serve.

African Food Practices and Beliefs

Graves were important sites of memory and therefore potential sites of resistance. According to Richard Watson, in Barbados around 1804, slaves "sometimes spread victuals on the graves of those who were recently dead, that their spirits might return and eat. I have often seen the graves made up with lime and stone in the form of a coffin, and a small earthen cup placed on the breast, for the purpose of containing meat or drink."[30] Watson also records an encounter with an elderly slave woman sitting on a grave and eating out of a calabash that she claimed, at the same time, to be using to feed the dead. In Haiti, sesame seeds (*Sesamum indicum*) were placed in the coffin. Known as *hoholi*, this offering was meant to provide the deceased with protection against malevolent sorcerers.[31] In eighteenth-century Suriname, Stedman observed the religious sharing of drink by slaves. This included the requisite acknowledgement of the departed, as Stedman witnessed: "were there one single dram of rum, he would divide it among the same number: this is not done, however, until a few drops are first sprinkled on the ground, as an oblation to the gods."[32] Libations were small "sips" of drinks poured on the ground from newly opened rum bottles. Such libations are still poured to "absent friends" at ordinary social gatherings and special occasions, such as funerals and weddings across the islands of the Caribbean.

Brought to Cuba in the sixteenth century, descendants of enslaved Calabari peoples (Efik and Ekoi or Efor) established a branch of a secret society known as Abakua (the Ekpe or leopard society). Abakua preserved the ceremony of the ancestor spirits, whose appearance allowed communication with dead elders as well as a cleansing and purifying of the living. Sharing food played a part in the ceremony of initiation in which initiates and devotees sat in a circle surrounding huge cooking pots of boiling water. These were used to cook fritters of cowpeas, corn, manioc, and pumpkin. A sacramental beverage was passed around in a gourd. Known as *aguanusoso*, the drink was made from aguadiente, salt, seven kinds of herbs, the grated bark or stalks of seven sacred plants, peanut, ginger, plantain, yam, and the blood of sacrificed goats and cockerels. *Uriabon*, the feast of yams, plantains, goat, cockerel, herbs, strands of tobacco, small bits of chalk, and powdered eggshell, followed.[33] Before eating, celebrants fed the spirits of the dead and the four winds found at the four cardinal points.

Many more slaves came to Cuba and other islands from Yorubaland in the nineteenth century (more than 130,000 went to Cuba between 1823 and 1865). Their beliefs centered on the Yoruba pantheon in the religion called Santeria. By then, food had become a systematic but secret means for communicating culture and spiritual ideals that were often feared and outlawed by the slave owners. The earlier religion known in Cuba as the Reglas de Palo was widely practiced by enslaved Africans. Its conceptual framework and powers were African-derived from the practices the enslaved captives brought from Angola and Kongo. Ritual foods were consumed in a circle formed around the cooks and their pots and pans.

Even when slaves were forced to convert to Christianity, they hid their

CUBAN ACARA OR COWPEA FRITTERS
(Abakua ceremony)

1 pound cowpeas (soaked overnight)
5 cloves of garlic
salt to taste
oil for frying

After soaking the beans overnight, rinse them several times, discarding skins. Drain; peel the remaining skins by rubbing the peas between your fingers. Mash with garlic until the beans are whipped to a creamy paste. (You can also use a food processor or blender, gradually adding up to 2 cups of water.) Add salt to taste. Shape the paste into little balls or croquettes, about the size of your finger. Deep-fry in hot oil in an iron frying pan.

Acara not intended for ceremonial use may be seasoned with ginger, pepper, basil, olive oil, or onions as desired. In Trinidad and the French Caribbean, acara are made with black-eyed peas. In Ghana, they are usually seasoned with dried shrimp. They are also eaten on Good Friday in the French Caribbean, where fritters are called "accras de zieu noi's." "Accras de Morue" (morue is an archaic term for "salt fish" and "prostitute") are made with salted cod and cassava used in place of the beans.

TRINIDAD ACARA
(annual New Year ceremony, Belmont)

3/4 cup flour
1/4 cup milk
1 can black-eyed peas, drained and ground (see above)
3 tablespoons onion, finely minced
salt, cayenne, and black pepper to taste
1 tablespoon baking powder
1 or 2 eggs, beaten
oil for frying

Mix all ingredients. Drop by spoonfuls into 1-inch of hot cooking oil. Fry until lightly browned, turning once or twice. Drain with slotted spoon on a paper towel.

In Brazil, acaraje is made for Yansa (Oya)—goddess of the Niger River and of tempests and winds—on the first Wednesday of every month. In Virginia, acara originated as a food from African-derived cuisines and became a favorite dish of upper-class whites on eighteenth-century plantations.

YEMAJA'S SOUP

6 cups cold water or broth
2 turnips, peeled and cut in 2-inch pieces
1 pumpkin, peeled and cut in 2-inch pieces
1 onion, chopped and browned in oil
1 bay leaf
1 sprig of parsley, finely chopped
1 cup uncooked rice
2 pounds meat (lamb, duck, or fish)
1 yam, peeled and cut in 2-inch pieces
1 sprig basil, chopped

Combine water or broth, turnips, pumpkin, golden brown onion, bay leaf, parsley, rice, choice of meat, and yam. Heat until the water starts boiling. Then whip the broth. Mash the pumpkin, rice, and yam, to thicken the broth. Garnish with fresh basil leaves.

memory of African deities in the guise of Catholic saints and Baptist ceremony. In this way, enslaved Africans resisted full assimilation, and African beliefs persisted. The nineteenth-century arrivals of Hinduism (with indentured laborers), the Kali-Mai (black mother) sect, and the Kabbalah (an esoteric set of Jewish and Christian teachings and practices) were no different. In time, their distinctive concepts and practices were merged and transformed by contact with African devotees. By the twentieth century, the adherents of the African-derived *orisha* religion of Trinidad sometimes embraced these systems into their own, both formally and informally helping to spread new ideas.[34] The Hindu deities most commonly found in *orisha* worship were Hanuman, Mahabir, Lakshmi, and Rama, all popular and known as freedom-seeking deliverers from sorrow or destroyers of injustice.

African-derived values and concepts were promoted through religious and ritual practice. They were communicated in the selection and preparation of foods as well. In the words of one food historian, these Yoruba deities, known as *orisha*, were "gourmet gods."[35] Colors, tastes, and allusions were significant factors in the choice of food for the gods. Alligator peppers seasoned yam flour with the fire of the Yoruba thunder god Shango's lightning. Yet one of Shango's praise songs claims that "[he is] cool when he eats."[36] Pepper grains are considered to be a particularly potent foodstuff. The association of pepper with heat, and therefore transformation, is paralleled by its nonfood uses in divination and other forms of spiritual activity. This otherworldly power is reflected in pepper's ability to cause tears and burning in the mouth and stomach.

The reddish colors of foods such as palm oil (*dende*), peppers, and *anatto* were powerful reminders of the links between food and life force. Soups were everyday foods savored across the Atlantic world and widely perceived to be the most nourishing of dishes that used every scrap of available nutrition. Observers of African cooking on a Trinidad estate in the early 1700s recorded a soup of meat with peppers and *eddoe* (an African tuber). This soup was not only palatable, but "indeed one of the great blessings of the West Indies."[37] John Atkins observed the West African use of palm oil in a dish he called "Black Soupee," a meat stew with peppers and okra.[38] Even when coconut milk was later substituted for the palm-oil-based broth in African soups, the milk was often colored red using anatto. There was no doubt among West Indians that ingesting a reddish meal prolonged life and promoted vitality. The favored color could also be achieved by adding pumpkin or red yam to soups, as in the ritual soup for Yemaya, the Yoruba goddess of the sea. In the Candomblé ceremonies of Brazil, the sacred preparation of foods can lead to a state of enhanced awareness and even spirit possession experienced by the cook.[39]

Gourmet Gods

All deities had food associations, some originating in the New World, some traceable to the African continent. The Yoruba deity Obatala was honored with white foods such as *eko*, fermented corn wrapped in plantain leaves. The white symbolized the purity with which Obatala, "King of Whiteness," was associated. Yellow or amber-colored foods such as honey, lemon, palm oil, and peppers represented Oshun, the goddess of love and wealth. Oshun's favorite dish in Cuba was *ochinchin*, shrimp prepared with greens that may grow near inland fresh water.[40] In an important religious story, honey features prominently in the successful wooing of the warrior Ogun by Oshun. Yemaya and Shango preferred male sheep, and their shared eating preferences symbolized the stories of their eternal bond; Oya eats only goat, a reflection of her divergence from the wishes of Yemaya. Plantains were also reserved for Shango, whereas Ogun was to be fed roasted yams and palm oil, salt, and cornmeal.

Initiates learned the most basic levels of spiritual and food knowledge first. The three principal deities were Elegua (the gatekeeper at the crossroads), Ogun (god of iron and warfare), and Ochosi (the archer, a hunter associated with the forest). These were the warrior orisas, essential for resistance and survival. They commanded larger-than-life appetites. In Trinidad, Ogun was fed rice and peas cooked with olive oil and left unsalted. In Haiti, Ogun was associated with the calabash tree; its leaves, fruit, and syrup were used medicinally to treat headaches, sunstroke, fever, whooping cough, asthma, and other ailments.[41] Moreover, the calabash was an essential utensil both in mundane food storage and preparation and in spiritual offerings. From the calabash, the priest's rattle was fashioned. Such a central association was in keeping with Ogun's strength and centrality as a powerful deity. In Brazil, Ogun's meal was known as *feijoada*, a stew of black beans and smoked meats, which became the national dish.

The deities were demanding gastronomes. They demanded skilled preparation and required their preferences be met with specificity, down to the very particular and peculiar details of preparation. The Candomblé cook was selected as a lead cook to oversee the preparation of foods required for the orisa. She was required to slice the okra in Ogun's soup in a certain manner and shape that differed from the slicing of the okra for Shango's *obeguirin*.[42] The various deities required five, six, nine, twelve, or sixteen pieces of food, arranged in a prescribed order on the plate. For example, sixteen eggs for Olokun would be placed with ten around the edge of the platter. The foods were considered pleasing and beautiful when evocative of the orisa. Libations or prayers to Ogun prefaced the wielding of iron kitchen utensils. Salt and seasonings were added or more often omitted as per the specific preference of the deity. The colors, textures, visual characteristics, and behavior of animals and plants all played a role in sacred selection. In the course of their preparation, foods acquired their complex layering of coded communication with unseen realms. Sacrifices were believed to initiate the discourse with ancestors and deities.

Similar formalization of food preparation practices was historically incorporated by the Abakua secret society of Cuba. Open to all races and based on Ekoi and Efik (of Nigeria's) highly militarized and patrilineal associations, the Cuban religion made food central in an all-male environment of resistance. The post of the *nkandembo* was particularly important. He provided ritual food for ceremonies and initiations. Particularly critical was his ability to measure ingredients and maximize the flavors of the food for deities and members.[43]

The religious foods mirrored and dictated health and social concerns registered in the diet. Deities were ignited or cooled with appropriate food and liquid. Ogun's iron utensils could not be cooled down with water but were to be washed with aguardiente (distilled sugar-derived alcohol). Feasts were held to honor particular deities, each of whom embodied a different constellation of divine powers. Family affairs, these feasts reinforced the familiarity with which most Africans interacted with deities, just as the deities interacted among themselves. People were considered daughters of Yemaya, sons of Ogun. Together they were a family, eating foods rich with meaning and history.

Ritual foods were closely associated with healing. The work of the orisas included their intervention in "diagnosing and suggesting cures for ills."[44] The slaves' medical knowledge consisted mostly of botanical cures. Rituals were thought to maintain the state of balance that characterized good health. Healing within a ritual occurred first; its actualization through the ingestion of prescribed foods or medicines might follow. Consequently the *babalu, santero, santera,* or priest in Santeria or other African-derived practices might become famous for his diagnostic skills and herbal treatments. His knowledge of foods, herbs, plants, and roots was a pharmacopeia of medicinal and spiritual power. This wisdom trickled down to the kitchen, where cooks understood which foods were most effective in treating stomachaches or heart problems. Not surprisingly, some famous "Voodoo" experts were also renowned as famous cooks, like Doctor John, whose powers were derived from Cuban and New Orleans culinary practices.[45]

Acara was a common ritual food with many religious associations. The Yoruba word for black-eyed peas was *ewa,* a pun on *ewa or wa,* meaning the essence of existence.[46] The peas could be boiled in water or with *dende* (palm oil), with or without salt, sometimes with tomatoes, peppers, or onions. Seaweed (or mustard greens) fried in palm oil might be added as a garnish when cooked for Oshun. Respect and worship, feeding and ritual observation, dominated the essential religious practice of the Yoruba world. The relationship between feeding, sustenance, and spiritual survival is visible in the New World altars to the Yoruba orisa (deities). From Cuba to Brazil and throughout most of the Caribbean, a soup pot held stones and other sacred elements that honored the orisa. Sacred vessels and plates held offerings of food and stored water. Inverted, the pots suggested the powers within.

Shrines and altars were placed within households and courtyards. They housed the remains of past feasts, providing a memorialized stratigraphy of repasts and rituals. A shrine required food to be spiritually active; likewise, spiritual action needed to be fed or charged. In African-derived belief systems, "food" or "medicine" (matter to be consumed by spirits or ancestors) was sometimes left for those in the unseen world and sometimes shared by

Rada shrine for Ogun, Belmont, Port of Spain, Trinidad
(Photograph by Candice Goucher)

devotees. For example, at a Rada shrine in Port of Spain, Trinidad, a plate of black-eyed peas cooked in olive oil was left at the altar of Ogun. At the end of the annual ceremonies, devotees took a handful of peas from this plate and ate them as they exited the shrine's compound.[47] In Jamaica, a *kumina* ceremony began with a table set for the spirits. A tablecloth was placed over a table and chairs were pulled up. Candles were lit. Bottles of clear liquid—soda and rum—were opened as an invitation to the invisible spirits to come and join the drumming and dancing during the evening.[48] Participants did not leave the compound without eating a plate of the foods prepared from the goat and the chickens that had been sacrificed during the evening's ceremony.

Other kinds of festivities were also cause for feasting with deities. In today's Cuba, a birthday party for Eleggua, the Yoruba messenger deity and guardian of the crossroads, attended by the author, is an occasion for drumming, dancing, and eating in a central Havana home. It is a festive occasion, filled with mirth and gaiety. The shrine room of a *babalu* (priest) is decorated in advance. At the altar or *panuelo* constructed for the deity's birthday, plants, objects, and foods play a major role in honoring the powers and potentialities of Eleggua and his followers. The altar is decorated with tree branches from which hang dolls and action heroes (toys of the trickster deity), plastic hot rods (perhaps an allusion to the crossroads), and balloons. A red plastic tub with candies wrapped in cellophane and bakery-bought frosted cakes join the baskets of fruit, money, flowers, and platters of savory ritual foods.[49] After altar blessings, drumming begins next door and one by one the deities are called over the next five hours to celebrate the birthday. Last to leave on this occasion (and the most bellicose) was the boastful Shango, that is, until Ogun returned and taunted women in the room for pesos. All over the city, devotees to Eleggua would be seen carrying cakes down the narrow neighborhood streets.

The deities controlled certain plants (including foods) that they called their own, although the deity of herbal medicines Osanyin controls all plants. The deities also dictated what and when people do or do not eat. The foods that deities preferred to eat were sometimes paralleled by what their followers were forbidden to eat. The daughters of Ochun may not eat pumpkin because of their shame at having been found in sexual relations with Ochun's brother-in-law in a pumpkin field. Babaluaye's children are forbidden to eat roasted corn until they feed the deity. Oya cut off her own ears so her husband, Shango, might eat them with *amala* (yam porridge), a reminder of the close association of food with violent action and sacrifice.

Fasting and Feasting: Christmas and Other Holidays

Sacrifice involving food was also important in the religion and culture brought to the Americas by European settlers during the Atlantic era. To take communion (in the Eucharist) was to partake of God in a mystical experience. For Christians, the wine was the blood of Jesus Christ and the bread was His flesh. Abstinence through Christian ritual was a means of preparing for the mystical experience, and fasting served as a regularly occurring renunciation of ordinary food that pointed the way to the food on the altar, the Eucharist. The ritual is believed to have roots in the pre-Christian Judaic world. Eating and not eating were central symbolic themes in European culture from medieval times, and these concepts traveled to the Caribbean.[50]

Like the sixteenth-century Yoruba, Native Americans, and peoples of South Asia, European Catholics believed in hot and cool foods. Because fish were considered "cool," fish could be consumed on the fasting days of their religious calendar. Hot foods were believed to confuse the mind and distract the eater from a spiritual path. In the eighteenth century, Stedman noted the similarities of food prohibitions among the slaves and their masters in Suriname: "[a]ny Negro will touch [the prohibited food handed down to him]; though I have seen some good Catholics eat roast-beef in Lent, and a religious Jew devouring a slice from a fat flitch of bacon."[51] Similar restrictions were in place for Muslims, both enslaved Africans and later indentured South Asians, who, together with Hindus, did not eat certain meats, if any at all. It was not always possible for adherents to follow religious observations as strictly as they may have wished. Violations of holy days both invited and incited revolts and rebellions.

On many islands, Europeans imposed their religion on enslaved and indentured laborers. They did so in ways that sometimes were inconsistent, ignoring some observances, activities, and prohibitions, while favoring the observance of the Christian calendar of holy days. When European slave masters celebrated Christmas, so did the enslaved African and, later, the indentured Asian. In 1724, the *Journal of a Lady of Quality* records the abundance of a Caribbean Christmas market, with goods carried by men and women in baskets on their heads:

> [H]ere a lamb, there a Turkey or pig, all covered in the same elegant manner. While others had the baskets filled with fruit, pine-apples reared over each other; Grapes dangling over the loaded basket: oranges, Shaddacks, water lemons, pomegranates, grandillas, with twenty others, whose names I forget.[52]

Later that century, William Beckford observed Jamaican festivities at Christmas, when the enslaved Africans collected provisions from the mountains and "the more wealthy sell poultry, or kill a hog (by which they make a considerable profit), or give an entertainment to their friends, or make a public assembly, at which every person pays a stipulated sum at his admittance." Peter Marsden also noted the special foods and the interactions between classes in Jamaica: "At Christmas the slaves are allowed three days holiday during which time they are quite at liberty, and have herrings, flour, and rum. The prime negroes and mulattoes pay a visit to the white people during the festivity, and are treated with punch."[53] Others received special allotments of rum, sugar, codfish, or salt meat. They had their Christmas cakes and, from the descriptions of slave owners, were thought to "abound in good things both to eat and drink."[54]

There was no doubt that feasting and excess were assumed to go hand in hand with the Christmas season, which was also the most common time of mischief, rebellions, and uprisings. Dancing, drinking, and masquerade balls occupied the plantocracy, and the added license afforded a select few among the enslaved population made the season of festivities an opportune time for resistance. The writer of the *Journal of a Lady of Quality* warned, "It is necessary however to keep a look out during this season of unbounded freedom; and every man on the island is in arms and patrols go around the different plantations as well as keep guard in the town."[55]

Still, the season was a time for familiar and recurring foods and smells: Portuguese garlic pork, Black Cake (a steamed English pudding corrupted with rum in the British territories) and anise seed or ginger drinks, pastelles (packets of cornmeal with savory or sweet additions steamed in banana leaves), to name a few of the holiday delicacies. The mood of resistance was never far removed. According to Cynric Williams, who spent Christmas in Jamaica at

CARIBBEAN BLACK CAKE

1 pound each of dark currants, raisins, and prunes
1 cup stout, plus enough other liquor to cover the fruit
1 pound plus 2/3 cup sugar
1 pound butter
12 eggs, beaten
2 1/4 cups flour
3 teaspoons baking powder
2 teaspoons vanilla essence
2 teaspoons each of nutmeg, allspice, and cinnamon
1/2 cup dark rum

At least a week in advance, soak the fruit in a glass jar, using 1 cup of stout and any leftover liquors available to cover the fruit mixture completely. Drain off the liquor but do not discard; add enough back to allow for grinding the fruit until fine. Do not allow the fruits to liquefy completely and lose their shape as distinct pieces. Set aside.

When ready to bake the cake, place 2/3 cup of refined white sugar in a large cast-iron skillet or pot over low heat. The sugar will begin to smoke and burn, darkening in the process. Add water, a little at a time, while constantly stirring the blackened sugar into a thick, dark syrup. Set aside. In a big bowl, cream the butter and 1 pound of sugar; add beaten eggs. Gradually add the flour, baking powder, and spices. The batter should be thick and creamy. Add the burnt sugar and, finally, the fruit. Turn into greased and floured pans, and bake at 350°F for about 90 minutes or until set. A fully baked black cake should be moist and very dark. The most common mistake is failure to achieve the correct balance of white flour and dark ingredients (hence the right color). After the cake has cooled and dried a bit, add dark rum until remoistened. Soaking in rum will preserve this cake for months, but a good black cake disappears far more quickly.

the beginning of the nineteenth century, "the merriment became rather boisterous as the punch operated, and the slaves sang satirical philippics against their master, communicating a little free advice now and then."[56] Christmas Day was the single most frequent choice for rebellions and uprisings.

Rastafarian organic farm, Jamaica, c. 1988
(Photograph by Candice Goucher)

I-tal Foods of the Rastafarians

In the Rastafarian religion of Jamaican resistance, food became an important symbol at the heart of that religion's cultural and social identity within the larger island society. The Rastafarian cuisine was one of the world's first antiglobalization diets. Rastafarian ideas emerged in the context of African-derived as well as Christian-Judaic religions carried to Jamaica and as part of the resistance to the white-dominated society. Rooted in protest, Rastafarianism was a messianic movement whose followers sought redemption through a peaceful and distinctive lifestyle, in which a spiritual birth was possible. In follower Samuel Brown's treatise on codes of behavior, diet is explained as basically vegetarian: "We [Rastafarians] are vegetarians, making scant use of certain animal flesh yet outlawing the use of swine's flesh in any form, shell fishes, scaleless fishes, snails, etc."[57] Small fish are consumed by some Rastafarians (and Cushitic Ethiopians), who trace the practice to Coptic versions of the scriptures, but other meats and large fish are believed to be contaminated and part of Babylon: the white man's establishment, believed to be a place where the big fish consume the little fish.[58] Rastafarians do not drink coffee, tea, milk, or alcohol, nor do they eat eggs. Liquids made from herbs, roots, and other plants are ingested for medicinal purposes. Ganja is considered a holy herb and is infused as well as smoked in rituals. I-tal refers to the natural essence of things, uncorrupted.

I-TAL DRINK

1 pound carrots, juiced
2 cups water, purified
1 cup soy or almond milk
3 tablespoons coconut cream
2 teaspoons nutmeg, freshly grated
1 teaspoon rosewater
molasses or raw sugar to taste

Mix all the ingredients in a blender, adding the sugar last to sweeten to taste. To vary the recipe, replace the carrots with the juice of available fresh fruits.

I-tal food is prepared according to strict rules, and no menstruating woman is permitted to cook food. Fasting is practiced and feasts are commonly part of religious ceremonies. I-tal food is cooked with no salt, part of a wider African-derived practice of ritual avoidance of salt. Haitians were forbidden to put salt in a slave spirit's (*zonbi*'s) food, and in Tobago it was believed that eating salt prevented the spirits of Africans from returning to Africa.[59] Coconut oil is sometimes used for cooking, but Rastafarians generally favor raw foods. Homegrown fruits and vegetables are preferred as I-tal foods. Among the most beloved of I-tal preparations is fresh fruit or vegetable juice.

Many Rastafarians grow their own food, taking pride in living off the land and being self-sufficient. A typical farm today will be used to grow organically their herbs, fruits, and vegetables. The Rastafarian farming techniques include using one plant to support another. Maroons passed down these techniques of intercropping. The persistence of growing local food, while shunning reliance on globalization, connected the Rastafarians to the traditions of runaway Africans, successfully isolated and independent in the mountains of Jamaica, and thus to generations of resistance.

Asian-Caribbean Religious Foods

The new Chinese and East Indian immigrants arriving in the mid-nineteenth century brought new religions to the islands, as well as distinctive foodways to the Caribbean cooking pot. Even the earliest indentured laborers grew familiar vegetables on small provision lands to supplement the meager foods provided in their often appalling living conditions—essentially the same as those endured by generations of enslaved Africans. Asians in urban slums had garden plots for vegetables such as cabbage, lettuce, garden eggs (a small fruit resembling eggplant), callaloo, and plantains.[60]

In Kingston, East Indian market gardens were known, since the 1890s, for their cultivation of vegetables and flowers: "nothing is wasted; there is strict economy everywhere and the most ordinary cultivation round the house is done with a certain rustic science that makes the most out of the soil and surroundings."[61] During the worldwide Depression of the 1930s, these Jamaican slum gardens became the site of controversy over land, water rights, and regulations. At the same time, more than a century after their arrival, Trinidadian East Indians, dressed as suffering "Canefarmers," protested their economic plight during the annual urban Carnival celebrations.[62] East Indians dominated the production of food for markets and for export in the Caribbean.

Colonizers had intended the indentured laborers as a buffer zone between Africans and Europeans. However, rather than becoming culturally divisive influences, the immigrants sometimes chose inclusion by finding commonalities among their cultures and foodways. Chinese in Jamaica marked gravesites as important places of identity building. The Hakka originally practiced the ritual known as Gah San as a form of ancestral worship.[63] Annual Qingming festivals in Jamaica became opportunities to honor spiritual connections by cleaning ancestors' graves in the cemetery. The occasions also perpetuated a sense of community and belonging among the living. Food offerings, given to strangers or guests in one's home, were important markers of politeness and inclusion. Offering food, incense, and money could mark a shrine where communication with and support from the spirit world were sought. Putting incense on a dining table was a continuing practice in Chinese-Jamaican homes, making the meal a sacred event and acknowledging ancestral interventions.

Religious beliefs also formed the basis for political resistance among the early East Indian populations in the Caribbean. In Trinidad, culture and religious beliefs were an amalgam of local practices from many parts of India. Public festivals and private life-cycle rites and ceremonies provided opportunities for expressing distinctive cultural flavors of Hinduism and Islam. As early as 1849, goats were being sacrificed for a *puja* (offering) in San Fernando, Trinidad, and in 1855 on Christmas Day, probably because this was a public holiday. In St. Lucia, East Indians prepared unsalted portions of dishes to be presented to ancestors as offerings.[64]

First celebrated in Trinidad in 1863, the Shi'ite Muslim observance of Muharram, the first month of the New Year, consisted of ten days of fasting, culminating in a procession. Public festivals such as Muharram, which included the observance of Hosay or *tadja* (as it was called in Guyana), were also occasions when large gatherings of non-Muslim East Indians sometimes turned into violent political demonstrations against the white colonial establishment. Other riots stemmed from the fierce competitions between estates. For example, when disturbances in the 1850s and 1860s erupted among Indians on Endeavor Estate and Woodford Lodge in Trinidad, Africans and Chinese loyal to each side joined in the fighting. In 1884, grievances aired during the festivities served as protests against the attempt by colonial authorities to regulate cultural practices. The violence claimed at least thirteen lives; more than a hundred persons were injured.[65] Tadja was not only celebrated by Indo-Caribbean peoples, but also observed by African-descendants or Creoles and Chinese since at least the 1860s.

Special foods were associated with the final stages of the Hosay processions. In Trinidad, ritual food was eaten each night. Before the last day's large procession in Jamaica, participants ate *malida*, a fried combination of burnt sugar, flour dough, and molasses.[66] The symbolic use of burnt sugar and molasses recalls the key elements of earlier Canbouley riots of Trinidad, where enslaved Africans rebelled against the brutality of the sugarcane fields. The Hosay events were also historical processions that commemorated events involving the grandchildren of the prophet Muhammad: the decapitation of Husayn and the poisoning of his brother Hasan, events in Islamic history remembered by some as inspirational martyrdoms.

In the twentieth century, Chinese and Indo-Caribbean people living under colonialism found inspiration in revolutions around the world. Double Ten Day marked the anniversary of the Wuchang Uprising on the tenth day of the tenth month (October 10, 1911). This revolt led to the end of dynastic rule in China. Halfway around the world, Chinese descendants celebrated with foods and parades. Sylvia Hunt's *Menus for Festivals and Daily Use*, published in Trinidad, included recipes for celebrating "with our Chinese community."[67] Hunt also included recipes and menus for Eid-ul-Fitr, marking the end of Ramadan and the sacrificial month of fasting for Muslims, and Divali, the Hindu celebration that recognizes the triumph of light over darkness in a sort of Congotay reckoning. For Chinese dishes to be served on Double Ten Day, Hunt insisted that a cook must have on hand the "required oriental spices such as Vetsin, soy sauce, seow [aged soy sauce used in stews], and ginger."[68] Similarly, Indo-Caribbean people followed the events of the Sepoy Mutiny (1857) and the later activities of the Indian nationalist movement with pride. They saw the revolts against the tyranny of the East India Company and British imperial rule. They watched the struggle from the 1920s on, witnessing the Indian National Congress' adoption of Mohandas Karamchand

Gandhi's policy of nonviolence and civil resistance that would create a mass movement and a nation-state.

Hidden at the Hearth

The cooking of food in every culture relied on pyrotechnological skills, the manipulation of fire. Danger was an acknowledged ingredient of food-preparation sites. Early Caribbean kitchens were usually situated at a distance from the living structures—in a courtyard or even a separate building—because of the threat posed by wood- or coal-burning cooking fires. At the same time, this distance from other activity provided cooks with some independence, which was frequently used in acts of resistance and empowerment. The architecture of cooking also separated the usually freestanding spaces where the activities of food preparation, cooking, bathing, and washing clothes and dishes took place. Sometimes the kitchen was nothing more than a circle of hearthstones in a communally shared outdoors.

Living conditions after slavery were not much better than those that existed in the appallingly crowded slave quarters. According to one observer in Trinidad in 1888, the plantation barracks were communal living spaces that seemed to lack kitchens altogether: "all noises and talking and smell pass through the open space . . . there are no places for cooking."[69] Cooking pots and cauldrons, even those serving the great houses of the slave masters, were often located in open courtyards. Plants grown in gardens near the kitchens were useful as medicines and as seasoning for food in cooking. In the Indo-Caribbean households, plants such as *tulsi* (*Ocimum sanctum*, a woody basil) were auspiciously planted in the front courtyard of every house, sometimes enshrined in a miniature temple.[70] Because *tulsi* initiated every *puja* or offering, it was considered sacred and thus demarcated the home and kitchen as sacred space. In Indo-Caribbean households it was customary not to taste food during preparation until an offering was first made to Agnidevata, the deity of fire.

Beliefs were never far away. Archaeologists note the continuities between cooking areas in slave quarters, the great house, and their African antecedents. Also, buried beneath the hearth were objects used in rituals derived from African beliefs. Archaeologists have uncovered these caches of intentionally placed small objects, such as pierced, round stones, metal rings, buttons, food, or drink offerings.[71] Such objects have been found under bricks and beneath or adjacent to the hearth areas. Charged with power to cure, protect, or divine the future, these ritual artifacts may have been hidden but potent reminders of the powers of the cook to transform matter and spirit both inside and outside the kitchen.

Cooking in the Caribbean was a ritual act: to offer food was to convey honor and respect. Above all, it was a form of symbolic communication. The recipes in this chapter have in common that they are message carriers. The poisonous and the bitter, the darkened and the sweet, all conveyed the possibility of resistance and the framework of ritual that could be transformed into meaningful action. Culinary knowledge was specialized and transmitted across generations, typically from mother to daughter and sometimes within religious contexts. It was knowledge that was embedded in a sacred structure of belief and practice. Each deity had a particular palate and predilection for certain colors, tastes, and textures of foods. Household and kitchen rituals remind us that spirituality was not reserved for a particular day of the week, but rather was a familiar and empowering part of daily life. Whether cooking for the gods or mere mortals, Caribbean women used food to resist their conditions and transcend the domestic and the ordinary.

Notes

1. Ulli Beier, ed., *Yoruba Poetry: An Anthology of Traditional Poems* (Cambridge: Cambridge University Press, 1970), 34.

2. K.T. Achaya, *Indian Food: A Historical Companion* (Delhi: Oxford University Press, 1998), 61.

3. Mavis C. Campbell, *The Maroons of Jamaica, 1655–1796: A History of Resistance, Collaboration and Betrayal* (Granby, MA: Bergin & Garvey, 1988), 222–223.

4. Robert Charles Dallas (1803), quoted in Frederick H. Smith, *Caribbean Rum: A Social and Economic History* (Gainesville: University of Florida Press, 2005), 162.

5. Engraving by Serge Daget, *An Englishman Tastes the Sweat of an African*, published in M. Chambon, *Le commerce de l'Amerique par Marseille* (Avignon, 1764), vol. 2, plate 11, facing 400.

6. Rosalind I.J. Hackett, *Art and Religion in Africa* (London: Cassell, 1996), 28 and 38.

7. Lady Maria Nugent, *Lady Nugent's Journal of Her Residence in Jamaica, from 1801 to 1805*, ed. Philip Wright (Kingston: Institute of Jamaica, 1966), 55.

8. See also Chapter 1 and Corporation for Public Broadcasting, *Africans in America Resource Bank*, www.pbs.org/wgbh/aia/part3/3h251.html.

9. See "Ackee," in *The Cambridge World History of Food*, ed. Kenneth F. Kiple and Kriemhild Conee Ornelas, 2 vols. (Cambridge: Cambridge University Press, 2000), 2: 1713–1714.

10. Bryan Edwards, *The History, Civil and Commercial, of the British Colonies in the West Indies* (London, 1793), 82–89.

11. Richard Robert Madden, *A Twelvemonth's Residence in the West Indies, During the Transition from Slavery to Apprenticeship . . .* vol. 2 (London: James Cochrane, 1835), 72.

12. Edward Long, *The History of Jamaica* (London: T. Lowndes, 1774), 2: 381.

13. See Wade Davis, *The Serpent and the Rainbow* (Toronto: Stoddart, 1985).

14. Melville Herskovits (1967), quoted in Suzanne Preston Blier, *African Vodun: Art, Psychology, and Power* (Chicago: University of Chicago Press, 1995), 409 n48.

15. Blier, *African Vodun*, 117.

16. Blier, *African Vodun*, 217.

17. Karen McCarthy Brown, *Mama Lola: A Vodou Priestess in Brooklyn* (Berkeley: University of California Press, 1991), 348.

18. Elizabeth McAlister, *Rara! Vodou, Power, and Performance in Haiti and Its Diaspora* (Berkeley: University of California Press, 2002), 225 n13.

19. Colonel C.L.G. Harris, "The True Traditions of My Ancestors," in *Maroon Heritage: Archaeological, Ethnographic, and Historical Perspectives*, ed. E. Kofi Agorsah (Kingston, Jamaica: Canoe Press/University of the West Indies, 1994), 57.

20. Mavis C. Campbell, *Back to Africa: George Ross and The Maroons, from Nova Scotia to Sierra Leone* (Trenton, NJ: Africa World Press, 1993), 37, 74.

21. David Barry Gaspar, "The Antigua Slave Conspiracy of 1736: A Case Study of the Origins of Collective Resistance," *William and Mary Quarterly*, 3rd ser., 35, no. 2 (1978): 322.

22. See Henry John Drewal and Margaret Thompson Drewal, *Gelede: Art and Female Power among the Yoruba* (Bloomington: Indiana University Press, 1990), 2, which discusses the market as a metaphor for the world's impermanence and spectacles.

23. W.M.L. Jay, *My Winter in Cuba* (New York: E.P. Dutton, 1871), 237–238.

24. Barbara Bush, *Slave Women in Caribbean Society: 1650–1838* (Kingston, Jamaica: Heinemann, 1990), 47–50.

25. Bush, *Slave Women*, 47–50.

26. Bush, *Slave Women*, 47–50.

27. Rev. J.S. Scoles, *Sketches of African and Indian Life in British Guiana* (Demerara, 1885), 56–57, quoted in Roger D. Abrahams and John F. Szwed, eds., *After Africa* (New Haven: Yale University Press, 1983), 92.

28. Richard Ligon, *A True and Exact History of the Island of Barbadoes*, 2nd ed. (London: Peter Parker and Thomas Guy, 1673 [1657]), 30.

29. Patricia B. Mitchell, *French Cooking in Early America* (n.p., 1995).

30. Richard Watson, *A Defense of the Wesleyan Methodist Missions in the West Indies* (London, 1817), 17, quoted in Abrahams and Szwed, *After Africa*, 144.

31. Leslie G. Desmangles, *The Faces of the Gods: Vodou and Roman Catholicism in Haiti* (Chapel Hill: University of North Carolina Press, 1992), 185.

32. Stedman [1796], quoted in Abrahams and Szwed, *After Africa*, 143.

33. Miguel Barnet, *Afro-Cuban Religions* (Princeton: Markus Wiener, 2001), 21–22.

34. James T. Houk, *Spirits, Blood, and Drums: The Orisha Religion in Trinidad* (Philadelphia: Temple University Press, 1995), 90–96.

35. Jessica Harris, *Tasting Brazil: Regional Recipes and Reminiscences* (New York: Macmillan, 1992), 59.

36. Recorded by Pierre Verger, *Notes sur le Culte des Orisa et Vodun* (Dakar, Senegal: I.F.A.N., 1957), quoted in Robert Farris Thompson, *Black Gods and Kings: Yoruba Art at UCLA* (Bloomington: Indiana University Press, 1976).

37. Mrs. (Alison) Carmichael, quoted in Cristine Mackie, *Life and Food in the Caribbean* (New York: New Amsterdam, 1991), 74.

38. Mackie, *Life and Food*, 74–75.

39. As observed by dance ethnologist Kimberly Miguel Mullen in a Bahian Candomblé kitchen, during food preparation (for Yemaya/Yemanja devotees); personal communication, Portland, Oregon, August 2008.

40. See David H. Brown, "Toward an Ethnoaesthetics of Santeria Ritual Arts: The Practice of Altar-Making and Gift Exchange," in *Santeria Aesthetics in Contemporary Latin American Art*, ed. Arturo Lindsay (Washington, DC: Smithsonian Institution Press, 1996), 135 n37.

41. Joan Dayan, *Haiti, History, and the Gods* (Berkeley: University of California Press, 1995), 94.

42. Interview with Maria de Lourdes Silvestre dos Santos, Los Angeles, California, May 2011.

43. Natalia Bolivar Arostegui and Carmen Gonzalez Diaz de Villegas, *Afro-Cuban Cuisine: Its Myths and Legends* (Havana: Editorial José Marti, 1998), 22 and 108.

44. Frances Henry, *Reclaiming African Religions in Trinidad: The Socio-Political Legitimation of the Orisha and Spiritual Baptists Faiths* (Kingston, Jamaica: University of the West Indies Press, 2003), 7.

45. Lafcadio Hearn, "The Last of the Voodoos," *Harper's Weekly*, November 7, 1885, 726–727.

46. Robert F. Thompson, *Face of the Gods: Art and Altars of Africa and the African Americas* (New York: Museum for African Arts/Prestel, 1993), 154, 181, 199.

47. Candice Goucher, field notes, Belmont, Port of Spain, Trinidad, February 2000.

48. Candice Goucher, field notes, Morant Bay, Jamaica, July 1991.

49. I am grateful to Miguelito Bernal, master drummer, for the invitation to attend this house celebration in Havana, Cuba, on March 18, 2002.

50. See Caroline Walker Bynum, *Holy Feast and Holy Fast: The Religious Significance of Food to Medieval Women* (Berkeley: University of California Press, 1987).

51. J.G. Stedman, *Narrative of a Five Year Expedition against the Revolted Negroes of Surinam* (Amherst: University of Massachusetts Press, 1971 [1796]), 364–366, quoted in Abrahams and Szwed, *After Africa*, 142.

52. Janet Shaw, quoted in Abrahams and Szwed, *After Africa*, 228.

53. Peter Marsden [1788], quoted in Abrahams and Szwed, *After Africa*, 229.

54. Alexander Barclay, *A Practical View of the Present State of Slavery in the West Indies* (London, 1826), quoted in Abrahams and Szwed, *After Africa*, 255; Barclay was speaking about Jamaica.

55. Abrahams and Szwed, *After Africa*, 229.

56. Cynric R. Williams, *A Tour Through the Island of Jamaica . . .* (London 1826), quoted in Abrahams and Szwed, *After Africa*, 250.

57. Leonard E. Barrett, *The Rastafarians* (Boston: Beacon Press, 1997), 140–142.

58. In his song *Guiltiness* (1977), Bob Marley sings, "These are the big fish / Who always try to eat down the small fish."

59. McAlister, *Rara!*, 108; Okonkon Essiet, personal communication, May 24, 1995.

60. Verene Shepherd, "Depression in the Tin Roof Towns: Economic Problems of Urban Indians in Jamaica, 1930–1950," in *India in the Caribbean*, ed. David Dabydeen and Brinsley Samaroo (London: University of Warwick, Centre for Caribbean Studies, 1987), 177–181.

61. MS 59, Livingstone Collection Scrap Book 1, National Library, Kingston, Jamaica.

62. Hollis "Chalkdust" Liverpool, *Rituals of Power and Rebellion: The Carnival Tradition in Trinidad and Tobago, 1763–1962* (Chicago: Research Associates School Times Publications, 2001), 413.

63. P. Pratap Kumar, *Religious Pluralism in the Diaspora* (Leiden, Netherlands: Brill, 2006), 64.

64. Kumar Mahabir and Mera Heeralal, *Caribbean East Indian Recipes* (Port of Spain, Trinidad: Chakra, 2009), x.

65. Kusha Haraksingh, "Control and Resistance among Indian Workers: A Study of Labour on the Sugar Plantations of Trinidad, 1875–1917," *India in the Caribbean*, ed. Dabydeen and Samaroo, 4.

66. Judith Bettelheim and John Nunley, "The Hosay Festival," in *Caribbean Festival Arts: Each and Every Bit of Difference*, ed. John Nunley and Judith Bettelheim (Seattle: Saint Louis Art Museum and University of Washington Press, 1988), 124.

67. Sylvia Hunt, *Sylvia Hunt's Menus for Festivals and Daily Use* (Port of Spain, Trinidad: Bank of Commerce, 1988), 5.

68. Hunt, *Menus*, 3; Vetsin was a product (monosodium glutamate) sold commercially.

69. Bettelheim and Nunley, *Caribbean Festival Arts*, 126, quoting Robert Guppy, a former plantation owner.

70. Rabindranath S. Lackhan, *Plants of Religious Significance: The Hindu Perspective*, 2nd ed. (Gasparillo, Trinidad: Revolution, n.d.), 84.

71. Mark P. Leone and Gladys-Marie Frye, "Conjuring in the Big House Kitchen: An Interpretation of African-American Belief Systems, Based on the Uses of Archaeology and Folklore Sources," *Journal of American Folklore* 112, no. 445 (1999): 372–403; of course, not all of these occurrences were necessarily intentional artifacts of African belief.

FIVE

For the Love of Food

Sexuality and the Caribbean Kitchen

> *You put the yam to bed in the ground*
> *[and] it will bring you money*
> *that will plant you on top of a beautiful woman.*
>
> —Yoruba poetry, collected by Ulli Beier[1]

> *Young men, I am warning you,*
> *Be careful when eating crab callaloo.*
>
> —"I Don't Want No Callaloo,"
> 1939 calypso by Growler (Errol Duke)[2]

Each year on the Feast Day of Saint Laurent, elegantly dressed cooks from all over the island of Guadeloupe assemble on the Rue d'Ennery at the Maison des Cuisinières in Pointe-à-Pitre for a colorful procession to the St. Peter and St. Paul Cathedral. Wearing "créole" dresses in bright cotton Madras plaid and flowery designs over lacy white petticoats, the women celebrate the historic Fête des Cuisinières. The cooks of the sponsoring association carry elaborately gathered and prepared créole foods—fruits, pastries, seafood—in baskets and on portable wooden "altars." In the cathedral, the foods and foodways are blessed, and then the participants move to a nearby celebratory community feast of magnificent proportions.

Later that afternoon, at the banquet's close, the costumed women dance to the traditional drums of a rural Guadeloupe village. African-style drumming reveals the survival of the complex cultural rhythms that extend back to slavery. While the celebration of food is at center stage, the unique role of women in the reproduction of society is remembered as reaching far beyond the kitchen. The eldest of the women—an eighty-four-year-"young" Madame Cuisinière in 2002—lifts her skirts and apron to the drums and mimics the

Dancing, Fête des Cuisinières, Pointe-à-Pitre, Guadeloupe
(Photograph by Candice Goucher)

sex act. She moves her buttocks in a frenzied vibrato, thrusts her pelvis for-
ward toward the drums, and sticks out her tongue at the man next to her. Her
body speaks to the memory of food as an essential life-giving force. In her
decidedly erotic dance, she joyously breathes life into the central meaning of
cooking: to cook is to reproduce and sustain the most intimate and significant
aspects of cultural identity.[3]

Food played an ambiguous role in Caribbean life and history. Food nour-
ished and made possible the unlikely survival of the enslaved and indentured

laborers. And while it thus prolonged the plantation system and its oppressive conditions, food also sustained the cultural identities of those enslaved and exploited. Food consumption was an important theater for social relations. Beyond the rations provided to laborers, food was given and exchanged to cement obligations; its display served as a marker of identity, gender, and status. The survival of Caribbean cooks, their cuisines, and those they fed necessarily played key roles in both the resistance to and the perpetuation of exploitative plantation systems.

Food and Family in the Caribbean

African-derived religions provided a framework for spiritual life conceived in terms of familial relationships. Food supported both the biological reproduction of the Caribbean family and also permitted the replication of an oppressive society and the unequal conditions under which enslaved families labored. This contradiction is most clearly recognizable in the plight of enslaved kitchen laborers. Like plantation domestic workers in general, those who worked in the kitchen were subject to extreme levels of subordination and sexual exploitation by overseers and slave masters by virtue of the enslaved workers' proximity to the whites and the forced cultural assimilation that followed their captivity. Those who cooked were frequently enslaved, indentured, or free women of color, whose positions were governed by gender inequality made worse under the oppressive racism of island plantation societies, both during and after slavery.

Enslaved African women in the Caribbean gave birth to enslaved children, who followed them into the fields by about the age of ten. Most slave families lived in relatively stable unions with two parents and their children in the same shared residence. Such unions, however, were not always possible. The Mesopotamia Plantation in Jamaica kept careful inventories of enslaved births between 1762 and 1833.[4] At Mesopotamia, there were two deaths for every birth, and the records indicate that the periodic purchase of slaves was the only means by which the population of laborers could be increased significantly. Almost half of the women at Mesopotamia had no children, and the childbearing women produced relatively small families. Historian Richard Dunn has suggested that the toxic environment of brutal labor regimes, disease, and food scarcity severely affected fertility rates and produced high infant mortality. There is also evidence that Caribbean women used their knowledge of medicines and poisons to prevent contraception and abort fetuses. Reverend Beame reports for Jamaica in 1826 that "herbs and powders" were given to them by obeah practitioners.[5] Typically, unless they were of mixed race, only women past their youth and childbearing age were removed from the fields and placed into domestic service in the great house. Once in close proximity to white men, women suffered rape and sexual exploitation. One enslaved woman, known only as Minny (1770–1826), spent nearly all of her working life on Mesopotamia as the overseer's housekeeper, bearing thirteen children (including five mixed-race, or "mulatto" children), an unusually large number of births.[6]

Women's positions in kitchens brought them opportunities through their increased access to food resources and at the same time imposed oppressive limitations through greater scrutiny of their behavior. Yet the enslaved cook was one room away from the fields, the agricultural realms where African-derived norms of communal sharing still held sway. In this way, the African cook was empowered to select menus, procure food, and decide the style of food preparation. Their control over food supplies could mean survival in times of scarcity even to the point of "redistributing" food. The common lament of plantation owners was that the masters were also victims and frequently taken advantage of by their servants, as William Bayley reported from Barbados in the early nineteenth century. Bayley, who accompanied his father to Barbados at the age of seventeen, wrote:

> In Barbados, however, as well as in other islands, masters are greatly plundered by their servants, of such things as poultry, porter, wine and sometimes money; for the purpose of carrying them to entertainments, which the negroes give among themselves. . . . After dancing, the group sits down to the supper table, the contents of which have all been stolen from the masters or mistresses of the different guests.[7]

The strategy of feasting to establish community and enhance status was a mainstay of African cultural survival. Sharing food was the most basic component of a shared humanity. African-Caribbean folktales are replete with lessons about sharing and theft of food. At the same time, one of the most heinous of historical punishment devices in the Caribbean was the one applied to slaves accused of stealing food from the kitchen. This iron-forged contraption was fitted to the head, preventing its victim from eating. This served as visible proof that the long, powerful arm of oppression could reach into the kitchen, a zone teetering between the opposite poles of ultimate vulnerability and potential empowerment.

Gender and the Caribbean Kitchen

The Caribbean kitchen existed as part of a gendered universe, and the designation of work roles included gender-specific restrictions. These specialized roles were based on learned cooking skills and esoteric knowledge, including such disparate culinary components as the procurement, cost, and chemical transformations, employed in the safe and healthful preparation of various foodstuffs. The tasks and activities surrounding food were clearly central to the survival of the individual and group. Ritual and prescriptive behavior in relation to food helped mark and define the contours of daily life.

Demography and Gender

Governing the way gender-specific cultural expectations were expressed in the Caribbean were, among other factors, the demographics of male and female populations as they intersected with racial and ethnic diversity. In no post-Columbian population group prior to the nineteenth century were the demographics natural; that is, among Europeans, Africans, and Asians, there were disproportionately more men than women in each group. The skewed demographics of the early European maritime community and later colonist populations were intentional. There were at most one or two women on board early ships, though women sometimes cross-dressed as pirates and sailors to gain berths on the Atlantic voyages. The seventeenth-century era of buccaneer and pirate homosexuality as argued by Barry Burg gave way to marine and island communities that increasingly came under the control of government and social mores that punished the buggery they had once condoned.[8] Foods that had been associated with the buccaneer era (roasted turtle and bushmeat) became taboo or were transferred to hypermasculine warrior subcultures of Caribbean society, including Maroon and male hunting activities.

Demographics also affected interracial socializing and sexuality. Subsequent colonial governments prior to the twentieth century actually discouraged women from joining their husbands in the colonies, and they discouraged (and sometimes forbade) officers from marrying.[9] Reliance on concubinage (liaisons between European men and enslaved or free women of color) was widely accepted, if not promoted in the Caribbean. Foods were symbols of the complex relationships that intertwined free and enslaved in sexual liaisons on the Caribbean plantation. When given by overseer or owner to the enslaved prostitute or exploited domestic servant, food was a token of an alternate sexual economy.

Among the enslaved populations in the circum-Caribbean, a persistent shortage of women existed. In studies of the sex distribution of slaves arriving in Havana and Jamaica in the late eighteenth century, women accounted for only 21 percent and 38 percent, respectively, of the enslaved adult populations.[10] In Saint Domingue, a male to female ratio of 180:100 in 1730 shifted to 120:100 by the 1780s. On other islands, on average about 60 percent of all slaves were men. While Europeans selected more male enslaved persons to be transported across the Atlantic and sold to plantations, local conditions rarely favored a natural expansion of the population. Scholars have shown that African merchants during the Atlantic slave trade were reluctant to part with females because women were preferred for their productive (not reproductive) capacity as enslaved members of society. Females were incorporated more easily into West and Central African states and households, sometimes even adopted into lineages. By contrast, European ideologies viewed women as vulnerable and less capable of hard labor than men. These divergent views of female suitability for labor resulted in more males being shipped as cargo to the Caribbean in the late seventeenth and early eighteenth century. Yet enslaved women were frequently assigned to the hardest labor gangs.

The peculiar status of enslaved women as somewhat rare and prized possessions certainly contributed to the general asymmetries of race, class, and gender as understood by men with power. Later nineteenth-century South Asian cargoes of indentured laborers repeated the skewed demographics, offering more males than females. With some exceptions, women were preferred for domestic labor.[11] Their presence in the intimate workings of the households of both those of privilege and those who were oppressed provided African women a major role in the processes of creolization and the durability of African cultural practices. Their domination of household and kitchen labors bridged racial, gender, and social divides. Ultimately, these women were the creators of the first global food cultures.

Binary Divides

Scholars have argued that whereas in Western cultural traditions, the association of male things with "culture" and female things with "nature" helped to distill gender inequalities, in African and other world traditions the culture/nature dichotomy was viewed as complementary rather than oppositional. Anthropologist Claude Lévi-Strauss has written extensively on cooking as a form of mediation, especially helping to bridge the gap between nature and culture, widely perceived by indigenous peoples of the Americas. In his classic work *The Raw and the Cooked*, Lévi-Strauss argued "not only does cooking make the transition from nature to culture, but through it and by means of it, the human state."[12] Animals eat raw food; only humans cook the food they consume.

Hispaniola's early importation of "raw" Africans (called literally *bozales* or unseasoned) suggested something of the European conceptualization of their unacculturated status. The same term was also noted for Trinidad's enslaved, probably derived from the Spanish period. Perhaps, because of their civilizing role, African women also derived power and status from their domestic activities. African-Caribbean women's gender-specific activities linked their resources and households in ways that confounded and blurred the dichotomies typical of the West.[13] Sexual strategies could and did play a significant role in strategies of survival and resistance, even while demarcating the boundaries of control that operated within a slave society.

Male and female categories flowed from the kitchen's activities. Women controlled the critical knowledge about what was safe and what was unsafe, what could cure or kill. Cooking transformed the raw, the inedible, and the poisonous. The most basic food preparation became symbolic code for the separation of realms. The cutlass was both life and death. The meeting of mortar and pestle mimicked the sex act. In Jamaican ghost stories, procuring food for a meal or placing a mortar in a bed could portend trickery, illness, and death. The meeting of mortar and pestle could also reflect the bridging of divides.

The traditional African-Guyanese marriage event was called *kweh-kweh*, which may be derived from the West African phrases (from the Ga language of coastal Ghana) *kwe-kwe*, meaning both sides are looking, or *kpe-kpe*, referring to a meeting in which two parties are getting together. The African-Guyanese kweh-kweh celebration included food, music, song, and dance on the night before a wedding that joined two families. After pouring libations to invoke the blessings of ancestors and spirits, a leader began a series of songs with the assembled community in the West African musical style of call-and-response. Dancing and singing focused on the sexuality, responsibilities, and commitments of married life. The rituals, teasing, and laughter brought the two families together on the eve of the wedding night (and provided instructions for the bridal couple) to ensure harmony in the years ahead. The mortar was a substitute for the female womb, as suggested by the kweh-kweh song lyrics, "ole lady, lend me your mortar/meh plantain run col' ahready."

Gendered Space

The kitchen itself was both a social and spatial realm. Symbolically, kitchens in the plantation great houses were zones that transcended the usual boundaries of enslaved and free. Slave kitchens were shared, open-air spaces down below the great house, situated in clearings between the enclosed sleeping quarters. While the cooking areas were visible from above, they constituted separate spaces where social interactions between enslaved Africans took place beyond the earshot of whites and where whites rarely ventured. Slave kitchens were racially segregated, whereas in the hilltop great house kitchens, cultural exchanges between whites and blacks were casual and unavoidable. Available foods in the great house naturally differed from those of the slave kitchens. Kitchen gardens behind the great house included fruits and herbs of bewildering varieties.[14] And while kitchens were associated with women, that association did not confine women indoors, nor did it isolate Caribbean women from access to more public spaces. Most cooking and other domestic affairs took place in the sociable presence of others. As in African traditions, the African-Caribbean cooking hearth was associated with female domains.

Evidence for the vibrancy of the kitchen as a distinct cultural space is found in the many uses of food-related sayings in Caribbean spoken languages and dialects. The hearth represents both a sense of continuity and change, owing to the transformations that take place therein. As in much of Africa and India, limestone ovens were commonly used in the Caribbean to bake bread and other food. These outdoor kitchens were the norm until the middle of the twentieth century. Despite its constancy, the hearth witnessed changes in technology and technique, such as the replacement of the clay cooking pot with iron pots. A proverb from Trinidad suggests one interpretation, "The clay-pot wishes to laugh at the iron pot," a kind of "pot calling the kettle black" piece of wisdom.[15] The material culture of kitchens and food preparation registered the strong social hierarchies. As this description from the Bahamas clearly suggests, kitchen activities and food preparation fueled the culture and language with rich metaphors that were widely shared:

> [In the outdoor hearths,] peas and rice were cooked in large cauldrons that were kept constantly heated. If there wasn't enough, more ingredients were simply added to the top. Eventually quite a crust would form at the bottom. The mongrel dogs, so abundant in the Bahamas, were fed the caked residue at the bottom of the pot. Hence, dogs without pedigree . . . are [still] called potcakes.[16]

The management of resources, the procurement of food, and the organization of labor and space in the service of Caribbean food-styles meant that much of the time women cooks did not actually occupy domestic space inside a residential structure. This pattern does not differ from other peasant populations across time and space. Almost 80 percent of the women's time was spent going to market and otherwise gathering foods outside the domestic cooking space we now call the kitchen. The persistence of communal food preparation areas in center courtyards is an African continuity. Described by Pieter de Marees in 1602, West Africans were observed to "link together three or four such Huts, standing next to each other so as to form a square, so that the women have a place in the middle where they work."[17] That this space was defined as a female domain is also an African continuity visible in the Caribbean. Archaeologists Douglas Armstrong and others have noted this

Food market, Antigua
(Photograph by Candice Goucher)

pattern in Jamaican slave villages attached to plantations. Alexander Barclay, an Englishman who went to Jamaica about 1805, described the evolution of houses containing a central communal kitchen area among individual sleeping spaces as "the room in the middle . . . the sitting apartment, and here the poorer class make fire and cook their victuals; the more wealthy have a separate kitchen at a little distance."[18] As was the case in West Central Africa,

Barclay noted that the individual rooms had a small cupboard for cups and dishes, iron pots and tin pans for cooking.

The activities of food preparation spanned the kitchen and field. They marked the spatial rhythm of Caribbean life. Families did not always have the opportunity to reside together on the same estate. Yet women cooked breakfast meals for their husbands and other men. They took or sent food to men the fields. They awakened first, a custom registered in the very first morning sounds of birdsong being identified with "bird-wife." In the following century, the travel writer Patrick Leigh Fermor described an early morning breakfast scene in Port-au-Prince, Haiti, around 1947:

> A small fire of logs and charcoal had been built on a sheet of tin in the centre of the floor, filling the upper half of the room with smoke. Round it squatted a peasant family, a man and three little girls of diminishing size, and an old woman who was cooking their breakfast. Their gourd-plates were being filled with ladlefuls of hot maize.[19]

Gendered Transmission of Knowledge

The symbolism of the female-identified hearth carries through as a theme in many West and Central African societies. Proverbs refer to the cooking hearth as a symbol of the home, stability, and security. The Akan symbol *fihankra* denoted this shared, central courtyard where cooking took place as a place of communal strength and family unity. The three stones that supported the cooking pot of the hearth expressed stability and continuity. Describing female rituals among the Mende (of Sierra Leone) in the 1970s, Sylvia Arden Boone noted that women shared their expertise and techniques for cooking during the initiation experience of the Sande secret society's "schools."[20] Young women were isolated in a distinct quarter, where cooking was a central activity that taught social values and conveyed the right of women to question inequalities and inadequacies of political and social institutions. Within this ritual space, the spread of food and the quantity eaten by women were unlike anything they would experience in the outer world. While the young girls were taught much more than cooking, inside the Sande experience was culinary training in which food was portrayed as both physical and spiritual nourishment. Relatives provided their tuition in the form of rice, oil, onions, pepper, dried fish, and provisions. And unlike the eventual outer world routine of cooking and presenting of dishes to husbands and other senior male guests, after which women themselves would eat, the Sande school encouraged the young women to consume whenever and however much they wanted. Boone observed the special savor of the food in this context of communal atmosphere.

A three-legged cooking pot was a popular symbol carved into the crowning top of the Sande masks. Other symbols included the chrysalis from which a butterfly emerges. Women wore the masks to express the secrets and ideals of beauty and positive life energy they gain during their initiation. The pot was associated with cooking, but it was equally the equipment of herbalists and sorcerers. Prayer stones and other valued items were placed inside a woman's pot. The mask's cooking pot became a reference to the healing social powers of female cooks once they left the privileges of this culinary school. But the most unique quality of the cooking pot imagery was that it could represent stability in spite of also being a portable symbol.

Like their African counterparts, cooks in the Caribbean relied on the oral transmission of food knowledge. This transfer occurred in female-dominated spaces. Caribbean house yards, because they contained hearths, ovens, and other domestic work areas, were traditionally defined as female spaces. Before abolition, they were not only organized according to African-derived patterns with women sharing resources and labor cooperatively, but also defined as places of female activity, founded by women and maintained as female-centered locations across postslavery generations. The trinity of cooking stones also defined the stable home life. By contrast, the breaking up of the three hearthstones (*pakuta meta* in Trinidadian Creole) was a sign of domestic disharmony signaling the end of a marriage.[21] Geographer Lydia Pulsipher observes that West Indian house yards were not places where men routinely met for informal interaction. In fact, if a Jamaican man entered another family's space before the arrival of the man of the house, he would proclaim the loud warning, "man 'a yard." Pulsipher suggests that, in the Caribbean, "space for interaction among men [tended] to be linked with public, leisure or non-productive activities in bars and on street corners."[22] The separation of male and female spheres of activities was reinforced by prohibitions surrounding their many interactions—especially those related to food and sex.

Liming

The gendered interpretation of social spaces for eating and drinking was most pronounced in the widespread Caribbean activity known popularly in the English-speaking Caribbean as "liming." Essentially a male activity, "liming" described the hanging out with a man's mates or "crews" (other men). No doubt derived from the British term "limey," which associated Royal Navy sailors with limes brought on board their ships to prevent scurvy over long voyages, a "lime" was indeed an opportunity to eat and drink (and socialize) outside the home sphere. A good lime had to have "plenty drink, good food and good conversation—from serious politics to crude nonsense."[23] The lime

Liming, Georgetown, Guyana
(Photograph by Candice Goucher)

lasted as long as it took to finish a bottle of rum. Like the environment of the ship, it was gender-specific. The rum shop and, to a lesser extent, the street corner, where men indulged in much "braggadocio" (to use Richard Burton's term), became the site of play, gossip, and mixing.[24] The menu of the rum shop typically included male-associated foods: fish tea (a broth), cowheel soup, doubles (an East Indian pea-stuffed fried bread), shark and bake (a sandwich of fried bread with shark and condiments), and souse (pickled pig's feet, tail, and organs).

Food and Procreation

Sexuality was brought to the kitchen not only through the obvious association of the childbearing woman as one who nourishes and reproduces society. Symbolic parallels between cooking, sexuality, and reproduction were widespread in African-derived religions. Among the Thonga (of Mozambique), children were thought to be born products of successful "firings," followed by ritual cooking in the womb, and a gradual cooling down. Food is frequently used metaphorically to convey complex ideas about technological and human processes. For example, the term for cold, cooked maize porridge was used to refer to an iron bloom, "half-cooked" in a smelting furnace and left to cool overnight.[25] Lévi-Strauss demonstrated the nearly universal complementarities, if not equivalence, of cooking and the sexual act. Even so, specific foods may be interpreted as aphrodisiacs, enhancing sexual appetites. Felipe Fernandez-Armesto goes one step further, pointing out that food and sex seem to be "mutually lubricating forms of sensuality, [although] every particular aphrodisiac is a kiss in the dark," and that "faith in aphrodisiacs has been maintained by food magicians in every society."[26]

Aphrodisiacs

Of the best-known aphrodisiacs in the region, chocolate figured prominently since the days of the Aztec and Spanish conquistador encounters. Cacao was used in an elite drink and formed the basis of many tribute arrangements. Observer Bernal Diaz del Castillo noted that the emperor Moctezuma consumed chocolate (rumored to be fifty glasses a day in the liquid form of *xaocatl*) before he retired, and "it was said to have aphrodisiac properties, but we did not pay any attention to this detail."[27] Whether or not this was true, other Europeans did pay attention to the rumors. Cortez brought cacao beans to the West Indies, and the Spaniards improved on the drink by adding sugar and hot water. By the eighteenth century, the reputation of chocolate was well established, but it was not universally consumed. From the Americas, the crop spread to West Africa and beyond. Eventually, chocolate returned to the Caribbean, where small-scale rural producers continue to grow it. "Wedding chocolate" was a popular drink served at traditional Puerto Rican weddings during the late nineteenth and early twentieth centuries. A euphemistic way of asking when a couple was to wed was to ask, "When are you going to offer us hot chocolate?"[28]

In some parts of the Caribbean, where cocoa beans were harvested locally, cooks roasted and prepared their own versions of either "chocolate tea" or "cocoa tea." In the early twentieth century, cocoa beans were sold in the Caribbean in big ninety- or hundred-pound sacks and then further marketed in smaller one- or five-pound bags to home cooks. The beans were roasted and their skins carefully removed to avoid burning. As soon as they were cool enough to handle, the beans would be poured out on a wooden board and crushed into a moist paste. Orange peel, cinnamon, nutmeg, and other spices were freshly ground and sifted into the cocoa. Finally the mixture was rolled out into logs and then cut into sticks or balls and allowed to dry. Women kept sticks in a tin and sometimes marketed their products to guesthouses. An individual cocoa stick would be placed in a cup of hot boiling water, with sugar and evaporated milk added to taste. That was cocoa tea, whereas the hot drink known as chocolate tea was made with cocoa powder.[29] Another dish

WEDDING CHOCOLATE

1/2 pound grated sweet chocolate
8 cups hot milk
1 can evaporated milk
1/4 cup sugar
2 egg yolks, beaten
4 tablespoons butter
vanilla to taste
freshly grated nutmeg, bay leaf, ginger to taste
zest of an orange or 1 orange peel (optional)

Melt the chocolate in hot milk in a double boiler. Add evaporated milk and sugar, stirring constantly. Just before serving, add the egg yolks, butter, and vanilla. Add the spices and orange, as desired. Beat for 2 minutes and serve in cups.

known as "matrimony" was described in Sullivan's late nineteenth-century cookbook, the earliest printed collection of recipes from Jamaica. It was a mixture of citrus, sugar, nutmeg, sherry, and local fruit creamy in flavor and texture, the star apple, to which was later added (after refrigeration) ice and milk. The term as defined in the *Oxford English Dictionary* was applied more widely as the "mixture of two comestibles or beverages," suggesting an "injudicious combination" in use as early as 1813.[30]

Many of the associative ideas about cooking and sexuality were the consequence of domestic arrangements in the Caribbean known as concubinage. Historically some concubines were slaves and others were free women of color. Sexual services and cooking were provided to European males through the web of desire, violence, racism, and ideas of European mastery and sexual inferiority. Back in European cities, colonial men had gained notorious reputations for enhanced sexual drives matched by enhanced desire in the tropics. Enslaved men—and by association, enslaved women—by the same token supposedly exhibited uncontrollable lust and "primitive" sexual urges. Such myths perpetuated racist stereotypes of the enslaved and supported male domination, oppression, and violence against women. Racially asymmetric and gender-specific rules and prohibitions governed Caribbean sex life even after the abolition of slavery. Both food and sexuality were part of the boundaries of privilege in the islands, and their twisted dialogue speaks to the processes of empowerment and resistance.

Concerns with fertility and motherhood dominated the identity politics of African women. Taboos were commonly associated with women's menstruation and food. Many African societies linked menstruation to the failure to conceive, and no condition could be worse in cultures where the ancestors are reborn. As Eugenia Herbert points out, the taboo that menstruating women should not cook, serve, or otherwise handle food was common in African societies. The prohibition was widespread and linked to associations between cooking and sexual activity. A woman was expected to cook for her husband when it was her turn (among multiple wives) to sleep with him, a practice ensuring that menstruating women could be prevented from handling the man's food. The prohibitions testified to "the incompatibility of menstruation as failed conception with activities that are construed as transformative."[31] An unknown number of African-Caribbean enslaved women suffered from amenorrhea (failed menses) due to harsh treatment and poor nutrition. The low fertility among women of reproductive age would have required an important shift in attitudes toward motherhood and female identity. Still the beliefs about sexuality were extended in African-Caribbean societies to tools or activities used to make things or to change one thing into another. Childbirth and fertility remained symbols of creativity and empowerment.

Cooking in the Caribbean was clearly an activity in which food was transformed into procreative and protective fuel. Enslaved African women controlled their sexuality through the ingestion of medicines and potions. They also used food to establish and influence relationships. Cooking for a man was tantamount to founding a sexual partnership. Indo-Caribbean immigrant practices also resulted in the separation of menstruating women from the household and sometimes prevented women from eating in front of men, except on special occasions. Generally, Hindu rituals provided an association between female sexuality and the prosperity or well-being of a household. Since married men and women were considered to be complementary parts of a whole, they could eat off each other's plates. In some parts of India, essences are believed to be transmitted to food through the preparation and cooking processes. In many West and Central African and South Asian traditions, feeding another the food of life was widely considered a magico-religious act, and the kitchen and dining table were by association ritual realms.

African-derived religions offered opportunities for preserving this conceptual universe of foodways. Followers of the Rastafarian religion in Jamaica were forbidden to handle food while menstruating. Some scholars might argue that these restrictions may even be universal. Cooking in pre-

Columbian societies in the Americas was often a gift of the gods, associated with, if not equivalent to, copulation and therefore not entirely associated with the "raw" and hot female domain.[32] On the other side of the Atlantic, the removal of European women from kitchen duties was perceived as an upper-class status indicator. The protection of Victorian sensibilities may also have been a more pragmatic precaution as elite female dress styles flaunted dangerously flapping sleeves meant to signal avoidance of any proximity to domestic cooking fires.

Menstruation, since it was often believed to represent the failure to conceive, was thus sometimes even considered to be at odds with culture and subject to suspicion. Such beliefs about menstruation were probably widespread in African-derived communities of the enslaved and may have influenced ideas associating women, witchcraft, and blood. Historian Barbara Bush suggests that herbal recipes were passed down from mother to daughter and could induce both abortion and menses.[33] Working in the Andes, Alison Krogel suggests that such associations with death and maleficent meals confirm beliefs at the other end of the spectrum of life and death, particularly that "the plate of food that a cook sets before her client or family contains both caloric and symbolic energy."[34]

Foods might heal, but they could also poison. The African duality of female mothers as nighttime witches was widespread in Caribbean folklore, replete with images of *duppies* (spirits), Soucouyant, and Ole-Higue. All were associated with mysterious places, dusk, darkness, streams, and trees. For example, Soucouyant sucks the blood of her victims at night. All were appeased through the use of food and drink. The threat of food magic or sorcery was commonplace during slavery. Slave owners rightly feared the ability of cooks to kill them by poisoning their meals. These ideas crossed racial lines in the case of Annie Palmer, an orphaned plantation owner, who was known as the "White Witch" of Rose Hall, Jamaica, after the death of three husbands and lovers. In a Jamaican folktale performed by Adina Henry in 1973, the evil slave mistress tries to poison John Do Good but inadvertently poisons her own children when John gives his poisoned journey cakes away.[35]

Beliefs in potentially maleficent meals also were reflected in the lingering Caribbean suspicion about women slipping menstrual blood into the food (sometimes called "sitting on the food"). The early calypsos of Trinidad refer to this supposed devious power of menstruating women who continued to cook. According to Growling Tiger's calypso *Marjorie*, "Yes, Sir, a girl named Marjorie/Giving me things in me food for matrimony." He goes on to allude to the placement of menstrual blood in food as a form of obeah to hold a man: "Look Marjorie, lord, leff [leave] me in peace/The rice looking nice but I 'fraid of the grease/Do Marjorie, lord, leff me in peace/The gravy

Dining room, Rose Hall, Jamaica
(Photograph by Candice Goucher)

too red and I 'fraid the grease."[36] According to Gordon Rohlehr, "sweet rice" was supposed to be a potent aphrodisiac employed to "tie" men.[37] Other likely ingredients of love potions were cocoa, callaloo (soup made from amaranth, dasheen, or taro leaves of *Colocasia esculenta*), and okra soup, all foods sharing a certain viscosity and luster. Boiled cornmeal and okra would be stirred over a fire until they congealed into a dish called *coocoo* in Barbados and *kuku* in Trinidad, where wedding songs conveyed a wish for compatibility by suggesting symbolic food combinations suggestive of male and female characteristics, colors, and qualities (bean sauce or melon seed sauce with *kuku* or sorrel with pounded yam).

Callaloo

Soups were savored across the Atlantic world, where their colors and tastes conveyed meaning and intentions. Observers of African cooking on a Trinidad estate in the early 1700s recorded a soup of meat with peppers and *eddoes* (starchy root vegetables). This soup was not only considered palatable but was "indeed one of the great blessings of the West Indies."[38] John Atkins observed

CRAB CALLALOO

1 habanero pepper, seeds and stem removed, finely minced
(for less heat, use 1/2)

1 medium onion, chopped

2 tablespoons butter or canola oil

3 cloves of garlic, minced

1 small tomato, diced

1 teaspoon each thyme, salt, and black pepper

3 bunches callaloo (or 1/2 pound spinach or other greens),
finely chopped

3 green onions, minced

2 cups chicken stock or water

1 cup okra, sliced (about 1/2 pound frozen, partially cooked 4
minutes in the microwave)

1/4 pound smoked salmon, flaked (or ham or shrimp, diced)

1 cup coconut milk

1/2 pound crabmeat, cooked

Sauté the pepper and onion in butter until transparent; add garlic, tomato, and spices. Add the callaloo, green onions, and stock. Cover and cook at low heat for about 15 minutes. Cool slightly and blend the soup with a hand blender directly in the pot until frothy and fragrant. Add the cooked okra and smoked salmon. Add coconut milk and simmer for about 20 minutes. Add crabmeat; reheat.

the West African use of palm oil in a dish he called "Black Soupee," a meat stew with pepper and okra. Okra was notoriously a slimy, green vegetable brought to the Caribbean from Africa. Ingesting a reddish meal was believed to prolong life and promote vitality.[39]

In much of the Caribbean, African descendants used anatto seed oil (*Bixa orellana*) to color their foods a yellowish-red, achieving a visual resemblance to African palm nut oil. In Cuba, this was accomplished by placing anatto seeds (actually the berries from the pod) in a gourd spoon with holes, using the spoon to stir the coloring directly into the cooking oil, stew, or soup. The gourd filled with anatto seeds could then be reused. Seeds could also be pulverized and ground into a fine powder. As the calypso warned, men who consumed such reddish food could never be certain of the source of the blood-red color and so needed to be careful about accepting a serving that might tie them to its cook.

Congo soup or callaloo invariably contained a medley of greens as its centerpiece ingredient. Callaloo was described as early as the seventeenth century by Sir Hans Sloane, physician and botanist in Jamaica. Botanists ever since have struggled with the confusion of similar leafy greens and their classification. Sloane thought that the leaves, when stripped from the stalk, "shred and boiled in pottages of all sorts," were among "the pleasantest I ever tasted, having something of a more fragrant and grateful taste, than any of these herbs I ever knew."[40] By the 1740s, the island's kitchen gardens grew "calloloe of three sorts, top-a-top, or the cocoa-calloloe; another sort grow like brocolli, and eats like spinach; and the mountain-callaloe."[41] A Spanish kind of callaloo was reputedly native, suggesting at least the use of the amaranth greens in soup prior to 1655. Associated with Africans, the soup represented the notion of many things entering the cooking pot. In the Malinke language, *kalalu* means "many things," and in Yoruba *ko ra lu* means "to mix several things together." The word "callaloo" was in particular used to describe a soup made of dasheen leaves, one of many spinach-like greens whose high-protein stalks and stems were cooked by the enslaved. In Cuba, the *calalu* was prepared with wild amaranth and all sorts of spices, making it "well-seasoned." On eighteenth-century Martinique, Charles de L'Yver's recipe for crab callaloo described a creolized "ragout," composed of different vegetables and crabs, seasoned with fiery spices. On other Spanish and some French islands, the thick soup was also known as *soncocho* or *sancoche*. In Jamaica, it was "rundown" or *pakassa*, and anatto coloring was added. In Guyana, the greens were omitted and the soup became the basis for *metagee*.

Callaloo soup was only one of the most famous of Caribbean aphrodisiacs, putting fear into the man offered "a taste," as the calypsonian Growler sang. Indeed, "give me a taste" can refer to sex in the British West Indies and beyond. In at least one language of coastal West Africa (Fanti), the words "to eat" and "to fornicate" are similar enough to be used in a continual punning relationship.[42] Many indigenous languages in the New World had similar equivalencies between foods and procreation.

Potent Food and Drink

In the Caribbean, it has been said, there were as many aphrodisiacs as there were cooks. Isabel Allende called them "the bridge between gluttony and lust."[43] Aphrodisiacs function through analogy, suggestion, and association, and their complex language of abundance rests in sharp contrast to the conditions of enslavement, hunger, and oppression. In the Caribbean, some aphrodisiacs, such as chocolate or avocado, were foods inherited from the indigenous peoples of the Americas. In Aztec, *ahuacatl*, the word for avocado, also meant "testicle," and Spanish conquistadors brought the fruit to Europe, boasting of its potential as a sexual stimulant. Other Caribbean foods and drinks are claimed to enhance potency and strength or variously described as "able to produce man child."

One well-known infusion came from the bark of trees found in the region (*Roupala montane, Richeria grandis*, and *Parinari campestris*) but now nearly extinct from overexploitation. One or two small pieces of bark are usually soaked in a quart-size bottle of white rum or cane juice, flavored with ginger, cloves, and cinnamon. In the nineteenth century, Father Michael de Verteuille vividly described the powerful effects of this 200-year-old version of Viagra, with "at least one [victim of aphrodisiacal overindulgence] having had to enclose the offending organ in a long tin can." De Verteuille recommended treatment in a "bed covered with a low tent . . . and also tolerance for the occasional unsuppressed snicker on the part of attendant nurses or visitors."[44] This concoction is still known as Boise Bande in the French Caribbean (*boise* translates from French to mean either "wood" or "stick" and is a common Caribbean slang term for the male sexual organ). The popular drug is sold today on both sides of the Atlantic.

Marriage rituals emphasized the concerns with potency and fertility. Traditional African-Guyanese kweh-kweh lyrics suggest that there were many remedies for impotence. One song asked what kind of man was the one who "cyan function" when the woman lies down. The groom was encouraged to seek help from herbal drinks: "Get Up, Stand Up," "Cappadula," "Sarsparilla," "Granny Backbone," and "Sweet Broom." The African-derived remedies intersected with European folk medicine. In Europe, pepper and spices such as nutmeg, cinnamon, and ginger had traditionally played a more important role in medicine than in cuisine. Since all of these grew in tropical areas, they were associated with exotic realms and with increased potency. They were used variously as powders applied topically to the penis and also were ingested by men. The nonnative spices were soon grown widely in the islands and became familiar local flavors in the hands of Caribbean cooks.

Other well-known aphrodisiac foods and drinks include fish tea (an aromatic broth) and various products made from sea moss, all considered to be particularly nourishing foods. Eating fish might explain a man's aggressive sexual appetite.[45] Sea moss is drunk in some places (e.g., Jamaica), and in other parts of the Caribbean (e.g., Antigua) it is made (for men only) in the form of ice cream. Sea-moss ice cream can be found on Sundays and most

---

FISH TEA

2 pounds fish heads
8 cups water or broth
1 tomato, chopped
1 sprig thyme
1 bay leaf
3 to 4 green onions, finely chopped
1 Scotch bonnet pepper (remove when flavors are hot enough)
salt and pepper to taste
4 green bananas, sliced lengthwise; or 3 small potatoes, cut into
   bite-sized pieces, if desired

Boil the fish in water or broth for about 30 minutes; strain off the stock
and save to return to pot. Remove the skin from the fish heads and
discard; remove the meat from the bones and return it to the stock.
Add all the other ingredients. Green bananas or potatoes may be added
to the soup at this stage. Continue cooking for another 30 minutes.
Serve piping hot.

---

holidays at the beach, where it is offered by women vendors. Made from the dried seaweed *Gracilaria verrucosa*, sea-moss jelly is flavored with rum, sugar, milk, and freshly grated nutmeg. Fish tea is simply a fish broth usually made from boiling the head of a fresh fish with herbs until the mixture forms a thick soup. Today, fish tea is commonly drunk, steaming hot from cups, by men in the small fishing villages of the Caribbean, from St. Lucea, Jamaica, to Scarborough, Tobago.

Cooking Transgressions

Under special circumstances, Caribbean men themselves served as cooks. After emancipation, they cooked for wages and became renowned as chefs on board ships and in Caribbean ports of call, including resorts. Earlier they had sailed as enslaved laborers or freed slaves. John Jae, an eighteenth-century freed slave, had been born on one side of the Atlantic but found himself on the other side. His abolitionist tract introduced his culinary skills and observations to a large reading audience. Often African-born cooks and kitchen workers were the only blacks employed on shipboard, as was the case of Joseph, the enslaved cook on the *Dragon*, a ship traveling between London, Jamaica, and Boston during the eighteenth century.[46] The presence—even predominance— of African descendants as stewards and cooks at sea was a by-product of the slave trade, even through the nineteenth and twentieth centuries. Although blacks worked hard at this thankless job, they dominated the trade for the relative independence it afforded them. As Jeffrey Bolster points out:

> At those ports . . . almost no white men filled the cooks' or stewards' berths— roles reserved for blacks. Aboard a man-of-war the cook had charge of a real galley below decks, with a substantial brick hearth and sizable kettles. Most cooks, however, sweated and swayed aboard tiny merchantmen, sloops or schooners from forty to sixty feet long manned by a sort of stunted sentry box lashed to the deck and sheltering a crude hearth on which he "dressed the Victuals" by boiling or roasting. Hunched in the swirling wood smoke and braced against the relentless motion of the ship, a merchantman's grimy cook coped with few utensils, monotonous prisons, and more abuse than glory at mealtime.[47]

There is even some evidence that the whites employing them considered black seamen cooks to occupy service-oriented, feminine roles. In the hyper-masculine world aboard ships, food-related roles were not defined by their physical or nautical skills. Male sea cooks were acculturated at the home hearths of Caribbean female cooks, but they usually learned their craft in hotels and restaurants. While they were often among the best-paid sailors on board a vessel, black cooks were wage-earning laborers, who provided for families back home. They were tainted by their association with what one writer described in 1852 as "West Indian [seaport] towns . . . generally notorious for immorality."[48] In the Caribbean, it was not uncommon for mulatto women to own and run establishments of ill repute, frequented by sailors and other travelers. The freed slave Rachael Pringle owned her notorious brothel in Bridgetown, Barbados, during the late eighteenth century. Yet her entertainment of transient seafarers "depended upon her subjugation of other women of African descent," including enslaved women.[49] Ironically, historian Paul Gilje called the drinking, treating, and whoring that characterized seamen's forays ashore the "sweets" of liberty.[50]

Maritime culture shaped life in port cities, reinforcing the contradictions of race and gender. A climate that tolerated homosexuality and bisexuality may have characterized the early maritime community, especially offering alternative lifestyles for pirates, buccaneers, and privateers of the Caribbean, where rank and class had a certain fluidity. Occupational norms aboard ships and in some restaurant establishments did not carry over to the seaports. At least as early as 1910, Trinidadians made fun of the male sailor-cooks, who were called "Bajans" (shortened from Barbadians, from Barbados, a popular tourist destination). Barbadians migrated to postemancipation Trinidad, where the local-born Creoles resented them as outsiders in competition for food and jobs. Popular music and performance arts targeted the Bajans and specifically Bajan cooks.

Carnival celebration was itself an inversion of the hierarchies of island life, celebrating unbridled desires and appetites prior to the deprivations of the Lenten season that followed Ash Wednesday in the Christian calendar. At the same time, the transgressions were temporary; Carnival reinforced the boundaries of social life when participants returned to their normal routines and society's conventional codes of behavior. Masqueraders observed the oppositional role of men as sailor-cooks and "played" Bajan cooks at Carnival time. Costumed revelers dressed in tall white chef's hats and white suits even constituted a favorite masque of white Trinidadians of the time.[51]

However, these male cooks were exceptional; more importantly, their cooking was associated not with the home but with travel, freedom, and the liminality of being situated between realms. The cooks were not associated with Caribbean kitchen space, owing to their very lack of residence and their association with movement from place to place, rather than any specific port of call. Male cooks masqueraded as females, when they dressed as cooks during Carnival. Carnival performances also transgressed norms, when *jamettes* (Creole from the French *diameter*), the working-class, urban women of Trinidad drank, sang, and confronted men for money in a public display that countered Victorian mores. In the 1874 Carnival, masked women also reportedly went about "in men's clothing, we cannot say how many hundred are flaunting their want of shame."[52]

Beyond the Afro-Creole cultural play such as that found in the rituals of carnival, cooking and food could be inverted and used to express the political in a more intimate and subtler metaphor. In Guadeloupe, writer Maryse Conde used "the taste of Bourbonnaise" to refer both to the flavors of a type of orange and to the ill-fated French monarchy, which would have been perceived as sweet on the tongues of monarchists during a revolutionary era on that island.[53] Archaeologist Ken Kelly has shown through architectural and spatial transformations that there were much greater mobility and transcendence of rigid class and race hierarchies in Guadeloupe after 1802. The 1805 singers from Port of Spain used the *belair* musical style (with its African-derived social commentary accompanied by a large drum) alongside food images of the Haitian Revolution when they sang, "The bread we eat/is the white man's flesh/The wine we drink/Is the white man's blood/He St. Domingo."[54] Political authority was also inscribed in the material world of freedom and slavery. Regardless of the presence of social or political turmoil, male authority dictated female subservience inside and outside of the kitchen. And personal politics flavored the production and consumption of meals.

Cooking was similarly associated with free women in the European-derived and Asian-derived domestic spheres of Caribbean society, regardless of class. Even upper-class women such as Lady Maria Nugent found themselves constantly concerned with the food they encountered daily in their social lives. They noted its abundance and they realized the interplay of the strange local food and the uncertainty of imported goods. These women did not necessarily prepare food themselves, nor did they dictate the content of menus served in their homes. Nonetheless, food-related spaces uniformly were defined as inherently female domains by all cultures arriving in the Caribbean. Particularly the women in multicultural relationships were expected to bridge the gap between home and exile abroad. Female domestic cooking was perceived as both a duty and a form of power. Simultaneously victims and beneficiaries of their domestic roles, female cooks most frequently found themselves at the heart of these dual aspects of food-related activities. Their choice of flavors and other key characteristics of ingredients altered the diets of men and established the cultural norms of a newly globalized community. As Jane Guyer has speculated, the universal association of women with cooking has nothing to do with physiology, yet everything to do with beliefs, symbolic meanings, and even cosmology.[55]

Dangerous Cooking, Dangerous Foods

Even if there were perceived dangers associated with receiving food from women, every Caribbean kitchen also offered its own threats to the maker and recipient of New World foods. Some but not all of these threats were the result of the meetings, crossings, and inversions of customary domains: enslaved feeding master, woman feeding man, poor feeding rich. While maintaining social control depended on mastery over the separate spheres of black and white, male and female, male slave masters were actually sometimes victims of the cultural fusion of food-styles taking place under watchful eyes in their own kitchens. The eventual arrival of European women in Caribbean kitchens creates a less flexible domestic colonialism, as Thomas Beidelman has argued for the African colony of Tanganyika.[56] The presence of European women did not reorder society either racially or sexually. After the Industrial Revolution, European women began to disassociate themselves from domestic chores if they could afford to do so. In the Caribbean kitchen, non-European women continued to feed and nurture a new Caribbean cuisine.

Fires also posed a constant and real danger to cooks, who endured hot steam, spills, and burns. Like the shattered hearthstones, a domestic fire signaled domestic conflict. Women cooks not only controlled fire, but also used dangerous knives and machetes, tools normally associated with male realms and male activities. In West and Central African as well as African-Caribbean cooking, the most basic stew relied on tough greens (like dasheen or taro leaves), requiring women to wield a sharp knife to slit the ingredients into fine slices for proper cooking and blending of flavors. In pre-Columbian traditions, there is another connection between mortality and the cooking fire. Lévi-Strauss explains the origins of fire as the jaguar gives a cooking lesson: "If you are in a hurry, light a fire, put the meat on a spit, and grill it; if you have time, cook it in an oven that has been hallowed out in the ground and previously heated; put foliage around the meat to protect it, and earth and hot ashes on top."[57]

Fire could be a dangerous weapon or a cultural tool. Attendant risks of household access across class and color lines led many cooks to bear the burden of blame for the mysterious deaths of household members. Accusations of food poisoning were as common as theft in slave society. Writing about the eighteenth century, the plantation owner Bryan Edwards describes the problem of poisons as a common thread in the history of the islands. It could be argued that women's role in relation to food enabled them to demonstrate their mastery over life and death and nature every day.

Dangerous Dining

In most African communities, men and women (and their children) ate their meals separately. Even in the multicultural communities of coastal West and Central Africa, African and mulatto women were retained as cooks for European men. This gendered practice of feeding expatriate communities and reinforcing the separation of genders largely carried over to the Caribbean. In conformity with European customs, European and Creole men and women sometimes might dine together, but after the meal they went their separate ways—the men to smoke and drink, the women to talk among themselves. Dining in the Caribbean could be a lavish and rather lengthy experience for the wealthy. The American traveler Julia Woodruff describes a nineteenth-century dining room on the Cuban plantation of San Benito:

> The guests at table number twenty-two—not including the dogs underneath the board, nor the parrots, pigeons, and chickens, that hover above and

around, to pick up the crumbs. Neither do I take into account a small army of cadaverous, squealing pigs, nor a scorpion that suddenly appears on a rough rafter, over Conchita's head, and is dispatched with some difficulty by the joint forces of three of the gentlemen, two of the servants, a cane, a riding-whip, an umbrella, and two brooms, in the midst of general confusion and dismay.[58]

Woodruff's observations romanticize the plantation cane fields, but also they reveal an assumed stratification of the diners by gender and class. After the meal, men smoked together. According to Lady Maria Nugent, women in Jamaica left the gentlemen and retired to bedrooms after dinner. This Lady Nugent did on April 1, 1802, "but [then she found herself] obliged to give audience to all the black and brown ladies in the parish, while . . . undressing."[59] Lady Nugent was extremely interested in what seemed to her the strange dietary and sexual habits of the New World. She thought that Jamaicans "lived to eat."[60] Because eating afforded slave masters a social occasion, meals were also seen as opportunities to create liaisons with local women. Meals could be preludes to sexual affairs. Such a dinner scene is humorously illustrated by William Holland's nineteenth-century cartoon *Johnny Newcome in Love in the West Indies*, in which the white plantation owner is made to look ridiculous. In his several amorous adventures, the women of color are depicted as sorcerers and prostitutes, as well as cooks and servants.

Interracial and gendered dining on some islands was considered provocative and even downright dangerous. In Trinidad, where racial tensions were heightened during an 1803 investigation of excessive violence against the enslaved, one member of the British governing commission came under suspicion for being overly sympathetic to the "Free Coloureds," those African descendants, who had purchased or been granted their freedom. A rumor circulated accusing his wife of seating a "dark mulatto" next to the presumably white Baron de Montalambert at her dining table. This rumor "dangerously excited" the locals until the baron made it quite clear that he would not have tolerated such an act.[61]

In stark contrast to the ruling class cuisine were the meals of enslaved Africans, which were combinations of rations and cultivated crops, eaten usually midway during the workday and sometimes after. Slaves worked from before daylight until after darkness. Their first meal was often hours into the day's labor. Mary Prince, an enslaved woman who lived in Bermuda, Turks Island, and, later, Antigua, described the regimen of dining outdoors:

I was given a half barrel and a shovel, and had to stand up to my knees in the water [mining salt], from four o'clock in the morning till nine, when

we were given some Indian corn boiled in water, which we were obliged to
swallow as fast as we could for fear the rain should come on and melt the
salt . . . we came home at twelve; ate our corn soup, called *clawly*, as fast as
we could, and went back to our employment till dark at night. . . . When we
returned to the house, our master gave us each our allowance of raw Indian
corn, which we pounded in a mortar and boiled for our suppers.[62]

In spite of the inclusive use of "we," it was the women who cooked for
men. Meals in the great house were taken in this order: breakfast tea upon
rising, second breakfast (brunch), and dinner (between 4 and 6 p.m.). Feasts
involving several neighboring plantations were described in the late eighteenth
century as "grandy balls," in which the enslaved "prepare a number of pots,
some of which are good and savory," including pork, poultry, salt beef, herring, and rats.[63] One observer of island life suggested that these extravagant
feasts were fashioned from goods taken from the plantation:

After dancing, the group sits down to the supper table, the contents of
which have all been stolen from the masters or mistresses of the different
guests . . . and the whole supper, even if it be not arranged upon the table
according to the strictest rules of etiquette and may not be called elegant,
is nevertheless a very substantial meal.[64]

After abolition, social dinners with neighbors and visitors could be quite
grand occasions, with feasting lasting well through the night. In country
districts, another gathering evolved: the tea meeting. This was based on the
widespread African-derived traditions of collecting a fee from the attendees
to cover the costs of the social affair. The clergyman and traveler Greville
John Chester warns in his *Transatlantic Sketches* that "these teas lead to a
great deal of immorality, and the evil is rather increased than lessened by the
vociferous singing of the most sacred hymns throughout the whole night."[65]
Tea meetings included food, singing, dancing, drinking, and speechmaking, in
an atmosphere controlled by a *master* of ceremonies. In this way, the domestic
meal was transformed from a woman-created occasion to a male-dominated
special event.

The Silence and Sounds of Food

As globalization encroached upon the diets of peoples around the world, a
silent web of dependency was spun from the threads of trade in imported foods
exchanged for plantation goods. The "invisible" women, who were situated
at the intersection of private and public spheres, also brought local foodstuffs

to the Caribbean table. They grew vegetables in private gardens and worked behind the scenes, in their private kitchens, fixing foods for consumption in the public sphere. Sometimes food formed a key commodity in an informal economy. Despite the myth of paradisiacal abundance, tropical fruits were preserved as jams and vegetables were pickled. Known as market gardeners, East Indian women in Jamaica sold their food to the Chinese shops in Kingston or piled them in baskets for door-to-door sales, an activity made illegal in the 1930s. One seller in the streets of the 1890s wore "heavy silver bangles" that "glistened pleasantly against the soft brown of her skin. . . . On her head was poised a basket laden with vegetables of every description; bunches of fresh lettuce, garden eggs (eggplants) and other similar products."[66] Presumably the sound of the bangles attracted attention to her wares. This was not the only instance of a hidden history of food. Not wishing to be seen in public, higher-status white women sometimes prepared baked breads or cakes for sale by lower-class black vendors in island towns. Annie Manville Fenn, in *Housekeeping in Jamaica* (1893), described such a door-to-door visit by an itinerant vendor with glass cases filled with cakes, tarts, fruit preserves, candies, and puddings:

> The next arrival, with a kind of double tray, is the cake woman. The top tray contains Jamaican sweet-meats—peppermint sticks and other tooth-destroying delicacies. She removes this and underneath are various kinds of spongey cakes and small basins of preserved pine [pineapple], mango, watermelon or other fruit. These confections are made, I am told, by Jewish ladies who employ the black women as sellers. I believe they do a thriving trade, especially with the hotels and lodging houses.[67]

The famous image of Rachael Pringle presented the notorious Creole brothel-owner seated in front of a sign advertising pickles and sweets. Pringle stares ahead silently while offering the "wares." Hidden layers of meaning in glass jars and on trays of delicacies serve us well as a metaphor for understanding the complexity of food history in the Caribbean. The African-Guyanese proverb reminds us "there is more in the mortar, than [is visible] on the pestle."

The hidden meanings of food could even be paraded down the public streets of an island without losing their nuanced capacity for coded expression. In Guadeloupe's Fête des Cuisinières, women use a wooden clapper seemingly to call attention to themselves and their foods. Yet, if one watches and listens more closely, the clapper appears to be played loudly only at crossroads, the dangerous intersections of the small, narrow streets, where the women change directions as they wind their way from the Maison des Cuisinières to

Selling foods, Trinidad
(Photograph by Candice Goucher)

the cathedral and then on to the community tables prepared on their behalf. The sounds are meant to warn the visible and invisible realms of their arrival. Men follow behind. They carry tall, wooden racks of cakes for distribution to the gathered crowds after the church service.

The elaborate process of dressing for the parade is a private affair for the women. Symbolic foods have been embroidered on their aprons—the fish, a Christian symbol, appears next to the letters "S" and "L" and a latched grill, a symbol of St. Laurent (a Christian martyr who was tied to a lattice and burned alive in the third century). St. Laurent, the patron saint of cooks, is associated with miracles of food multiplying to feed the poor and a Catholic feast day celebrated in August. The fish is also the symbol associated with the African (Yoruba) deity Yemaya, goddess of the sea and an omen of fertility

Procession to the cathedral, Fête des Cuisinières, Pointe-à-Pitre, Guadeloupe
(Photograph by Candice Goucher)

and abundance. The women's headscarves are knotted in styles that quietly show whether they are married or not, whether their hearts are "available" or "unavailable." Heirloom gold jewelry is both visible and hidden, pinned on undergarments or worn as earrings or beads under scarves tied around the neck.

Originally formed as a mutual-assistance association, the Cuisinières provide financial help for funeral or health expenses of their members in need. But food is the intentional focus of the festival, which recognizes the creativity of cooks and their role in preserving cultural identity. And foods there are aplenty—salt-fish salad, curried chicken, creamy stewed dasheen, stuffed christophene (a Caribbean squash), blood pudding, steamed fish and lobster, peas and rice, and freshly baked breads and cakes. The association began in 1916, a time of great suffering, hunger, and widespread poverty in the French colony, where sugar remained the only export of any value long after slavery had ended. Today, it is widely recognized that the cuisine that survived yet another century is at the heart of Guadeloupe's spiritual and material culture.

The dancing cooks of Guadeloupe recall another aspect of the collective memory of Caribbean food. Their erotic gestures bring into the public sphere the unspoken, if obvious, connection between the sex act and the bodily ingestion of food. In any culture, food interacts with a sphere that includes the most intimate of bodily actions. Many West and Central Africans still masticate the food for young children and transfer it from their mouth to the child's, mingling their body fluids in an intimate gesture of cultural and chemical transmission. Sexual activity also constitutes such a hidden transfer in both its cultural and biological aspects. As embodied behavior, eating and copulating share much in common. The separation of individual and social memory is as unthinkable and meaningless as the separation of food from the body it enters and becomes.[68]

Global Food Fusion in Caribbean History

The triangular trade that connected Africa, Europe, and the Americas (and, by later extension, Asia) had a cultural dimension that flowed through the kitchens of the Caribbean, generation after generation. Shared foods helped fuse Caribbean culture, and out of the ingredients and inspiration of four continents a truly global cuisine first appeared. Its fusion relied both on force and resistance to oppression. Food was the ultimate substance of power. What greater power than the ability of women to give birth to children and transmit cultural memory to each new generation? The recipes of this chapter reflect desire and procreation, as well as empowerment; their aphrodisiac elements, including chocolate, callaloo, and fish tea, span the sweet and the savory, the indigenous and the borrowed. In Caribbean foodways as in life, "as though spinning on two separate axes distinguished by different activities, the world of men and the world of women mesh and articulate."[69] Moreover, food represented the remembered essence of a past embodied in cultural expression. Like the eloquent movements of the Guadeloupe cook, food memory was expressed in repeated bodily actions and verbal morsels associated with both its preparation and ingestion. As the edible vocabulary of ritual and belief, food allowed women cooks to claim the first and last word of each and every day in Caribbean history.

Notes

1. Ulli Beier, *Yoruba Poetry: An Anthology of Traditional Poems* (Cambridge: Cambridge University Press, 1970).

2. Gordon Rohlehr, *Calypso and Society in Pre-Independence Trinidad* (Port of Spain: Gordon Rohlehr, 1990), 260, 586; the calypso was also called "Roast Saltfish."

3. I had the pleasure of sharing this meal with food writer Jessica Harris, in Pointe-à-Pitre, Guadeloupe, August 10, 2002.

4. Richard S. Dunn, "The Demographic Contrast between Slave Life in Jamaica and Virginia, 1760–1865," *Proceedings of the American Philosophical Society* 151, no. 1 (2007): 43–60.

5. Quoted in Barbara Bush, *Slave Women in Caribbean Society, 1659–1838* (Kingston, Jamaica: Heinemann, 1990), 139.

6. Dunn, "Demographic Contrast," 52 n10.

7. F.W.N. Bayley, *Four Years' Residence in the West Indies*, 3rd ed. (London, 1833), 69–71, quoted in Roger D. Abrahams and John F. Szwed, eds., *After Africa* (New Haven: Yale University Press, 1983), 305.

8. B.R. Burg, *Sodomy and the Pirate Tradition: English Sea Rovers in the Seventeenth Century Caribbean* (New York: New York University Press, 1983).

9. Ann Laura Stoler, "Carnal Knowledge and Imperial Power: Gender, Race, and Morality in Colonial Asia," in *Gender at the Crossroads of Knowledge: Feminist Anthropology in the Postmodern Era*, ed. Micaela di Leonardo (Berkeley: University of California Press, 1991), 51–101.

10. Paul E. Lovejoy, *Transformations in Slavery: A History of Slavery in Africa* (African Studies Series 36) (Cambridge: Cambridge University Press, 1983), Table 3.8.

11. Michael A. Gomez, *Reversing Sail: A History of the African Diaspora* (Cambridge: Cambridge University Press, 2005), 93; Gomez suggests that male cooks were preferred in Saint Domingue, where women, however, dominated local markets and food rations were regulated by the Code Noir (1685).

12. Claude Lévi-Strauss, *The Raw and the Cooked: Introduction to a Science of Mythology*, vol. 1 (New York: Harper and Row, 1969), 164.

13. See, for example, the discussion by Riva Berleant-Schiller and William M. Maurer, "Women's Place Is Every Place: Merging Domains and Women's Roles in Barbuda and Dominica," in *Women and Change in the Caribbean: A Pan-Caribbean Perspective*, ed. Janet Momsen (Kingston, Jamaica: Ian Randle, 1993), 65–79.

14. Lady Maria Nugent, *Lady Nugent's Journal of Her Residence in Jamaica from 1801 to 1805*, ed. Philip Wright (Kingston: Institute of Jamaica, 1966 [1907]), 26.

15. Lafcadio Hearn, *Gombo Zhebes: Little Dictionary of Creole Proverbs, Selected from Six Creole Dialects* (New York: Will H. Coleman, 1885), 13.

16. Shelley Boyd Calone and Richard Campbell Roberts, *Nostalgic Nassau: Picture Postcards, 1900–1940* (Nassau, Bahamas: Nassau Nostalgia, 1991), 57.

17. Pieter de Marees, *Description and Historical Account of the Gold Kingdom of Guinea (1602)*, ed. Adam Jones, transl. Albert van Dantzig (London: British Academy, 1987), 76.

18. Barclay (1826), in Abrahams and Szwed, *After Africa*, 346.

19. Patrick Leigh Fermor, *The Traveller's Tree: A Journey Through the Caribbean Islands* (New York: New York Review Books, 1950), 247.

20. Sylvia Arden Boone, *Radiance from the Waters: Ideals of Feminine Beauty in Mende Art* (New Haven: Yale University Press, 1986), 52–63, 215.

21. Maureen Warner-Lewis, *Guinea's Other Sons: The African Dynamic in Trinidad Culture* (Dover, MA: Majority Press, 1991), 95.

22. Lydia Mihelic Pulsipher, "Changing Roles in the Life Cycles of Women in Traditional West Indian Houseyards," in *Women and Change in the Caribbean*, ed. Momsen, 57.

23. Joseph Lambert, personal communication, May 21, 2001.

24. Richard D.E. Burton, *Afro-Creole: Power, Opposition, and Play in the Caribbean*, (Ithaca: Cornell University Press, 1997), 161; see also Gary Brana-Shute, "Drinking Shops and Social Structure: Some Ideas on Lower-Class West Indian Male Behavior." *Urban Anthropology* 5, no. 1 (1976): 53–68.

25. David Killick, quoted in Eugenia W. Herbert, *Iron, Gender, and Power: Rituals of Transformation in African Societies* (Indianapolis: Indiana University Press, 1993), 87.

26. Felipe Fernandez-Armesto, *Near a Thousand Tables: A History of Food* (New York: Free Press, 2002), 32–33.

27. Christine McFadden and Christine France, *The Cook's Guide to Chocolate* (Oxford: Sebastian Kelly, 1997), 60.

28. Berta Cabanillas and Carmen Ginorio, *Puerto Rican Dishes* (San Juan: University of Puerto Rico, 2002), 100.

29. Personal communication, Joseph Lambert, Berbice, Guyana, February 12, 2004.

30. Caroline Sullivan, *The Jamaica Cookery Book* (Kingston, Jamaica: Aston W. Gardner, 1893), 78; see the discussion by Barry Higman, *Jamaican Food: History, Biology, Culture* (Kingston, Jamaica: University of the West Indies Press, 2008), 202–204.

31. Herbert, *Iron, Gender, and Power*, 226.

32. See, for example, the widespread association of women with nature and cooking with culture in the circum-Caribbean region, as discussed by Lévi-Strauss, *Raw and the Cooked*, 269.

33. Bush, *Slave Women*, 141–142.

34. Alison Krogel, *Food, Power, and Resistance in the Andes: Exploring Quechua Verbal and Visual Narratives* (New York: Lexington Books, 2011), 141.

35. Laura Tanna, *Jamaican Folktales and Oral Histories* (Kingston: Institute of Jamaica, 1984), 65–68.

36. Rohlehr, *Calypso and Society*, 258–259.

37. Rohlehr, *Calypso and Society*, 259.

38. Mrs. (Alison) Carmichael, quoted in Cristine Mackie, *Life and Food in the Caribbean* (New York: New Amsterdam, 1991), 74.

39. Mackie, *Life and Food*, 74.

40. Hans Sloane, 1707, quoted in Higman, *Jamaican Food*, 107.

41. *The Importance of Jamaica to Great Britain, Consider'd* (1740) quoted in Higman, *Jamaican Food*, 104.

42. Kwaku Mensah, personal communication, October 20, 2003.

43. Isabel Allende, *Aphrodite* (New York: HarperPerennial, 1999), 29.

44. Michael de Verteuille, cited in Rosemary Parkinson, *Culinaria, The Caribbean: A Culinary Discovery* (Cologne, Germany: Konemann, 1999), 244.

45. The Mighty Chalkdust's 2010 calypso claims to explain President Bill Clinton's affair with Monica Lewinsky by revealing that "Is Ah Fish He Eat" when he went to St. Thomas.

46. W. Jeffrey Bolster, *Black Jacks: African American Seamen in the Age of Sail* (Cambridge, MA: Harvard University Press, 1997), 30.

47. Bolster, *Black Jacks*, 33.

48. Henry Highland Garnett, writing from Jamaica and quoted in Bolster, *Black Jacks*, 160.

49. Marisa J. Fuentes, "Power and Historical Figuring: Rachael Pringle Polgreen's Troubled Archive," *Gender & History* 22, no. 3 (2010): 564.

50. Paul A. Gilje, *Liberty on the Waterfront: American Maritime Culture in the Age of Revolution* (Philadelphia: University of Pennsylvania Press), 2003.

51. Burton, *Afro-Creole*, 211.

52. *Chronicle* (1874) editorial quoted by John Cowley, *Carnival, Canboulay, and Calypso: Traditions in the Making* (Cambridge: Cambridge University Press, 1996), 73.

53. Maryse Conde, *In the Time of the Revolution*, translated from the French by Doris Y. Kadish and Jean-Pierre Piriou, *Callaloo* 25, no. 2 (2002): 467 n43.

54. Cowley, *Carnival, Canboulay, and Calypso*, 14; see also Hollis "Chalkdust" Liverpool, *Rituals of Power and Rebellion: The Carnival Tradition in Trinidad and Tobago, 1763–1962*, (Chicago: Research Associates School Times Publications, 2001), 149.

55. Jane Guyer, *The Raw, the Cooked, and the Half-Baked* (Boston: Boston University, African Studies Center Working Papers, 1981).

56. Thomas Beidelman, *Colonial Evangelism* (Bloomington: Indiana University Press, 1982), 13.

57. Ribeiro, quoted in Lévi-Strauss, *Raw and the Cooked*, 129.

58. W.M.L. Jay, *My Winter in Cuba* (New York: E.P. Dutton, 1871), 241.

59. Nugent, *Lady Nugent's Journal*.

60. See Sylvia Wynter, "Lady Nugent's Journal," *Jamaica Journal* 1, no. 1 (1967): 25–27.

61. Reported in Bridget Brereton, *A History of Modern Trinidad, 1783–1962* (Kingston, Jamaica: Heinemann, 1981), 50.

62. Moira Ferguson, ed., *The History of Mary Prince, A West Indian Slave: Related by Herself* (Ann Arbor: University of Michigan Press, 1993), 61–62.

63. J.B. Moreton, *Manners and Customs in the West India Islands* (London, 1790), 152–153, 155–158, quoted in Abrahams and Szwed, *After Africa*, 290.

64. Bayley, *Four Years' Residence in the West Indies*, quoted in Abrahams and Szwed, *After Africa*, 305.

65. Greville John Chester, *Transatlantic Sketches in the West Indies . . .* (London, 1869), 80.

66. Quoted in Verene Shepherd, "Depression in the 'Tin Roof Towns': Economic Problems of Urban Indians in Jamaica, 1930–1950," in *India in the Caribbean*, ed.

David Dabydeen and Brinsley Samaroo (London: Hansib/University of Warwick, Center for Caribbean Studies, 1987), 178.

67. Quoted in Norma Benghiat, *Traditional Jamaican Cookery* (London: Penguin Books, 1985), 133.

68. Paul Connerton argued for this artificial separation of analytical categories in his work on cultural memory, *How Societies Remember* (Cambridge: Cambridge University Press, 1989).

69. Brana-Shute, "Drinking Shops," 60.

SIX

Caribbean Hunger

Food, Politics, and Globalization

Hunger makes a person lie down
And count the rafters in his roof . . .
I have eaten yesterday
Does not concern hunger.
There is no god like one's stomach:
We must sacrifice to it every day.

—Yoruba song[1]

An empty sack cannot stand up.

—Proverb from Martinique[2]

The print of hunger wanders in the land.
. . . The huts of men are fused in misery.

—Martin Carter, *University of Hunger*[3]

Father Jean-Baptiste Labat, a plump Dominican priest, sailed from France to the island of Martinique at the end of the seventeenth century. Once in the Caribbean, he investigated the soil, local plants, and foods, eventually establishing a sugar works that relied on slave labor. By the time he returned to Europe more than a dozen years later, Labat had traveled to many of the Dutch, French, Spanish, and English islands of the Antilles, sampling the foods of each place. He gathered his information in an eight-volume series on the Americas. His works were translated into many European languages and became something of the equivalent to a runaway best seller. Caribbean culinary tourism was born.

In his *Nouveau Voyage aux isles Françoises de l'Amérique* (1722), Père Labat described the cuisines he encountered at ship tables and in ports of call.

His gastronomical comments were influential in shaping the image of the Caribbean as a paradise of plenty, abundantly stocked with exotic fruits, meats, and spices. As he settled into Caribbean life, Labat tasted island delicacies such as turtle, lizard, manatee, and iguana. He ate with other Europeans, indigenous Amerindians, and enslaved Africans. He became part of the creolization of culinary habits, mixing French and local foods and techniques of preparation.

Labat perceived the new as framed by the familiar. For example, he describes the lizard *en fricassée*, likening its taste to chicken, tender and delicate. He likened the avocado to "a marrow pie" and the taste of peppery artichokes. The turtle breast was prepared with chili peppers, lime juice, cloves, salt, and pepper, much like the typical marinade of Caribbean fish. Labat also combined traditional French ingredients and local spices in an outdoor feast of the meat of two large sea turtles prepared in the manner of the buccaneers ("A Turtle Boucan"), the meat mixed with hard-boiled egg yolks, fines herbes, lemon juice, salt, and chili pepper and then stuffed back into one of the shells and slow cooked in the ground.[4] The land crabs might be prepared in *taumalin* sauce, with lime juice, salt, and peppers added, or even as a casserole with egg, onion, parsley, orange peel, and nutmeg. In this way, Labat applied local culinary ideas to familiar European patterns of fasting and feasting.[5]

Feasts and Famines

The feasting experienced by the friar stands in stark contrast to the hunger and famine experienced by many others in the Caribbean before, during, and after the seventeenth century. After Columbus, the settling of the Caribbean became a model for globalization, creating distinctive and widening gaps between the haves and the have-nots. Ongoing processes of globalization have revealed further the intertwined roles of hunger and identity in Caribbean historical perspective. The many explorers and the many slave ships too frequently arrived in the Caribbean with nothing left of their original victuals and with the captain and crew eyeing flying fish and sea birds for their cooking pots, while the valuable cargoes of slaves were being fed the last miserable rations. As the Caribbean region became a veritable chessboard for global strategic positioning by imperial design, its tables repeatedly suffered from food embargos and ill-planned reliance on imports. Even for tavern and hotel cuisines that catered to tourism, going global while maintaining local identities was a macabre dance of dueling identities.

The culinary tastes of the region were anchored in a gastronomy that wavered between the opposing poles of singular native palates and homogenizing hungry tourists, between devastating famines and groaning feasts. This dialectic was abundantly clear from the earliest encounters with Europeans.

Mimi Sheller has observed the juxtaposition of images of abundance and the constant dangers of starvation endemic to the earliest experience of the Caribbean. Columbus admitted his immediate dependence upon local foods: "this food was so nutritious as to prove a great support to all of us after the privations we endured at sea."[6] From the letters of Columbus in which the New World was portrayed as a "veritable Cockaigne," a magical land of plenty, Judeo-Christian culture was a "paradise cult," with religious depictions serving as expressive motivations in secular terms. Columbus revised his view of the earth using imagery of female breast and pear-shaped fecundity, signaling a forbidden paradise.[7] Amid the persistent depiction of enormous trees laden with fruits and flowers, the tropics held out the possibilities of luxuriant excess and severest limitation.

In the seventeenth century, it had been nearly impossible to avoid the seafaring cuisines of salted pork and salt fish common to every voyage and frequently the substance of imported island food, from the Sandwich Islands (Hawaii) to the Antilles. Richard Ligon lived on the island of Barbados between 1647 and 1650. His *True and Exact History of the Island of Barbadoes* (1657) described in great detail the foods and their specific methods of cultivation, including sugar, ginger, guava, citrus, melons, papaya, peppers, pineapple, and plantains. They were viewed as tropical luxuries, but in fact were critical to the strategies for survival employed by early residents, both enslaved and free.[8] Travelers themselves were sources of globalization. Ligon carried seeds, animals, and people on his voyages. He traveled with cattle and horses. His "Rosemary, Time, Winter Savory, Sweet Margerom, Pot Marjerom, Parsley, Penniroyall, Camomile, Sage, Tansie, Lavender, Lavender Cotten, Garlicks, Onyons, Colworts, Cabbage, Turnips, Redishes, Marigolds, Lettice, Taragon [and] Southernwood" prospered in their new island home.[9] In Ligon's time, going to the Caribbean was meant to be a culinary adventure, although available accounts of the first centuries of encounters seemed to contradict the notion of a sought-after adventure, as it gave way to the realities of exploitation, enslavement, and conquest.

By the eighteenth century, the realities of geopolitical and economic forces had also begun to encourage the enslaved toward the pragmatic reliance on local rather than global foods. "Local foods" did not mean indigenous. In Martinique, onions, chives, thyme, and other familiar seasonings from Europe and North America were growing in island kitchen gardens alongside the native plant *Pimenta racemosa* (*bois d'Inde*, the aromatic bay leaf) for use in Creole cooking.[10] A century after Labat's arrival in Martinique, the Caribbean region was engulfed in war and its aftermath. Food supplies became devastatingly erratic, especially during the American War of Independence. The West African ackee fruit, the breadfruit from the Pacific, and the mango from the Indian Ocean arrived at this critical point, but even they were not enough to save local diets from despairing times. From the 1770s, planters faced difficulties both in shipping their consumable products (sugar, molasses, and rum) and in receiving food imports (rice, meat, and fish). In Barbados, the price of flour more than doubled in 1775, the first year of the American War of Independence, when the British were barred from trade with Americans and there was a danger of starvation when hurricanes and tsunamis struck. The slave populations declined by roughly 12 percent in a decade. Island food trade also suffered from the irregularities of privateering, while a continual number of captured sloops illegally carrying goods such as flour were documented in the early nineteenth century.[11] By the second decade of the nineteenth century, Barbados was exporting sugar and poultry, but still relied on flour and salt fish imports from North America.[12]

Three devastating hurricanes struck Jamaica in 1784, 1785, and 1786. More than 15,000 slaves died due to widespread famine. Overreliance on imports led the 1791 Jamaica Assembly to encourage local substitutions of "Yams, Cocos, Maize, Plaintains and such products as the Breadfruit, Nutmeg, Cloves, Cinnamon . . . and Coffee: it being believed that the cultivation of such exotics would, without doubt, in the course of a few years, lessen the dependence of the sugar islands on North America for food and necessaries; and not only supply subsistence for future generations, but, probably, furnish fresh incitements to Industry, new improvements in the Arts, and new subjects of Commerce."[13] According to locals, the cuisine of Martinique could not survive without fruit de pain. Before breadfruit, cassava and yams had anchored the diet. The local substitutions began to define the contours of a unique Caribbean culinary tradition. Who better equipped than the enslaved Africans carrying their sustainable foodways from tropical realms?

The poles of hunger and excess found their way into proverbs and popular songs. Lafcadio Hearn thought the "Congo" song about indulgence in the absence of the slave master to be one of the very few Creole songs with a purely African refrain still sung in New Orleans in the 1880s. Its satirical tone and subversive subject matter may have clung to African vocabulary in order to go undetected as social commentary. The song's theme revolved around the word *macaya*, meaning to stuff oneself or to eat at all hours:

> [In the song's refrain] *Ouende, ou-nde, macaya* . . . The theme seems to be that, the master and mistress of a house being absent, some slave is encouraging a slave-friend to eat excessively, to "stuff himself" with wine, chicken, etc. "They are gone, friend: eat, fill yourself; I'm not a bit ashamed; stuff yourself!—I'm drinking good wine; stuff yourself!—I'm eating good chicken; gorge yourself."[14]

Just as certain foods (chicken and imported wine) were associated with excess, others were the foods of hungry times, scarcity, and famine. For example, in eighteenth-century Jamaica, the indigenous breadnut (not to be confused with the breadfruit) characterized the diet of enslaved Africans and poor whites "and proved a wholesome and not unpleasant food."[15] Likened to the European chestnut (which was also maligned as poor people's food), roasted breadnut provided a substantial meal between July and September and in the aftermath of hurricanes. John Lunan (1814) promoted the plant's use beyond provisioning as "a rich resource in times of scarcity, or famine, as food for the negroes."[16]

Harvest Feasts

African harvest celebrations marked the period of the year when foods were abundant again. For example, among the Ibo people of West Africa, the Festival of the New Yam was a time of feasting, songs, and games. Yet even at a time of abundance, the departed were not forgotten. Nigerian novelist Chinua Achebe used the festival for the backdrop of his novel *Things Fall Apart*:

> The Feast of the New Yam was approaching and Umuofia was in a festival mood. It was an occasion for giving thanks to Ani, the earth goddess and the source of all fertility. Ani played a greater part in the life of the people than any other deity. She was the ultimate judge of morality and conduct. And what was more, she was in close communion with the departed fathers of the clan whose bodies had been committed to earth.
>
> The Feast of the New Yam was held every year before the harvest began, to honor the earth goddess and the ancestral spirits of the clan. New yams could not be eaten until some had first been offered to these powers. Men and women, young and old, looked forward to the New Yam Festival because it began the season of plenty—the new year. On the last night before the festival, yams of the old year were all disposed of by those who still had them. The new year must begin with tasty, fresh yams and not the shriveled and fibrous crop of the previous year. All cooking pots, calabashes and wooden bowls were thoroughly washed, especially the wooden mortar in which yam was pounded. Yam foo-foo and vegetable soup was the chief food in the celebration. So much of it was cooked that, no matter how heavily the family ate or how many friends and relatives they invited from neighboring villages, there was always a large quantity of food left over at the end of the day. The story was always told of a wealthy man who set before his guests a mound of foo-foo so high that those who sat on one

side could not see what was happening on the other, and it was not until late in the evening that one of them saw for the first time his in-law who had arrived during the course of the meal and had fallen to on the opposite side. It was only then that they exchanged greetings and shook hands over what was left of the food.[17]

A large store of food meant that the farmer had been industrious and the ancestors and spirit world had blessed the family. Under slavery, a different rationale prevailed since the enslaved were celebrating the slave owner's bounty. In Cuban houses of Santeria, parties were hosted on corresponding feast days of Catholic saints. On the feast of San Juan, African participants paid homage to Ogun, the god of iron, farmers, and war. Ogun was known for his voracious appetite. His feasting table should be set with cockerel, guinea fowl, dove's breast, *hutia* (a large rodent), goat meat, and fresh fish.[18] Only by properly preparing Ogun's favorite foods could his excessive hunger be satiated.

Funerary Foods

Death may have brought a welcomed end to the suffering of severely weakened, diseased, and half-starved laborers. Not only did enslaved African cooks use herbs and potions for healing, but also sometimes the same herbs were used in washing and burying the dead, providing protection in the afterlife. In mid-twentieth-century Trinidad, J.D. Elder recorded Yoruba dirges sung at funerals by African descendants. The song "Eweya" recalled the use of *egbesi* leaves (*ewé*), which are mentioned in punning relationship to children (*èwe*), the only difference being tonal: "Children of our mother/Egbesi leaves/ Are what we use for the burial of our mother/By the riverside."[19] Feasting followed the initial period of sorrow. Food and food symbols conveyed the cycle of life, since children were ancestors reborn. The womb was likened to a calabash. A metaphor for death might thus be seen or even heard as a calabash falling to the ground and spilling its contents. Elder recorded another African-Trinidadian funeral song, probably sung by a third-generation Yoruba at the death of a baby or young child:

> Hear!
> It fell from my hands, alas!
> The round gourd I took to the stream
> It fell from my hands, alas!
> The round gourd we took to the stream
> It fell from our hands, alas![20]

Funeral celebration, Ghana, c. 1979
(Photograph by Candice Goucher)

Not only song, but also food and drink were among the ceremonial components that characterized the funerals of the enslaved. African-derived rituals
ensured the transformation of the deceased into an ancestor, thus remaining an
active member of the community's spiritual life. In the seventeenth century,
one visitor to Jamaica noticed that the burial itself received offerings and as
soon as the grave was filled, they "eat and drink thereon."[21] In 1740, Charles
Leslie observed of slave burials that the enslaved were buried with "a pot
of soup at the head, and a bottle of rum at the feet."[22] According to Edward
Long, the eighteenth-century funeral celebrations themselves were occasions
that included "drinking, dancing and vociferation."[23] Food and drink were
powerful lubricants of social bonding, representing the acknowledgement of
spiritual realms, while enabling the reweaving of society after loss.

Women and Proverbial Hunger

Foods were classified by the enslaved in terms of what was necessary rather
than superfluous. At all costs, warned the African-Martinique proverb, one
must avoid becoming "an empty sack that cannot stand up." Another Creole
proverb, *Si moin te gagnin moussa, moin te mange gombo* ("If I had some
moussa, I would eat some *gombo*"), expressed the perceived difference
between provision (corn mush) and the more refined and even extravagant

soups.[24] That the majority of Caribbean proverbs relate to food or animals may reflect the hungry person's preoccupation with finding sufficient nourishment. The abundance of food-related proverbs suggests that women used the kitchen as a venue for promoting folk wisdom and moral advice. It also may explain how Caribbean cooks became early critics of globalization. After all, they bore the primary responsibility for food procurement. If foods were scarce, women were blamed. Their judged culpability was reflected in the widespread Creole proverb recorded in the 1880s in Martinique: "Too much jewelry, empty cupboard."[25]

Globalization and Food

The globalization of foodstuffs had promised to make foods more widely available and alleviate the problems of scarcity in any one place. Far from that, globalization encouraged the stockpiling of foods for profit. In West Africa, African merchant princes began to cultivate crops to supply the slave ships with needed food. Recognizing the cycles of dry season shortages and even famines, they withheld supplies at critical times, driving up the prices to artificially high levels. Investing their profits, they became rival entrepreneurs. Once seen as exhibiting an exercise in acculturation, the merchant prince was a harbinger of capitalist production and consumption in the late seventeenth and early eighteenth centuries. Sometimes male and often female, the creolized sensibility of these entrepreneurs provided a threat and boon to economic and political change in the Atlantic world. Around 1720, one such successful merchant, John Conny, may have inspired an Atlantic reputation for his fancy dress and powerful dealings at Axim on the Gold Coast.[26] Another independent trader based at Komenda on the Gold Coast, John Kabes brokered labor and supplies, including food he had grown and offered to sale to the Europeans, not just the British, but also Dutch and French traders, who were in frenzied competition for provisions.

Across the Atlantic, enslaved and free Africans had used provision grounds to grow their own food and also to market local produce. Not only the product of insufficient food supplied by plantations, their labors engaged in a critique of global food sourcing by eschewing imported foods and embracing the local system, which they controlled. Economic crises brought on by natural disasters and warfare created environments in which the exercise of food sovereignty worked to contest the plantation legacy. Geographer Benjamin Timms has argued that the official economic policy in the early colonial period centered on the mercantilist doctrine of market protection, a strategy that attempted to create a favorable balance of trade by importing raw materials from the colonies and exporting manufactures to the colonies. In maintaining such a "balance,"

Production of foodstuffs in the colonies was discouraged as resources were focused on tropical export products while sustenance needs were met through importation of agricultural products produced in the temperate regions of the metropole. There were contrary voices calling for diversified domestic production in the Caribbean, and a proposal to ban imported foodstuffs to force domestic production in the colonies was put before the British Parliament in 1698. Predictably, this proposal was rejected on the basis that it would decrease land devoted to the prize tropical product of the period; namely sugar.[27]

Even after emancipation, the continued denial of the access to land for local needs forced the majority of the freed labor to continue to work on behalf of the metropoles. Despite the role of Africans in small-scale food production, the island populations remained dependent on food imports throughout the colonial period. Only a small and largely neglected sector of peasant farming survived into the twentieth century. The global agricultural and industrial revolutions had made possible food systems that increasingly came under the control of global corporations and imperial governments. What visitors ate began to differ from the foods locals consumed at the beginning of the nineteenth century.

Culinary Travels

For European sojourners across the Atlantic but resident in the Caribbean, exploratory travel around their own island homes and to neighboring islands meant opportunities to visit family, friends, and military and business colleagues, with whom they also dined. Touring Jamaica in 1802, Lady Nugent describes her visit to the botanical garden at Bath, a thermal spring acquired by the island government in 1699. The town of Bath was several hours away (at a distance of about forty miles) from the Nugent residence in Spanish Town. Its hillside vegetation was sufficiently lush to attract Lady Nugent's eye. The breadfruit, cabbage tree, jackfruit, cinnamon, star-apple, and Otaheite apple were among the plants "as curious and extraordinary as they are beautiful." The prepared food was also perceived to be remarkable, despite its proximity to the Nugent home. Lady Nugent emphasized the "local" African and Maroon influences in the Bath countryside. The "strange dishes" encountered included fried conch, barbecued hog, and black crab "pepper-pod" soup, "which was very good indeed."[28]

A century after Père Labat, merchant John Huggins built the Bath Hotel in Nevis also adjacent to warm springs situated about half a mile south of the island's main town. Constructed in 1778, entirely of local, hand-cut stone, with forty or fifty accommodations, the hotel soon operated as a vacation-ing spot for European and Caribbean travelers, aristocrats, and royalty. The hotel was the residence of Samuel Taylor Coleridge's nephew and editor, Henry Nelson Coleridge, for a number of weeks. The younger Coleridge had no doubt heard about St. Nevis from his uncle's writings around the turn of the century, when the elder Coleridge claimed that "St Nevis [was] the most lovely as well as the most healthy island in the West Indies."[29] Travel to this inexpensive colonial outpost attracted many from the European continent. In the case of the younger Coleridge, he went abroad in search of a cure for rheumatism. Sailing from Montserrat in 1825, he found "the appearance of Nevis is perhaps the most captivating of any island in the West Indies. . . . It is green as any heart can conceive, perfectly cultivated, and enlivened with many old planters' houses of a superior style and churches peeping out in the most picturesque situations imaginable."[30]

Coleridge traveled to fifteen islands during a period of about six months. Like many nineteenth-century travelers after him, he ignored the economic conditions that had brought about the abandonment of sugar works and left behind waves of hunger, but, more importantly for Coleridge, produced quaint ruins for his pleasure. He expected and received abundance, although surely there was scarcity around him. His concerns were culinary. He noted the turtles on the beach that ended up on the dinner table of the Government House, where one of them "was excellent and dressed with extraordinary care."[31] He also described the finest oranges and pineapples, guava jelly, as well as European vegetables grown locally. The admixture of a cuisine that was at once local and global did not bother Coleridge, since he remarked that "indeed I have reason to believe that if any persons thought it worth their while to make the experiment with a proper attention to soil and situation, a large proportion of the valuable trees and culinary vegetables of countries lying in very different latitudes might be interchangeably transplanted."[32] According to Coleridge, the cure was successful: "Whether I ate, drank or sweated it out, I cannot say; but the fact is, I am well and flexible in all my limbs, and if the West Indies cured me, I am very much obliged to the West Indies for the favour."[33]

Medicine and Botanical Science

Sir Hans Sloane (1660–1753) had done much the same for the reputation of Jamaica, while furthering his own professional and personal agenda. As president of the Royal Society from 1727 to 1741, he described the flora and fauna, giving special attention to climate, agriculture, and medicinal plants.[34] Sloane had been personal physician to the governor of the island and collected plants for scientific study. While in Jamaica, he cultivated key relationships (including with the family of his future wife) that would help him to amass a huge fortune used to support his science. He also gathered information about the plants from local "Inhabitants, either Europeans, Indians or Blacks." Among the 800 plants Sloane collected was *Theobroma cacao*, "food of the gods." His volumes, published in the first quarter of the eighteenth century, spurred interest in the further conquest of new islands and their cuisines.

European women similarly traveled in the circum-Caribbean in order to engage in bioprospecting, recording the local plants and foods. Some itineraries were determined by the demands of family and others were undertaken independently. In the eighteenth century, naturalist Maria Riddell accompanied her father William Woodley, governor of Saint Kitts and the Leeward Islands. German-born botanist Maria Sibylla Merian (1647–1780) was the only known European woman of her time to travel out on her own in pursuit of scientific knowledge. She had divorced her husband and established herself as an artist and businesswoman, when she first sailed toward the circum-Caribbean at the age of fifty-two. There she sketched and painted her quarry and returned with specimens, as well as recipes for a variety of exotics, including cassava bread and medicinal cures from Suriname.[35] In France, the eighteenth century witnessed the rise of agricultural societies in which research and colonial prospecting were intertwined practices. Above all, the tone was set for the scientific and economic conquest of the Caribbean botanical world, its labors and its fruits.

The late nineteenth-century collapse of the sugar industry (in part due to the competition from other tropical colonies and the sugar beet production in temperate zones) triggered interest in searching for replacement plants. In 1897, the British Royal West Indies Commission reassessed the needs of the Caribbean colonies. The commission recommended the creation of botanical gardens on each island. If the Caribbean could focus on economically valuable plants, a small, local agricultural sector might be profitably developed. Yet colonial governments continued to ignore domestic agriculture and, except during the world wars, self-sufficiency seemed out of reach. In the meantime, culinary tastes continued to be shaped by global markets.

Ice Apples and Banana Boats

Consuming the Caribbean was not limited to the local acquisition of foods and plants for culinary and medicinal purposes. During the eighteenth and nineteenth centuries, products found their way to other global locations for consumption by imperial design and commercial gain, for scientific study and culinary delight. Père Labat claimed to have brought the citrus to new island homes. Turtle soup was popular in the Western world, which coveted and drove to near extinction the natural populations of turtles from Belize to the Bahamas. Spices and fruits were prized by the wealthy in Europe and Asia. African products like palm oil were introduced to the Caribbean and then developed for reexport to African consumers. The negative consequences of tropical exploitation were deforestation, overgrazing, erosion, and irreparable habitat loss.

By the late nineteenth century, refrigerated ships were regularly transporting "ice apples" (North American-grown fruit preserved on ice) and smoked hams of the cold north to the Caribbean. Pineapples, oranges, bananas, and other local delights were shipped to the Northern Hemisphere. Industrial-scale fruit production relied on Western chemicals and factory technologies. Banana boats carried both the laborers and the fruits that the laborers produced from one end of the Caribbean to the other. The United Fruit Company was forged from the merging of two companies in 1899, just after the end of the Spanish-American War, and it became a powerhouse pushing large-scale agricultural plantation operations. From navy surplus, a formidable fleet of commercial steamships was formed. It was known as the Great White Fleet because the once-gray ships were painted white. The fleet also symbolized the triumphalism of the era in which Uncle Sam's imperialist motives were expressed in racist paternalism directed against peoples the United States now influenced in the Philippines, Haiti, Cuba, and Puerto Rico. Soon West Indian agricultural workers replaced the Italian and Chinese laborers, who earlier had replaced enslaved Africans. Workers then tried unsuccessfully to lobby for better working conditions in a racist environment. The companies opposed any collective labor strikes and turned again to former slaves and their descendants. Hundreds of thousands of black workers from Jamaica, St. Kitts, and other islands arrived in Costa Rica, Honduras, and Cuba to grow bananas, other fruits, and sugar until the eventual collapse of the global market in the twentieth century. The capitalist remapping of the post-Columbian world had introduced exotic plants and foods to Europe and the Americas, forever altering island cuisines as well as transforming the gastronomic tastes and experiences of people far from the Caribbean.

Caribbean Tourism

The steamships also carried tourists, whose romanticized visions of the Caribbean lured them through ports such as New Orleans, the "Gateway to the Tropics." Caribbean foods were touted as "delicious cuisine" suitable for the luxury passengers aboard. Yet the fare listed on a 1915 menu of The Great White Fleet's SS *Tivives* (owned by the United Fruit Company Steamship Ser-

Cruise ship menu, Alcoa Steamship Company, c. 1950
(Collection of Candice Goucher)

vices) suggests some maritime continuity. Breakfast included fried haddock, kippered herring, salt mackerel, and tropical fruits. By the 1940s, postwar companies used similar prewar requisitioned ships for cruising. Travel writer Patrick Leigh Fermor boarded a ship in England and headed for the Caribbean, where he dined with Maroons on a simple meal of eggs, cassava, yam, and pineapple. He noted the "absolute splendor of breakfast" in Jamaica—a tropical cornucopia.[36] Not everyone agreed.

Fermor himself complained that the "hotel cooking in the island [of Trinidad in the 1940s)] is so appalling that a stretcher may profitably be ordered at the same time as dinner."[37] On the seas, the midcentury meals reflected limits of commoditization and captive diners. The Dominican Republic became involved in cruising when the Flota Mercante bought the SS *New Northland*

and sailed it with Dominican navy sailors as crew. In 1953, the renamed and refurbished ship *Nuevo Dominicano* was chartered out of Miami, sailing between Ciudad Trujillo, Nassau, and Jamaican ports. At least one North American passenger was not impressed by the cruise line's food, writing in 1953 on a postcard, "Dear Lou & Irv, Don't book anyone on the S.S. *Nuevo Dominicano*. . . . The ship is infected with rats, ants, and cockroaches, and the food is plain lousy and in very short variety."[38]

Modern tourists since the early twentieth century have sought to "get away" to the Caribbean as a destination intended to leave behind the familiar. Yet the familiar social divisions typically hovered nearby. African-American writer Langston Hughes ate local seafood with boiled bananas and "Spanish rice," but failed to escape the color line on a Cuban beach in 1930.[39] Among West Indians, class divisions were omnipresent. In 2000, Winston Bailey (The Mighty Shadow) sang, "Without money to buy honey/You're headin' for misery/She want hairdo and callalloo/And you ent have nothing."[40]

Not only food shortages were experienced in the Caribbean. Water supply had always been a problem on some islands. In Trinidad, the Water Riots of 1903 led to a number of deaths when police shot into crowds angry about increased water rates. The riots occurred at the seat of Parliament, the government Red House, which protesters completely gutted. Thirty years after Hughes, African-American writer Amiri Baraka went to Cuba to hear then Prime Minister Fidel Castro speak. Baraka recalled that he "hadn't had any water since early morning, and the heat and the excitement made my mouth dry and hard. . . . Most of the masses of Cubans had canteens or vacuum bottles, but soon someone had forgotten to tell the Americans (North and South) that there'd be no water." Baraka drank the local water and came down with dysentery.[41]

Food-borne illness was actually uncommon in the Caribbean. According to Haitian cook Claudette Eugene, savvy cooks know that all ingredients should be washed in vinegar and salt or scrubbed with lemon, lime, or other citrus. Molly O'Neill has argued that the "Haitian cook's habit of rinsing, marinating, rubbing, cooking, and re-cooking actually added to the complexity of flavors, [since] seasoning is added at each stage."[42] Caribbean cooks, like their African counterparts, favored large pots of stews that were brought to a boil periodically to reduce contamination. The widespread use of smoking and salting and a preference for pickled foods, papaya, and cassava (as cassareep) also preserved foods in the heat and humidity common to the region. However, water-borne diseases were leading causes of death in the twentieth-century Caribbean, where the shortage of water plagued many island communities.

Why then did the world clamor to consume the Caribbean through its tourism? Nineteenth-century steamers that shared available on-board space between passenger cabins and large holds for cargo goods gave way to cruise ships devoted entirely to passenger service. Cruise ships in the Caribbean developed out of the transatlantic passage, a sailing that was limited to the months of warm weather, avoiding the coldest winter months in the northern Atlantic, and thereby made large ships available for winter sailings in the southern waters beginning about 1900. From this time and prior to the end of Prohibition laws in the 1930s, the Caribbean island of Cuba, with its free-flowing rum and close proximity to the United States, was a particularly popular tourist destination. Three-quarters of a century later, *The Love Boat* television series (1977–1986) helped make cruising appealing for the middle-class American, who was attracted to the endless seas of food served buffet-style. Twenty-first-century cruise ships plying the Caribbean now boast of ice-skating rinks aboard and restaurants that feature diverse culinary offerings, including 1950s-style American or Italian cuisine, thus having lost any pretense of presenting an authentic experience of Caribbean culture and cuisine.[43]

Caribbean Cookbooks

Local Caribbean cooking reflected the fervent interest in food as cultural expression and marker of status. As early as 1856, a Cuban treatise on island cuisines was careful to distinguish Cuban from Spanish cooking.[44] Cookbooks offered advice on creating creolized identities thought to confer elevated social status. In Jamaica, the earliest known cookbook is Caroline Sullivan's *The Jamaica Cookery Book* (1893).[45] Its audience included the middle-class and European newcomers, for whom the cookbook offered to reveal native dishes. According to one reviewer, Jamaican cooking was moving toward a new phase:

> The art of cookery in these islands has hitherto been carried on by tradition and empirical rule and we welcome an attempt to place it on a definite basis and to introduce some method and principle as a point from which future conquests on behalf of tropical humanity may be made.[46]

At about the same time, Cuban cook Felicia Mendoza de Arostegui was writing her *Arte Culinario* (1896) and Lafcadio Hearn was assembling his *La Cuisine Creole* (1885). Across the Caribbean, these authors emphasized the cosmopolitan nature of the cuisine that had emerged after emancipation. According to Hearn, ignorance, a lack of hygiene, and a recognized discontinuity with the past rendered the urban housewife in need of advice. Furthermore, food preparations now distinguished Creoles from freed Africans, since the "Creole housewife often makes delicious *morceaux* (morsels) from the things usually thrown away by the extravagant servant."[47]

The distinctiveness of a singular Caribbean regional cuisine was recognized in Linda Wolfe's *The Cooking of the Caribbean Islands* (1970), a Time-Life book in the series *Foods of the World*. The principal consultant was Elisabeth Lambert Ortiz. The book painted a picture of a cuisine with indigenous roots that was "enticing, exotic, and above all, experimental."[48] More recently, the well-researched cookbooks of writer Jessica Harris finally have emphasized the African side of the Caribbean culinary heritage.

Urban Cauldrons

While African-Caribbean cuisine may be said to have emerged in the rural countryside on the provision grounds of the enslaved, the nineteenth and twentieth centuries witnessed a shift to more urbanized crucibles of culinary arts. Shaped by hunger and shantytown struggles, the Caribbean city itself reflected a new stage in the globalization of food. Procuring food and water no longer relied solely on access to grown provisions. The little food produced by a peasantry on interior landholdings found its way to city markets and coastal ports through a network of rural roads. Buying city food meant necessary entanglement in the web of capitalist deprivation and underdevelopment. The resultant hunger of the city haunted people and poets. In the poem "Pan Recipe," Guyanese poet John Agard (born 1949) used the cookbook-style jargon adopted from the colonizer to explore the impact of pain and rage in the urban cauldron. His verbs mix rape and simmer, whip and stir, evoking the shantytown experience about to explode.[49] For other writers, the cookbook was synonymous with a romanticized longing for food by Caribbean emigrants in exile.[50]

Caribbean Fast Food

Not only tourists, but also fast food enterprises invaded the Caribbean in the twentieth century. As elsewhere in the world, street foods became widespread as a first consequence of urbanization. The transformation of *roti* into popular fast food in Trinidad occurred in Port of Spain. But the setting was an impoverished urban crucible in which few barrack households had knives and forks, so the wrapped, to-go meal was welcome.[51] Later fast-food restaurants were indicators of economic transformations, conforming to the homogeneity predicted by George Ritzer's "McDonaldization thesis."[52] Global chains such as Kentucky Fried Chicken offered unique island-flavored foods to local residents at high prices as early as the 1970s. The plight of the local man, who became undesirable as a marriage partner because he was unable to afford "box chicken" (take-out food), became the target of song lyrics in Trinidad.

Winston Bailey (The Mighty Shadow) sang the lament in 2000: "Friday evening people passing / With box of fried chicken / Yuh looking for horn [you're setting yourself up to be cheated on]."[53] Historically, calypso had served as a vehicle for sharing consistent concerns about economic needs as expressed in food. After the Second World War, the Mighty Duke (1932–2009) in his calypso "Trinidad" observed:

> Beef gone up, Dasheen leaf gone up
> Chicken wing gone up . . .
> To get food to eat
> We have to send ah S.O.S.[54]

The military occupation of islands further linked food supplies to the interplay of local and global forces. Particularly during the postwar years, the economic plight was felt in terms of basic foodstuffs. Another calypsonian, The Mighty Viking, also sang about the shifting class lines and altered food preferences owing to price controls:

> The things are getting harder every day
> No rice, no flour the controller say
> We used to make distinctions
> Between yam and other provisions,
> Now women well dressed and men in saga suits [fashionable, narrow-lapelled, very long suit jacket with tapered pants]
> Bullying one another to buy breadfruits.[55]

Atilla and Executor were two other calypsonians who sang about food price control, corruption, and scandals. Ethnomusicologist Gordon Rohlehr has portrayed the conditions of deprivation, suffering, and food scarcity as culturally defining features of Trinidadian life since the 1930s. Themes of hunger and survivalism entered into personal relationships and can be viewed in both the hostility and hospitality of food encounters among different ethnic groups.[56] The creation of black markets soon followed the intrusive price controls, exacerbating disparities with the fact that "some people doing well/While others catching hell."[57]

Postcolonial Government Interventions

In the circum-Caribbean nation of Guyana, the Burnham socialist government attempted to reduce reliance on food imports in order to control prices in the 1970s. Cultural cuisines suffered when wheat flour and other imports (potatoes, currants, raisins, prunes) were restricted. Afro-Guyanese cooks were deprived of ingredients for their black cake, and Indo-Guyanese could not make daily breads such as roti. According to Guyana government official Rampersaud Tiwari, the governments of both Cheddi Jagan (of East Indian heritage) and Forbes Burnham (an Afro-Guyanese) actually "regulated imports and distribution based on the availability of foreign exchange."[58] This, in effect, was banning of selected imports. Elsewhere, agricultural policy also took control away from the small farms. Without actually banning imported food, Caribbean governments saw that local fruits such as guarana, sapadilla, and carambola were given increased awareness and promoted as local substitutes for imported carbonated soda drinks on some islands. The embargo of Cuba after the Revolution similarly saw that meat was tightly rationed, although the spirits were still being fed in African-derived rituals.[59] These experiences suggest that food restrictions, rather than reducing distinctive cultural practices, actually enhanced their local value and meaning.

The postcolonial policies of Caribbean governments were often linked to the International Monetary Fund and other global banking strategies and requirements. Dependent on developed nations for trade, economic assistance, and financial investment, the Caribbean economies increasingly were linked to global structures and challenges. Between 1961 and 2009, the Caribbean Basin spent an average of $2 billion per year on imported food. Structural adjustment and neoliberal fixes have worsened the future outlook on food sovereignty. Local agricultural production has steadily declined over time, and economies have become increasingly dependent on global food sources. United Nations data from the Food and Agricultural Organization confirm the inadequacy of domestic food production, with the significant result that "most countries are net food importers and in some food categories—staples in particular—the gap between domestic consumption and domestic production is quite significant, with consumption two to nearly four times greater than production."[60]

The importance of tourism for Caribbean economies may be limited to increased income for locals. In spite of foreign hotel chains importing foods for their menus, most tourists stay only a week or less, and their presence has had little impact on the levels of local food imports.[61] Yet at the same time, the Caribbean's demand for US foods increased 5 percent in 2010. This made the Caribbean Basin the seventh-largest export market for US consumer-oriented foods.

In Barbados, sometimes derisively called "Little England," local residents have competed with global food imports by trying to raise their own chickens to sell to the local Kentucky Fried Chicken franchise.[62] In Jamaica, local fast-food establishments in downtown Kingston and at other locations, including the airport, have offered *bammie* (cassava flatbread), jerk chicken,

Local market, Port of Spain, Trinidad
(Photograph by Candice Goucher)

and the like, testing the foreign formulas for successfully capturing the urban take-out market and exiting tourists. Meanwhile, Jamaican-owned and operated hotels, such as the Courtleigh Hotel and Suites in Kingston, have taken salt fish and boiled banana off the breakfast menu, but are well-stocked to prepare a traditional local breakfast if called upon to do so.[63] Ironically, the most quintessentially national cuisine of all African-Jamaican meals—salt fish and ackee—is unaffordable and now beyond the average Jamaican's budget.

Jamaicans and other local farmers increasingly have turned away from production of foodstuffs for local needs to produce for overseas markets. However, overseas Jamaicans can purchase salted cod, pepper sauce, and canned ackee in stores occupying less likely and distant refuges, from Portland, Oregon, to Miami, Brooklyn, Toronto, and London.

Scarcity and Hunger

Scarcity of imported food inevitably caused shifts in food habits and helped to homogenize the tastes and cuisines that lived under the influence of African traditions. Growing food on provision grounds helped to alleviate the hunger of the enslaved produced by insufficient rations. Still, frequent hurricanes and captured ships created widespread conditions of deprivation and famine across the islands. In African communities, periodic scarcity typically invoked the historical memory of hunting and gathering foodways from earlier generations, the reliance on knowledge of wild plants and behavior remembered from prehistoric times. In the Caribbean, the enslaved's use of gathered wild greens added essential nutrients to a meat-scarce diet.

Changing Ecologies

The Columbian Exchange wrought powerful changes in the ecosystems of Caribbean islands. Societies and their landscapes still bear the scars of colonialism and slavery. Deforestation and species loss have been constant reminders of the imperialism of land use strategies and the loss of habitats given over to plantation crops. Among the most devastating challenges have been the destruction of mangrove swamps that protect island life and the irrevocable loss of coral reefs and their ecologies. Large-scale catastrophes, such as hurricanes, volcanic eruptions, and earthquakes, have resulted in mass depopulation and acute awareness of the fragility of the island resource base in postcolonial Caribbean society. For example, Hurricane Hugo (1989) flattened 90 percent of Montserrat's infrastructure. Mount Chance's eruptions since 1995 further extended the reliance of local populations on imported food and aid and contributed to the erasure of cultural identities.

Invasive species introduced by colonizers opened island habitats to centuries of destruction. Yet without the wild pigs, freedom-fighting Maroons might not have flourished. On the island of Jamaica, a new threat appeared in the form of the tropical lionfish, native to the Indian Ocean and invasive to Caribbean coastal waters, where it has few natural predators. Local fishermen are organizing to eradicate the species. The Bluefields Bay Fishermen's Friendly Society in Jamaica was established to educate its members in sustain-

Captured iguanas, Bourda Market, Georgetown, Guyana
(Photograph by Candice Goucher)

able fishing practices and other "alternatives that will enhance the quality of life and preserve the natural environment of Bluefields."[64] Local consumption of the lionfish is being encouraged. In 2012, the local cooperative created a government partnership to establish a coral reef sanctuary intended to enhance sustainability efforts and increase snapper and lobster yields.

Taking Back the Land

Dirt eating was another practice brought by African immigrants to the New World. Specialized clays became an important dietary supplement, especially for women. Geophagy, as the practice is called scientifically, may have provided otherwise deficient diets with much-needed sources of minerals, including calcium and iron. According to Timothy Johns, "Earth may not be to everyone's taste, but it is one of the oldest tastes known to humankind."[65] Guadeloupean writer Maryse Condé described her Caribbean island home as "a galette of an island that the sun cooked over and over again in its oven."[66] Condé intended her use of food-related metaphors to be read not as actual recipes, but rather as "a kind of food painting."[67] Nonetheless, the edible island became a reality.

Caribbean slave owners referred to the widespread practice of dirt eating as "Cachexia Africana," which was thought to be a disorder leading to suicidal death. Enslaved Africans were observed eating "charcoal, chalk, dried mortar, mud, clay, sand, shells, rotten wood, shreds of cloth or paper, hair, or occasionally some other unnatural substance." Some scholars have theorized that the syndrome was a response to diets that left the enslaved malnourished. Another theory is that geophagy served to counter gastrointestinal responses to toxic plants (perhaps some wild plants not regularly consumed) and hunger. One means of dealing with the habit of dirt eating was to force slaves "to wear cone-shaped mouth locks, tin masks that covered the entire face."[68] Twenty-first-century observations of the continued practice of dirt eating in Haiti suggest the addition of dirt to bread dough was an economic strategy in order to "stretch" food supplies in a time of scarcity and extreme hunger.

Both catastrophic and inexorable changes have furthered the globalization of Caribbean cuisines. Resorting to geophagy was a commonplace practice among impoverished families in Haiti before the January 2010 earthquake. Although famine relief efforts were immediately welcomed after the quake, the efforts also threatened to alter the culinary cultures of Haitians by providing North American foods to replace local crops and interfere with local food markets. Indeed, beyond the crisis, food aid may do more harm than good by making self-reliance next to impossible on an ecologically devastated island still swirling in a sea of imperialism.

Food Memories and Globalization

A Creole proverb collected by Lafcadio Hearn credited the flourishing of Creole culture and cuisine to the end of slavery, suggesting the key role that food played in expressing freedom after emancipation: *Azourdi tout marmites dibout labaut dife* ("All the cooking pots are on the fire now").[69] Yet memories of slave food persisted in highly valued, if not romanticized cuisines of salted pigtail and breadfruit, "provision" and cowheel soup. And time will tell whether or not inaccessibility and hunger will erase or crystallize the cultural memories of the African culinary heritage. Born in the crucible of cultural encounters at the birthplace of modern slavery and capitalism, Caribbean food, hunger, and satisfaction have remained tethered to the economic forces of globalization.

A Conclusion in Which Anancy Makes Dinner

Anancy wants the last word. Did he not learn his lesson when he tried to collect all the wisdom of the world in his own calabash, only to spill its contents and scatter knowledge across the diaspora? Despite his voracious spider appetite, Anancy avoids the kitchen. Too much pot bangin,' and boilin,' and fry-up danger. No, we find him perched high above the dining table, resting off his hungry belly, ready to pounce, and thinking hard-hard about his next culinary adventure.

His spider reverie is too soon interrupted by his spider wife. She'd finished cooking the soup since morning, although it was Anancy's turn to cook. All this while Anancy still sleepin,' so he didn't have h'opportunity to smell, let alone taste Mrs. Anancy's fine-seasoned pot. Yes, she thinks it's time to pull Anancy's leg and serve him a trick.

She says, "Anancy, time fuh dinner. You best go to work."

"What's fuh dinner, 'ooman?" asks Anancy, without looking up, like he didn't hear her question.

"What you tink? You don' add nuttin' to s'up pot. No sal' pork, no labba, no 'guana. So is jus' greens you muss be growin' 'n gathering up for 'ome?"

Anancy yawned a spider yawn, saying quiet-like, "Res' yourself, 'ooman. Soon come."

Now Anancy friends were well acquainted with his spider ways, such as visitin' them just at mealtime so. But friend is friend. They grudgingly tolerated the spider appetite and each friend made the expected contribution. So it was that very afternoon that Anancy visited Tortoise, who was serving river fry fish, stuffed with herbs and chopped scallions, and Rabbit, who was making fiery callaloo, and friend Cow, who was preparing roasted yam. Yes, Anancy visited all his other animal friends, dipping into each and every one of their cooking pots.

And so Anancy arrived home not only in time to eat, but also with all the fixin's for the evening meal. Even Anancy was surprised how quickly a likkle dis and a likkle dat made a big ras feast, the first course of which Mrs. Anancy had warming on the fire. She couldn't help but smile her wifely smile.

Anancy had learned the lesson of hard times. Sharing mitigated hunger. And Anancy shared the food from all his friends with his wife and family. And that's why I'm sharing it with you.

Notes

1. Yoruba song collected by Ulli Beier, *Yoruba Poetry: An Anthology of Traditional Poems* (Cambridge: Cambridge University Press, 1970), 75.

2. Lafcadio Hearn, *Gombo Zhebes: Little Dictionary of Creole Proverbs, Selected from Six Creole Dialects* (New York: Will H. Coleman, 1885), 33.

3. Martin Carter and Gemma Robinson, *University of Hunger: Collected Poems and Selected Prose* (London: Bloodaxe Books, 2006).

4. Suzanne Toczyski, "Jean-Baptiste Labat and the Buccaneer Barbecue in Seventeenth-Century Martinique," *Gastronomica* 10, no. 1 (2010): 65–66.

5. Toczyski, *Jean-Baptiste Labat*, 61.

6. Christopher Columbus was probably describing South American yams, which he likened to turnips.

7. The phrase "paradise cult" is used by Frank E. and Fritzie P. Manuel, "Sketch for a Natural History of Paradise," in *Myth, Symbol, and Culture*, ed. Clifford Geertz, (New York: Norton, 1971), 83 and 119.

8. Richard Ligon, *A True and Exact History of the Island of Barbadoes*, (London: Peter Parker and Thomas Guy, 1673).

9. Londa Schiebinger, *Plants and Empire: Colonial Bioprospecting in the Atlantic World* (Cambridge, MA: Harvard University Press, 2004), 14, 30–35.

10. Vincent Huyghues-Belrose, "Avant le fruit de pain: La cuisine martiniquaise au XVIIIᵉ siècle," in *Sur les chemins de l'histoire antillaise*, ed. Jean Bernabe and Serge Mam Lam Fouck, (Paris: Ibis Rouge, 2006), 207.

11. Lady Maria Nugent, *Lady Nugent's Journal of Her Residence in Jamaica, from 1801 to 1805*, ed. Philip Wright (Kingston: Institute of Jamaica, 1966), 34–35 n1.

12. Henry Nelson Coleridge, *Six Months in the West Indies, in 1825* (New York: G. & C. Carvill, and E. Bliss & E. White, 1826), 45.

13. Quoted in J.H. Parry and P.M. Sherlock, *A Short History of the West Indies*, 2nd ed. (London: St. Martin's Press, 1965), 140–141.

14. Hearn, *Gombo Zhebes*, 38.

15. Patrick Browne (1756), quoted in Barry W. Higman, *Jamaican Food: History, Biology, Culture* (Kingston, Jamaica: University of the West Indies Press, 2008), 200.

16. Higman, *Jamaican Food*, 200.

17. Chinua Achebe, *Things Fall Apart* (New York: Anchor Books, 1994), 36–37.

18. Natalia Bolivar Arostegui and Carmen Gonzalez Diaz de Villegas, *Afro-Cuban Cuisine: Its Myths and Legends* (Havana, Cuba: Editorial Jose Marti, 1998), 86.

19. Maureen Warner-Lewis, *Yoruba Songs of Trinidad* (London: Karnak House, 1994), 151.

20. Warner-Lewis, *Yoruba Songs*, 146–147.

21. John Taylor, cited in Richard D.E. Burton, *Afro-Creole: Power, Opposition, and Play in the Caribbean* (Ithaca: Cornell University Press, 1997), 18.

22. Charles Leslie, *A New and Exact Account of Jamaica* (Edinburgh: A. Kincaid, 1739), 307–310.

23. Edward Long, *The History of Jamaica*, 3 vols. (London: T. Lowndes, 1774), 421–422.

24. Hearn, *Gombo Zhebes*, 34.

25. Hearn, *Gombo Zhebes*, 37.

26. Judith Bettelheim, "The Afro-Jamaican Jonkonnu Festival: Playing the Forces and Operating the Cloth" (PhD diss., Yale University, 1979). Jonkonnu or John Canoe is remembered from the Bahamas to Jamaica.

27. Benjamin Timms, "Development Theory and Domestic Agriculture in the Caribbean: Recurring Crises and Missed Opportunities," *Caribbean Geography* 15, no. 2 (2008): 102.

28. Nugent, *Lady Nugent's Journal*, 67–68; Captain Bligh reportedly brought both the breadfruit and the Otaheite or Malay apple to Jamaica in 1793, but this was not the first arrival.

29. Quoted in Tilar J. Mazzeo, "Coleridge's Travels," in *The Oxford Handbook of*

Samuel Taylor Coleridge, ed. Frederick Burwick (Oxford: Oxford University Press, 2009), 100.

30. Coleridge, *Six Months in the West Indies*, 171.

31. Coleridge, *Six Months in the West Indies*, 179.

32. Coleridge, *Six Months in the West Indies*, 178.

33. Coleridge, *Six Months in the West Indies*, 293.

34. Hans Sloane, A *Voyage to the Islands, Madera, Barbados, Nieves, S. Christophers and Jamaica* . . . (London: Printed by B.M. for the author, 1707–1725).

35. See Schiebinger, *Plants and Empire*, 25–35.

36. Patrick Leigh Fermor, *The Traveller's Tree: A Journey Through the Caribbean Islands* (New York: New York Review Books, 1950), 369 and 335.

37. Fermor, *Traveller's Tree*, 157.

38. Postcard, Cruising the Past, http://cruiselinehistory.com/the-dominican-republic-steamship-line-and-the-s-s-nuevo-dominicano/.

39. Quoted in Alan Ryan, ed., *The Reader's Companion to Cuba* (New York: Harcourt Brace, 1997), 86–88.

40. Winston ("Shadow") Bailey, Yuh Lookin' for Horn. On *Just for You* [CD]. (Leander, TX: Crossroads Records, 2000).

41. Ryan, *Reader's Companion to Cuba*, 205.

42. Molly O'Neill, "Spice Island: Haitian Food Layers the Sweet against the Bitter to Stand Up to Summer Heat," *New York Times Magazine*, July 16, 2000, 73–74.

43. Royal Caribbean International, www.royalcaribbean.com.

44. *Handbook for Cuban Cooks* (Havana, Cuba: Spencer, 1856), cited in Arostegui and Diaz de Villegas, *Afro-Cuban Cuisine*, 12.

45. Higman, *Jamaican Food*, 49–50.

46. *Gleaner*, December 18, 1893, 2.

47. Lafcadio Hearn, *La Cuisine Creole: A Collection of Culinary Recipes from Leading Chefs and Noted Housewives, Who Have Made New Orleans Famous for Its Cuisine [1885]*, (Carlisle, MA: Applewood Books, 2008), Introduction.

48. Linda Wolfe and the Editors of Time-Life, *The Cooking of the Caribbean Islands* (New York: Time-Life Books, 1970), 11.

49. John Agard, "Pan Recipe," in *Man to Pan* (Havana, Cuba: Ediciones Casa de las Américas, 1982), 9.

50. See, for example, the excellent cookbook by Cynthia Nelson, *Tastes Like Home: My Caribbean Cookbook* (Kingston, Jamaica: Ian Randle, 2011). Jamaican poet Louise Bennett writes of the longing for comfort foods of home ("Me dah dead fi drink some coaknut water") and the irony of "home" meaning food, not family, in the poem "Homesickness," in *The Heinemann Book of Caribbean Poetry,* ed. Ian McDonald and Steward Brown, comps. (Oxford: Heinemann, 1992), 11.

51. See the autobiography of Eric Williams, *Inward Hunger: The Education of a Prime Minister* (London: Andre Deutsch, 1969), 17.

52. George Ritzer, *The McDonaldization Thesis: Explorations and Extensions* (London: Sage, 1998).

53. Winston ("Shadow") Bailey, Yuh Lookin' for Horn. On *Just for You* [CD]. (Leander, TX: Crossroads Records, 2000).

54. Randolph Chase, "Protest in West Indian Folk Poetry," Kola (2009), www.thefreelibrary.com/Protest+in+West+Indian+folk+poetry-a0204205449.

55. Quoted in Hollis Liverpool, *Kaiso and Society* (Diego Martin, Trinidad: Juba, 1990), 61.

56. Taunts against East Indians and Afro-Caribbean food preferences abound in calypsos as well as popular jingles; see Gordon Rohlehr, *Calypso and Society in Pre-Independence Trinidad* (Port of Spain: Gordon Rohlehr, 1990), 254–256.

57. As Beginner sang in the calypso "Black Market," quoted in Rohlehr, *Calypso and Society*, 228.

58. R. Tiwari, former attaché in the Foreign Ministry, Guyana, personal communication, March 2010.

59. Mark Kurlansky, "The Babalawo and the Birds," in *Reader's Companion to Cuba*, ed. Ryan, 351.

60. Lurleen M. Walters and Keithly G. Jones, "Caribbean Food Import Demand: Influence of the Changing Dynamics of the Caribbean Food Economy," paper presented at the annual meeting of the Southern Agricultural Economics Association, Birmingham, Alabama, February 4–7, 2012, http://purl.umn.edu/119724, 4.

61. Walters and Jones, "Caribbean Food Import Demand," 14.

62. Interview in Bridgetown, Barbados, with local farmers, Inez Simon and family, August 1991.

63. In 2008, the hotel restaurant typically offered an all-inclusive American-style buffet and also made available a menu of alternatives. An unusual omelet with salt fish and ackee did appear on the breakfast menu in 2008.

64. Bluefields Bay Fishermen's Friendly Society, Official Website http://bluefieldsbayfishers.wordpress.com/.

65. Timothy Johns, "Well-Grounded Diet," *The Sciences* 31, no. 5 (September/October 1991): 38–43.

66. Maryse Condé, *Victoire: My Mother's Mother* (Simon & Schuster, 2010), 8.

67. Melissa Clark, "The Kitchen and the Quill: Maryse Condé in Conversation with Melissa Clark," Center for the Humanities, Graduate Center, CUNY, December 1, 2010.

68. Susan Allport, "Women Who Eat Dirt," *Gastronomica: The Journal of Food and Culture* 2, no. 2 (2010): 28–37.

69. Hearn, *Gombo Zhebes*, 8.

Bibliography

Abrahams, Roger D. *Singing the Master: The Emergence of African-American Culture in the Plantation South*. New York: Penguin Books, 1992.

Abrahams, Roger D., and John F. Szwed, eds. *After Africa*. New Haven: Yale University Press, 1983.

Achaya, K.T. *Indian Food: A Historical Companion*. Delhi: Oxford University Press, 1998.

Achebe, Chinua. *Things Fall Apart*. New York: Anchor Books, 1994.

Agard, John. *Man to Pan*. Havana, Cuba: Ediciones Casa de las Américas, 1982.

Agorsah, E. Kofi. *Maroon Heritage: Archaeological, Ethnographic, and Historical Perspectives*. Kingston, Jamaica: Canoe Press/University of the West Indies, 1994.

Allende, Isabel. *Aphrodite*. New York: HarperPerennial, 1999.

Allport, Susan. "Women Who Eat Dirt." *Gastronomica: The Journal of Food and Culture* 2, no. 2 (2010): 28–37.

Allsopp, Jeannette. *The Caribbean Multilingual Dictionary of Flora, Fauna, and Foods in English, French, French Creole, and Spanish*. Kingston, Jamaica: Arawak, 2003.

Andrews, J.B. "Ananci Stories." *Folk-Lore Record* 3, no. 1 (1880): 53–55.

Arkell, Julie. *Classic Rum*. London: Prion, 1999.

Armstrong, Douglas V. *The Old Village and the Great House: An Archaeological and Historical Examination of Drax Hall Plantation, St. Ann's Bay, Jamaica*. Champaign: University of Illinois Press, 1990.

Arostegui, Natalia Bolivar and Carmen Gonzalez Diaz de Villegas. *Afro-Cuban Cuisine: Its Myths and Legends*. Havana, Cuba: Editorial José Marti, 1998.

Avins, Lyn, and Betsy Quick. *Central Nigeria Unmasked: Arts of the Benue River Valley (A Curriculum Resource for Teachers)*. Los Angeles: Fowler Museum, UCLA, 2011.

Awang, Sandra S. "Reinterpreting Afrocentric Resistance in the Diaspora: Slave Women Higglers in the Commonwealth Caribbean." Paper presented at the African Studies Association annual meeting, Seattle, Washington, 1992.

Bailey, Winston ("Shadow"). Yuh Lookin' for Horn. On *Just for You* [CD]. Leander, TX: Crossroads Records, 2000.

Barbot, John. *A description of the Coasts of North and South Guinea*. London 1746.

Barnet, Miguel. *Afro-Cuban Religions*. Princeton, NJ: Markus Wiener, 2001.

Barrett, Leonard E. *The Rastafarians*. Boston: Beacon Press, 1997.

Bascom, William R. *Ifa Divination: Communication Between Gods and Men in West Africa*. Bloomington: Indiana University Press, 1969.

Beidelman, Thomas. *Colonial Evangelism*. Bloomington: Indiana University Press, 1982.

Beier, Ulli. *Yoruba Poetry: An Anthology of Traditional Poems*. Cambridge: Cambridge University Press, 1970.

Benghiat, Norma. *Traditional Jamaican Cookery*. London: Penguin Books, 1985.

Bennett, Norman R., and George E. Brooks, eds. *New England Merchants in Africa: A History Through Documents, 1802–1865*. Boston: Boston University Press, 1965.

Berleant-Schiller, Riva, and William M. Maurer. "Women's Place Is Every Place: Merging Domains and Women's Roles in Barbuda and Domina." In *Women and Change in the Caribbean: A Pan-Caribbean Perspective*, ed. Janet Momsen. Kingston, Jamaica: Ian Randle, 1993.

Bernault, Florence. "Body, Power and Sacrifice in Equatorial Africa." *Journal of African History* 47 (2006): 207–239.

Berry, Jack, and Richard A. Spears. *West African Folk Tales*. Evanston, IL: Northwestern University Press, 1991.

Bettelheim, Judith. "The Afro-Jamaican Jonkonnu Festival: Playing the Forces and Operating the Cloth." PhD diss., Yale University, 1979.

Bettelheim, Judith, and John Nunley, eds. *Caribbean Festival Arts: Each and Every Bit of Difference*. Seattle: Saint Louis Art Museum and University of Washington Press, 1988.

Blier, Suzanne Preston. *African Vodun: Art, Psychology, and Power*. Chicago: University of Chicago Press, 1995.

Bluefields Bay Fishermen's Friendly Society. Official Website http://bluefieldsbay-fishers.wordpress.com.

Bolster, W. Jeffrey. *Black Jacks: African American Seamen in the Age of Sail*. Cambridge, MA: Harvard University Press, 1997.

Boone, Sylvia Arden. *Radiance from the Waters: Ideals of Feminine Beauty in Mende Art*. New Haven: Yale University Press, 1986.

Bosman, Willem. *A New and Accurate Description of the Coast of Guinea, Divided into the Gold, the Slave, and the Ivory Coasts*. London: J. Knapton et al., 1705.

Brana-Shute, Gary. "Drinking Shops and Social Structure: Some Ideas on Lower-Class West Indian Male Behavior." *Urban Anthropology* 5, no. 1 (1976): 53–68.

Brathwaite, L. Edward ("Kamau"). *The Development of Creole Society in Jamaica: 1770–1820*. Oxford: Clarendon Press, 1978.

Brereton, Bridget. *A History of Modern Trinidad, 1783–1962*. Kingston, Jamaica: Heinemann, 1981.

Briggs, Richard. *The New Art of Cookery, According to the Present Practice*. Philadelphia: W. Spotswood, Campbell and Johnson, 1792.

Brown, David H. "Toward an Ethnoaesthetics of Santeria Ritual Arts: The Practice of Altar-Making and Gift Exchange." In *Santeria Aesthetics in Contemporary Latin American Art*, ed. Arturo Lindsay. Washington, DC: Smithsonian Institution Press, 1996.

Brown, Karen McCarthy. *Mama Lola: A Vodou Priestess in Brooklyn*. Berkeley: University of California Press, 1991.

Brown, Thomas. *The Works of Mr. Tho. Brown, . . .* , vol. 2. London: Benjamin Bragg, 1708.

Buckley, Roger Norman. *The British Army in the West Indies: Society and the Military in the Revolutionary Age*. Gainesville: University Press of Florida, 1998.

————. *Slaves in Red Coats: The British West India Regiments, 1795–1815*. New Haven: Yale University Press, 1979.

Burg, B.R. *Sodomy and the Pirate Tradition: English Sea Rovers in the Seventeenth Century Caribbean*. New York: New York University Press, 1983.

Burnard, Trevor. *Mastery, Tyranny and Desire: Thomas Thistlewood and His Slaves in the Anglo-Jamaican World*. Chapel Hill: University of North Carolina Press, 2003.

Burton, Richard D.E. *Afro-Creole: Power, Opposition, and Play in the Caribbean*. Ithaca: Cornell University Press, 1997.

Bush, Barbara. *Slave Women in Caribbean Society: 1650–1838*. Kingston, Jamaica: Heinemann, 1990.

Bynum, Caroline Walker. *Holy Feast and Holy Fast: The Religious Significance of Food to Medieval Women*. Berkeley: University of California Press, 1987.

Byock, Jesse, et al. "A Viking-Age Valley in Iceland: The Mosfell Archaeological Project." *Medieval Archaeology* 49 (2005): 194–218.

Cabanillas, Berta, and Carmen Ginorio. *Puerto Rican Dishes*. San Juan: University of Puerto Rico, 2002.

Calone, Shelley Boyd, and Richard Campbell Roberts. *Nostalgic Nassau: Picture Postcards, 1900–1940*. Nassau, Bahamas: Nassau Nostalgia, 1991.

Campbell, Mavis C. *Back to Africa: George Ross and The Maroons, from Nova Scotia to Sierra Leone*. Trenton, NJ: Africa World Press, 1993.

————. *The Maroons of Jamaica, 1655–1796: A History of Resistance, Collaboration and Betrayal*. Granville, MA: Bergin & Garvey, 1988.

Carmichael, Mrs. (Alison). *Domestic Manners and Social Customs of the White, Coloured, and Negro Population of the West Indies*, vol. 2. London, 1833.

Carney, Judith. *Black Rice: The African Origins of Rice Cultivation in the Americas*. Cambridge, MA: Harvard University Press, 2001.

————. "Rice, Slaves, and Landscapes of Cultural Memory." In *Places of Cultural Memory: African Reflections on the American Landscape*. US Department of the Interior, National Park Service, Conference Proceedings, Atlanta, Georgia, May 9–12, 2001.

Carter, Martin, and Gemma Robinson. *University of Hunger: Collected Poems and Selected Prose*. London: Bloodaxe Books, 2006.

Chambon, M. *Le commerce de l'Amerique par Marseille*, 2 vols. Avignon, 1764.

Chase, Randolph. "Protest in West Indian Folk Poetry." Kola, 2009. www.thefreelibrary.com/Protest+in+West+Indian+folk+poetry-a0204205449.

Chester, Greville John. *Transatlantic Sketches in the West Indies . . .* London, 1869.

Chowdhury, Amitava. "Horizons of Memory: A Global Processual Study of Cultural Memory and Identity of the South Asian Indentured Labor Diaspora in the Indian Ocean and the Caribbean." PhD diss., Washington State University, 2008.

Clapperton, Hugh. *Hugh Clapperton into the Interior of Africa: Records of the Second Expedition, 1825–1827*. Edited by Jamie Bruce-Lockhart and Paul E. Lovejoy. Leiden, Netherlands: Brill, 2005.

Clark, Melissa. "The Kitchen and the Quill: Maryse Condé in Conversation with Melissa Clark." Center for the Humanities, Graduate Center, CUNY, December 1, 2010.

Coe, Sophie D. *America's First Cuisines*. Austin: University of Texas Press, 1994.

Cogeshall, Captain Daniel. Letter from Captain Daniel Cogeshall to Abraham Redwood, March 19, 1726, Newport Historical Society, Abraham Redwood Papers, Book 2, MS #644, v. 1.

Cole, Herbert M., and Chike C. Aniakor. *Igbo Arts: Community and Cosmos*. Los Angeles: Museum of Cultural History, UCLA, 1984.

Cole, Herbert M., and Doran H. Ross. *The Arts of Ghana*. Los Angeles: Museum of Cultural History, UCLA, 1977.

Coleridge, Henry Nelson. *Six Months in the West Indies, in 1825*. New York: G. & C. Carvill, and E. Bliss & E. White, 1826.

Collingham, Lizzie. *Curry: A Tale of Cooks and Conquerors*. Oxford: Oxford University Press, 2006.

Condé, Maryse. *In the Time of the Revolution*. Translated by Doris Y. Kadish and Jean-Pierre Piriou. *Callaloo* 25, no. 2 (2002): 454–493.

———. *Victoire: My Mother's Mother*. New York: Simon & Schuster, 2010.

Connerton, Paul. *How Societies Remember*. Cambridge: Cambridge University Press, 1989.

Coughtry, Jay. *The Notorious Triangle: Rhode Island and the African Slave Trade, 1700–1807*. Philadelphia: Temple University Press, 1981.

Cowley, John. *Carnival, Canboulay, and Calypso: Traditions in the Making*. Cambridge: Cambridge University Press, 1996.

Crosby, A.W. *The Columbian Exchange: Biological and Cultural Consequences of 1492*. Westport, CT: Greenwood, 1972.

Dabydeen, David, and Brinsley Samaroo, eds. *India in the Caribbean*. London: University of Warwick, Centre for Caribbean Studies, 1987.

Daniels, John, and Christian Daniels. "The Origin of the Sugarcane Roller Mill." *Technology and Culture* 29 (1988): 483–535.

Davidson, Osha Gray. *Fire in the Turtle House: The Green Sea Turtle and the Fate of the Ocean*. New York: PublicAffairs, 2001.

Davis, Wade. *The Serpent and the Rainbow*. Toronto: Stoddart, 1985.

Day, Charles. *Five Years Residence in the West Indies*, vol. 1. London, 1852.

Dayan, Joan. *Haiti, History, and the Gods*. Berkeley: University of California Press, 1995.

DeCorse, Christopher R. *An Archaeology of Elmina: Africans and Europeans on the Gold Coast, 1400–1900*. Washington, DC: Smithsonian Institution Press, 1998.

Delle, James A., Mark W. Hauser, and Douglas V. Armstrong, eds. *Out of Many, One People: The Historical Archaeology of Colonial Jamaica*. Tuscaloosa: University of Alabama Press, 2011.

De Marees, Pieter. *Description and Historical Account of the Gold Kingdom of Guinea (1602)*. Edited by Adam Jones. Translated by Albert van Dantzig. London: British Academy, 1987.

Desmangles, Leslie G. *The Faces of the Gods: Vodou and Roman Catholicism in Haiti*. Chapel Hill: University of North Carolina Press, 1992.

Donnan, Elizabeth. *Documents Illustrative of the History of the Slave Trade to America*. Vol. 3, *New England and the Middle Colonies*. Washington, DC: Carnegie Institution of Washington, 1932.

Drewal, Henry John. *Mami Wata: Arts for Water Spirits in Africa and Its Diasporas*. Los Angeles: Fowler Museum, UCLA, 2008.

———. "Mami Wata Shrines: Exotica and the Construction of Self." *Proceedings of the May 1988 Conference and Workshop on African Material Culture*, Joint Committee on African Studies, American Council of Learned Societies and the Social Science Research Council, 1988.

———. *Sacred Waters: Arts for Mami Wata and Other Divinities in Africa and the Diaspora*. Bloomington: Indiana University Press, 2008.

Drewal, Henry John, and Margaret Thompson Drewal. *Gelede: Art and Female Power among the Yoruba*. Bloomington: Indiana University Press, 1990.

Drewal, Henry John, and John Pemberton III with Rowland Abiodun. *Yoruba: Nine Centuries of African Art and Thought*. New York: Center for African Art/Harry N. Abrams, 1989.

Dunn, Richard S. "The Demographic Contrast Between Slave Life in Jamaica and Virginia, 1760–1865." *Proceedings of the American Philosophical Society* 151, no. 1 (2007): 43–60.

———. *Sugar and Slaves: The Rise of the Planter Class in the English West Indies, 1624–1713*. Chapel Hill: University of North Carolina Press, 2000.

Edwards, Bryan. *The History, Civil and Commercial, of the British Colonies in the West Indies*, 2 vols. Dublin 1793.

Edwards, Jonathan, Jr. *Injustice and Impolicy of the Slave Trade and of the Slavery of Africans . . .* New Haven, CT: Thomas & Samuel Green, 1791.

Ehret, Christopher. "Africa in History." Presentation at the Conference on Understanding African Poverty over the Longue Durée, The Weatherhead Center for International Affairs (WCFIA, Harvard University) in Partnership with the International Institute for the Advanced Study of Cultures, Institutions and Economic Enterprise (IIAS), Hephzibah Christian Center, Peduase, Ghana, on July 15–17, 2010. http://www.wcfia.harvard.edu/sites/default/files/Ehret%20Africa%20in%20History%205-5-10.pdf.

Elder, J.D. *Song Games from Trinidad and Tobago*. Port of Spain, Trinidad: National Cultural Council, 1973.

Equiano, Olaudah. *The Interesting Narrative of the Life of Olaudah Equiano, Written by Himself* (1789). Edited by Robert J. Allison. Boston: Bedford/St. Martin's, 2007.

Ferguson, Moira, ed. *The History of Mary Prince, a West Indian Slave: Related by Herself*. Ann Arbor: University of Michigan Press, 1993.

Fermor, Patrick Leigh. *The Traveller's Tree: A Journey Through the Caribbean Islands*. New York: New York Review of Books, 1950.

Fernandez-Armesto, Felipe. *Millennium: A History of the Last Thousand Years*. New York: Scribner, 1995.

———. *Near a Thousand Tables: A History of Food*. New York: Free Press, 2002.

Fields-Black, Edda L. *Deep Roots: Rice Farmers in West Africa and the African Diaspora*. Bloomington: Indiana University Press, 2008.

Foote, Andrew H. *Africa and the American Flag*. New York, 1854.

Fuentes, Marisa J. "Power and Historical Figuring: Rachael Pringle Polgreen's Troubled Archive." *Gender & History* 22, no. 3 (2010): 564–584.

Fuson, Robert H., trans. *The Log of Christopher Columbus*. Camden, Maine: International Marine Publishing, 1987.

Gaspar, David Barry. "The Antigua Slave Conspiracy of 1736: A Case Study of the Origins of Collective Resistance." *William and Mary Quarterly*, 3rd ser., 35, no. 2 (1978): 308–323.

Geertz, Clifford, ed. *Myth, Symbol, and Culture*. New York: Norton, 1971.

Gilje, Paul A. *Liberty on the Waterfront: American Maritime Culture in the Age of Revolution*. Philadelphia: University of Pennsylvania Press, 2003.

Gomez, Michael A. *Reversing Sail: A History of the African Diaspora*. Cambridge: Cambridge University Press, 2005.

Goody, Jack. *Cooking, Cuisine, and Class: A Study in Comparative Sociology*. Cambridge: Cambridge University Press, 1982.

Goucher, Candice. "African Metallurgy in the Atlantic World." In *Archaeology of Atlantic Africa and the Atlantic Diaspora*, ed. Toyin Falola and Akin Ogundiran. Bloomington: Indiana University Press, 2007.

Goveia, E.V. *The West Indian Slave Laws of the 18th Century (Chapters in Caribbean History 2)*. Aylesbury, UK: Caribbean Universities Press, 1970.

Grossman, Anne, and Lisa Thomas Grossman. *Lobscouse and Spotted Dog*. New York: W.W. Norton, 1997.

Guyer, Jane. *The Raw, the Cooked, and the Half-Baked*. Boston: Boston University, African Studies Center Working Paper, 1981.

Hackett, Rosalind I.J. *Art and Religion in Africa*. London: Cassell, 1996.

Haraksingh, Kusha. "Control and Resistance Among Indian Workers: A Study of Labour on the Sugar Plantations of Trinidad, 1875–1917." In *India in the Caribbean*, ed. David Dabydeen and Brinsley Samaroo. London: University of Warwick, Centre for Caribbean Studies, 1987.

Harris, Jessica B. *Beyond Gumbo*. New York: Simon & Schuster, 2003.

———. *Tasting Brazil: Regional Recipes and Reminiscences*. New York: Macmillan, 1992.

Hauser, Mark W. "Routes and Roots of Empire: Pots, Power, and Slavery in the 18th-Century British Caribbean." *American Anthropologist* 113, no. 3 (2011): 431–447.

Hearn, Lafcadio. *La Cuisine Creole: A Collection of Culinary Recipes from Leading Chefs and Noted Housewives, Who Have Made New Orleans Famous for Its Cuisine [1885]*. Carlisle, MA: Applewood Books, 2008.

———. *Gombo Zhebes: Little Dictionary of Creole Proverbs, Selected from Six Creole Dialects*. New York: Will H. Coleman, 1885.

———. "The Last of the Voodoos." *Harper's Weekly*, November 7, 1885, 726–727.

———. *Two Years in the French West Indies*. New York: Harper, 1903.

Henige, David. "John Kabes, an Early African Entrepreneur and State Builder." *Journal of African History* 18, no. 1 (1977): 1–19.

Henry, Frances. *Reclaiming African Religions in Trinidad: The Socio-Political Legitimation of the Orisha and Spiritual Baptists Faiths*. Kingston, Jamaica: University of the West Indies Press, 2003.

Herbert, Eugenia W. *Iron, Gender, and Power: Rituals of Transformation in African Societies*. Indianapolis: Indiana University Press, 1993.

Heywood, Linda M., and John K. Thornton. *Central Africans, Atlantic Creoles, and the Foundation of the Americas, 1585–1660*. Cambridge: Cambridge University Press, 2007.

Higman, Barry W. *Jamaican Food: History, Biology, Culture*. Kingston, Jamaica: University of the West Indies Press, 2008.

Hodges, Graham Russell, ed. *Black Itinerants of the Gospel: The Narratives of John Jea and George White*. Madison, WI: Madison House, 1993.

Horst, G., Donald B. Hoagland, and C. William Kilpatrick. "The Mongoose in the West Indies: The Biogeography and Population Biology of an Introduced Species." In *Biogeography of the West Indies: Patterns and Perspectives*, ed. Charles Arthur Woods et al., 2nd ed. 409–424. Boca Raton, FL: CRC Press, 2001.

Houk, James T. *Spirits, Blood, and Drums: The Orisha Religion in Trinidad*. Philadelphia: Temple University Press, 1995.

Hughes, R.E. "Scurvy," in Kenneth F. Kiple and Kriemhild Conee Ornelas, eds., *The Cambridge World History of Food*, vol. 1, IV.D.8, 988–1000. Cambridge: Cambridge University Press, 2000.

Hulme, Peter, and Neil L. Whitehead, eds. *Wild Majesty: Encounters with Caribs from Columbus to the Present Day*. Oxford: Clarendon Press, 1992.

Hunt, Sylvia. *Sylvia Hunt's Menus for Festivals and Daily Use*. Port of Spain, Trinidad: Bank of Commerce, 1988.

Huyghues-Belrose, Vincent. "Avant le fruit de pain: La cuisine martiniquaise au XVIIIᵉ siècle." In *Sur les chemins de l'histoire antillaise*, ed. Jean Bernabe and Serge Mam Lam Fouck. Paris: Ibis Rouge, 2006.

Jane, Lionel Cecil, trans. *Select Documents Illustrating the Four Voyages of Columbus*. Nendeln, Liechtenstein: Kraus Reprint, 1967 (originally published by the Hakluyt Society, 1930).

Jay, W.M.L. *My Winter in Cuba*. New York: E.P. Dutton, 1871.

Jekyll, Walter, coll. and ed. *Jamaican Song and Story: Annancy Stories, Digging Sings, Ring Tunes, and Dancing Tunes*. London: David Nutt, 1924.

Johns, Timothy. "Well-Grounded Diet." *The Sciences* 31, no. 5 (September/October 1991): 38–43.

Johnson, Kim. *Descendants of the Dragon: The Chinese in Trinidad, 1806–2006*. Kingston, Jamaica: Ian Randle, 2006.

Kashyap, Arunima, and Steve Weber. "Harappan Plant Use Revealed by Starch Grains from Farmana, India." *Antiquity* 84, no. 326 (2010) http://antiquity.ac.uk/projgall/kashyap326/.

Keeler, Mary Frear, ed. *Sir Francis Drake's West Indian Voyage, 1585–86*. Hakluyt Society, 2nd ser., no. 148 (1975).

Kelly, K.G. "The Archaeology of African-European Interaction: Investigating the Social Roles of Trade, Traders, and the Use of Space in the Seventeenth and Eighteenth Century Hueda Kingdom, Republic of Benin." *World Archaeology* 28, no. 3 (1997): 77–95.

———. Current Research in the French West Indies. Department of Anthropology, University of South Carolina, 2008. www.cla.sc.edu/anth/faculty/KGKelly1/guadeloupe.html.

Kimball, Eric. "'The Meat of All the Slaves in All the West Indies': How Fishermen from Salem and Marblehead Sustained the Plantation Complex in the 18th-Century Caribbean." Paper presented at the World History Association annual meeting, Salem State College, Salem, Massachusetts, June 26, 2009.

Kiple, Kenneth F., and Kriemhild Conee Ornelas, eds. *The Cambridge World History of Food*, 2 vols. Cambridge: Cambridge University Press, 2000.

Krogel, Alison. *Food, Power, and Resistance in the Andes: Exploring Quechua Verbal and Visual Narratives*. New York: Lexington Books, 2011.

Kumar, P. Pratap, ed. *Religious Pluralism in the Diaspora*. Leiden, Netherlands: Brill, 2006.

Kurlansky, Mark. *Cod: A Biography of the Fish That Changed the World*. New York: Penguin Books, 1997.

———. *Salt: A World History*. New York: Walker, 2002.

Lackhan, Rabindranath S. *Plants of Religious Significance: The Hindu Perspective*. 2nd ed. Gasparillo, Trinidad: Revolution, n.d.

Lengel, Edward G., ed. *The Papers of George Washington: The Revolutionary War Series (December 1777–February 1778)*, vol. 13. Charlottesville and London: University of Virginia Press, 2003.

León-Portilla, Miguel. *The Broken Spears: The Aztec Account of the Conquest of Mexico*. Boston: Beacon Press, 2008.

Leone, Mark P., and Gladys-Marie Frye. "Conjuring in the Big House Kitchen: An Interpretation of African-American Belief Systems, Based on the Uses of Archaeology and Folklore Sources." *Journal of American Folklore* 112, no. 445 (1999): 372–403.

Leslie, Charles. *A New and Exact Account of Jamaica*. Edinburgh: A. Kincaid, 1739.

Lévi-Strauss, Claude. *The Raw and the Cooked: Introduction to a Science of Mythology*, vol. I. New York: Harper and Row, 1969.

Lewis, M.G. *Journal of a West Indian Proprietor*. London, 1834.

Ligon, Richard. *A True and Exact History of the Island of Barbadoes*. 2nd ed. London: Peter Parker and Thomas Guy, 1673 [1657].

Linebaugh, Peter, and Marcus Rediker. *The Many-Headed Hydra: Sailors, Slaves, Commoners, and the Hidden History of the Revolutionary Atlantic*. Boston: Beacon Press, 2000.

Liverpool, Hollis "Chalkdust." *Kaiso and Society*. Diego Martin, Trinidad: Juba, 1990.

———. *Rituals of Power and Rebellion: The Carnival Tradition in Trinidad and Tobago, 1763–1962*. Chicago: Research Associates School Times Publications, 2001.

Long, Edward. *The History of Jamaica*, 3 vols. London: T. Lowndes, 1774.

Look Lai, Walton. *The Chinese in the West Indies: A Documentary History, 1806–1995*. Kingston, Jamaica: University of West Indies, 1998.

Lovejoy, Paul E. *Salt of the Desert Sun: A History of Salt Production and Trade in the Central Sudan*. Cambridge: Cambridge University Press, 1986.

———. *Transformations in Slavery: A History of Slavery in Africa* (African Studies Series 36). Cambridge: Cambridge University Press, 1983.

Mackie, Cristine. *Life and Food in the Caribbean*. New York: New Amsterdam, 1991.

MacLean, Rachel, and Timothy Insoll. "Archaeology, Luxury, and the Exotic: The Examples of Islamic Gao (Mali) and Bahrain." *World Archaeology* 34, no. 3 (2003): 558–570.

———. "The Social Context of Food Technology in Iron Age Gao, Mali." *World Archaeology* 31, no. 1 (1999): 78–92.

Madden, Richard Robert. *A Twelve Month's Residence in the West Indies, During the transition from Slavery to Apprenticeship . . .* , vol. 2. London: James Cochrane, 1835.

Mahabir, Kumar, and Mera Heeralal. *Caribbean East Indian Recipes*. Port of Spain, Trinidad: Chakra, 2009.

Mansur, Anita. *Culinary Fictions: Food in South Asian Diasporic Culture*. Philadelphia: Temple University Press, 2010.

Mason, John. *Orin Orisa*. New York: Yoruba Theological Archministry, 1992.

Mazumdar, Suchea. "The Impact of New World Food Crops on the Diet and Economy of China and India, 1600–1900." In *Food in Global History*, ed. Raymond Grew, 71–72. Boulder: Westview, 1999.

Mazzeo, Tilar J. "Coleridge's Travels." In *The Oxford Handbook of Samuel Taylor Coleridge*, ed. Frederick Burwick, 89–106. Oxford: Oxford University Press, 2009.

McAlister, Elizabeth. *Rara! Vodou, Power, and Performance in Haiti and Its Diaspora.* Berkeley: University of California Press, 2002.

McCann, James C. *Maize and Grace: Africa's Encounter with a New World Crop, 1500–2000.* Cambridge, MA: Harvard University Press, 2005.

———. *Stirring the Pot: A History of African Cuisine.* Athens: Ohio University Press, 2009.

McDonald, Ian, and Steward Brown, comps. *The Heinemann Book of Caribbean Poetry.* Oxford: Heinemann, 1992.

McFadden, Christine, and Christine France. *The Cook's Guide to Chocolate.* Oxford: Sebastian Kelly, 1997.

Miller, Joseph C. *Way of Death: Merchant Capitalism and the Angolan Slave Trade, 1730–1830.* Madison: University of Wisconsin Press, 1988.

Mintz, Sidney. *Sweetness and Power: The Place of Sugar in Modern History.* New York: Elisabeth Sifton/Viking, 1985.

Mitchell, Patricia B. *French Cooking in Early America.* n.p., 1995.

Munasinghe, Viranjini. *Callaloo or Tossed Salad? East Indians and the Cultural Politics of Identity in Trinidad.* Ithaca: Cornell University Press, 2002.

Nelson, Cynthia. *Tastes Like Home: My Caribbean Cookbook.* Kingston, Jamaica: Ian Randle, 2011.

Niane, D.T. *Sundiata: An Epic of Old Mali.* New York: Longman, 2005.

Nugent, Lady Maria. *Lady Nugent's Journal of Her Residence in Jamaica, from 1801 to 1805.* Edited by Philip Wright. Kingston: Institute of Jamaica, 1966.

O'Neill, Molly. "Spice Island: Haitian Food Layers the Sweet against the Bitter to Stand Up to Summer Heat." *New York Times Magazine*, July 16, 2000.

Park, Mungo. *Travels in the Interior Districts of Africa: Performed in the Years 1795, 1796, and 1797.* Reprinted New York: Dutton, 1960.

Parkinson, Rosemary. *Culinaria, The Caribbean: A Culinary Discovery.* Cologne, Germany: Konemann, 1999.

Parry, John H. "Plantation and Provision Ground: An Historical Sketch of the Introduction of Food Crops into Jamaica." *Revista de Historia de America* 39 (1955): 1–22.

Parry, John H., and P.M. Sherlock. *A Short History of the West Indies.* 2nd ed. London: St. Martin's Press, 1965.

Pezzarossi, Guido, Ryan Kennedy, and Heather Law. "Hoe Cake and Pickerel: Cooking Traditions, Community, and Agency at a Nineteenth-Century Nipmuc Farmstead." In *The Menial Art of Cooking: Archaeological Studies of Cooking and Food*, ed. Sarah R. Graff and Enrique Rodriguez-Alegria, 201–230. Boulder: Colorado University Press, 2012.

Pollard, Velma, ed. *Anansesem: A Collection of Folk Tales, Legends and Poems for Juniors.* Kingston, Jamaica: Carlong, 1985.

Pendergrast, Mark. *Uncommon Grounds: The History of Coffee and How It Transformed Our World.* New York: Basic Books, 1999.

Pulsipher, Lydia Mihelic. "Changing Roles in the Life Cycles of Women in Traditional West Indian Houseyards." In *Women and Change in the Caribbean: A Pan-Caribbean Perspective*, ed. Janet Momsen, 50–64. Kingston, Jamaica: Ian Randle, 1993.

Quinlan, Marsha B., and Robert J. Quinlan. "Balancing the System: Humoral Medicine and Food in the Commonwealth of Dominica." In *Eating and Healing: Exploration of Wild and Domesticated Plants and Animals as Food and Medicine*, ed. Andrea Pieroni and Lisa Leimar Price, 197–212. Binghamton, NY: Haworth Press, 2005.

Rahamut, Wendy. *Curry, Callaloo, and Calypso: The Real Taste of Trinidad and Tobago*. Oxford: Macmillan, 2011.

Randolph, Mary. *The Virginia House-Wife, with Historical Notes and Commentaries by Karen Hess*. Columbia: University of South Carolina Press, 1984.

Redhead, J. *Utilization of Tropical Foods: Sugars, Spices and Stimulants*. FAO Food and Nutrition Paper 47, no. 6 (1989).

Rickford, John R. *Dimensions of a Creole Continuum: History, Texts, and Linguistic Analysis of Guyanese Creole*. Palo Alto, CA: Stanford University Press, 1987.

———. "Pidgens and Creoles." In *Oxford International Encyclopedia of Linguistics*, ed. William Bright, 3: 224–228. New York: Oxford University Press, 1992.

———. "Preface and Editing of Two Papers by S.R. Richard Allsopp, 'The Case for Afrogenesis' and 'The Afrogenesis of Caribbean Creole Proverbs.'" *Society for Caribbean Linguistics Occasional Papers*, nos. 33–34 (2006): 3–52.

Ritzer, George. *The McDonaldization Thesis: Explorations and Extensions*. London: Sage, 1998.

Roberts, Lissa. "Geographies of Steam: Mapping the Entrepreneurial Activities of Steam Engineers in France during the Second Half of the Eighteenth Century." *History and Technology* 27, no. 4 (2011): 417–439.

Roberts, Mary Nooter, and Allen F. Roberts. *Memory: Luba Art and the Making of History*. New York: Museum for African Art/Prestel, 1996.

Rodney, Walter. *A History of the Upper Guinea Coast, 1545–1800*. New York: Monthly Review Press, 1970.

Rohlehr, Gordon. *Calypso and Society in Pre-Independence Trinidad*. Port of Spain: Gordon Rohlehr, 1990.

Ross, Doran H. *Fighting with Art: Appliqued Flags of the Fante Asafo*. UCLA Pamphlet Series 1, no. 5. Los Angeles: Museum of Cultural History, 1979.

Ryan, Alan, ed. *The Reader's Companion to Cuba*. New York: Harcourt Brace, 1997.

Ryder, Alan. *Benin and the Europeans, 1485–1897*. New York: Humanities Press, 1969.

Salkey, Andrew. *Anancy's Score*. London: Bogle-L'Ouverture, 1973.

Samaroo, Brinsley. "Two Abolitions: African Slavery and East Indian Indentureship." In *India in the Caribbean*, ed. David Dabydeen and Brinsley Samaroo, 25–41. London: Hansib/University of Warwick, Center for Caribbean Studies, 1987.

Sandiford, Keith A. *The Cultural Politics of Sugar*. Cambridge: Cambridge University Press, 2000.

Schiebinger, Londa. *Plants and Empire: Colonial Bioprospecting in the Atlantic World*. Cambridge, MA: Harvard University Press, 2004.

Sharpe, Jenny. *Allegories of Empire: The Figure of Woman in the Colonial Text*. Minneapolis: University of Minnesota Press, 1987.

Shepherd, Verene A. "Depression in the Tin Roof Towns: Economic Problems of Urban Indians in Jamaica, 1930–1950." In *India in the Caribbean*, ed. David Dabydeen and Brinsley Samaroo, 173–188. London: University of Warwick, Centre for Caribbean Studies, 1987.

Shepherd, Verene A., and Glen L Richards, eds. *Questioning Creole: Creolisation Discourses in Caribbean Culture*. Kingston, Jamaica: Ian Randle, 2002.

Sheridan, Richard B. "The Crisis of Slave Subsistence in the British West Indies During and After the American Revolution." *William and Mary Quarterly* 33 (1976): 615–641.

Shimada, Ryuto. *The Intra-Asian Trade in Japanese Copper by the Dutch East India Company*. Leiden, Netherlands: Brill, 2005.

Sloane, Hans. *A Voyage to the Islands, Madera, Barbados, Nieves, S. Christophers and Jamaica* . . . London: Printed by B.M. for the author, 1707–1725.

Smith, Frederick H. *Caribbean Rum: A Social and Economic History*. Gainesville: University of Florida Press, 2005.

Smith, Sydney. *Wit and Wisdom of the Rev. Sydney Smith*. New York: Redfield, 1856.

Spary, E.C. *Eating the Enlightenment: Food and the Sciences in Paris, 1670–1760*. Chicago: University of Chicago Press, 2012.

Stedman, John. *Narrative of a Five Years' Expedition Against the Revolted Negroes of Surinam*. Amherst: University of Massachusetts Press, 1971 [1796].

Stoler, Ann Laura. "Carnal Knowledge and Imperial Power: Gender, Race, and Morality in Colonial Asia." In *Gender at the Crossroads of Knowledge: Feminist Anthropology in the Postmodern Era*, ed. Micaela di Leonardo, 51–101. Berkeley: University of California Press, 1991.

Sullivan, Caroline. *The Jamaica Cookery Book*. Kingston, Jamaica: Aston W. Gardner, 1893.

Tanna, Laura. *Jamaican Folktales and Oral Histories*. Kingston: Institute of Jamaica, 1984.

Tannahill, Reay. *Food in History*. New York: Stein and Day, 1973.

Thompson, Robert Farris. *Black Gods and Kings: Yoruba Art at UCLA*. Bloomington: Indiana University Press, 1976.

———. *Face of the Gods: Art and Altars of Africa and the African Americas*. New York: Museum for African Arts/Prestel, 1993.

Thornton, John. *Africa and Africans in the Making of the Atlantic World, 1400–1800*. London: Cambridge University Press, 1998.

Timms, Benjamin. "Development Theory and Domestic Agriculture in the Caribbean: Recurring Crises and Missed Opportunities." *Caribbean Geography* 15, no. 2 (2008): 101–117.

Toczyski, Suzanne. "Jean-Baptiste Labat and the Buccaneer Barbecue in Seventeenth-Century Martinique." *Gastronomica* 10, no. 1 (2010): 65–66.

Tompkins, Kyla Wazana. "Everything 'Cept Eat Us: The Antebellum Black Body Portrayed as Edible Body." *Callaloo* 30, no. 1 (2007): 201–224.

———. *Racial Indigestion: Eating Bodies in the 19th Century*. New York: New York University Press, 2012.

Unsworth, Barry. *Sacred Hunger*. New York: Norton, 1992.

van Dantzig, Albert. *Forts and Castles of Ghana*. Accra, Ghana: Sedco, 1980.

Vines, Richard. Letter from Richard Vines to John Winthrop, July 19, 1647, *Winthrop Papers*, 6 vols. (Boston: Massachusetts Historical Society, 1929.

Walters, Lurleen M., and Keithly G. Jones. "Caribbean Food Import Demand: Influence of the Changing Dynamics of the Caribbean Food Economy." Paper presented at the annual meeting of the Southern Agricultural Economics Association, Birmingham, Alabama, February 4–7, 2012. http://purl.umn.edu/119724.

Ward, Edward. *The Wooden World Dissected in the Character of a Ship of War*. 2nd ed. London, 1708.

Warner-Lewis, Maureen. *Guinea's Other Sons: The African Dynamic in Trinidad Culture*. Dover, MA: Majority Press, 1991.

———. *Yoruba Songs of Trinidad*. London: Karnak House, 1994.

Wilk, Richard. *Home Cooking in the Global Village: Caribbean Food from Buccaneers to Ecotourists*. Oxford: Berg, 2006.

Williams, Eric. *Documents of West Indian History: 1492–1655*. Port of Spain, Trinidad: PNM, 1963.

———. *From Columbus to Castro: The History of the Caribbean, 1492–1969*. New York: Vintage Books, 1984.

———. *Inward Hunger: The Education of a Prime Minister*. London: Andre Deutsch, 1969.

Wolfe, Linda, and the Editors of Time-Life, *The Cooking of the Caribbean Islands*. New York: Time-Life Books, 1970.

Woods, Charles Arthur Lewis, et al., eds. *Biogeography of the West Indies: Patterns and Perspectives*. 2nd ed. Boca Raton, FL: CRC Press, 2001.

Wright, Donald R. *The World and a Very Small Place in Africa: A History of Globalization in Niumi, The Gambia*. Armonk, NY: M.E. Sharpe, 2010.

Wynter, Sylvia. "Lady Nugent's Journal." *Jamaica Journal* 1, no. 1 (1967): 25–27.

Index

Note: Page numbers in italics indicate illustrations.

About the Author

Candice Goucher, PhD, is a professor of history at Washington State University, Vancouver, where she has taught since 2000. She has conducted historical and archaeological research in Ghana, Togo, Nigeria, the Caribbean, and Mauritius. She was one of two lead scholars for the project *Bridging World History* (Annenberg/Corporation for Public Broadcasting), a twenty-six-part video series and interactive website.